Automated Librai

Supplements to Computers in Libraries

Automated
Library
Systems

A Librarian's Guide
and Teaching Manual

Beverly K. Duval
and
Linda Main

Meckler
Westport • London

Library of Congress Cataloging-in-Publication Data

Duval, Beverly K.
    Automated library systems : a librarian's guide and teaching
manual / Beverly K. Duval and Linda Main.
        p. cm. -- (Supplements to Computers in libraries ; 64)
    Includes bibliographical references and index.
    ISBN 0-88736-873-5 : $
    1. Libraries--Automation. 2. Retrospective conversion
(Cataloging) 3. Microcomputers--Library applications. 4. CD-ROM-
-Library applications. 5. Catalogs, On-line. I. Main, Linda.
II. Title. III. Series.
Z678.9.D82   1992
025.3'0285--dc20   92-41406
                                                          CIP

British Library Cataloguing-in-Publication Data

Duval, Beverly K.
    Automated Library Systems: Librarian's
    Guide and Teaching Manual. -
    (Supplements to Computers in Libraries
    Series)
    I. Title II. Main, Linda III. Series
    025.04

    ISBN 0-88736-873-5

Meckler Publishing, the publishing division of Meckler Corporation,
    11 Ferry Lane West, Westport, CT 06880.
Meckler Ltd., 247-249 Vauxhall Bridge Road, London SW1V 1HQ, U.K.

Printed on acid free paper.
Printed and bound in the United States of America.

Contents

Preface

Automated Library Systems: A Librarian's Guide and Teaching Manual has been jointly written as:

(1) a self-paced guide for librarians and paraprofessionals new to the field of automated library systems and those interested in upgrading automated library systems;

(2) a textbook for instructors in both Master of Library Science (MLS) programs and Library Technical Assistant (LTA) programs.

We feel that there is a definite need for a *single teaching guide* that will help to familiarize librarians and library staff with the growing market for automated library systems, what to know, and how to interact in the field. The decision to initially automate or to upgrade an outdated automated library system is one of the most important activities that a library will undertake.

The teaching manual is divided into nine chapters with the following purposes in mind:

Chapter 1: **AUTOMATED LIBRARY SYSTEMS: AN OVERVIEW** introduces and concisely defines the terms and jargon associated with automated library systems. It is intended to get the reader up to speed in the world of automated library systems so that he or she can converse intelligently and act as a prudent negotiator in the automated library systems marketplace.

Chapter 2: **KEY PLAYERS/LEADERS IN THE FIELD: PAST AND PRESENT** briefly outlines historical trends and shifts in the industry, discusses the importance of the marketplace, highlights the primary vendors, and suggests sources for further reading.

Chapter 3: **THE PLANNING PROCESS** identifies and details each of the planning stages of automating a library and the steps involved. Planning is a complex, time consuming, and costly process which requires extensive investigation, discussion and decision-making. Each step should be carefully considered.

(a) Justification for automating/migrating
(b) Committee process, who is involved and how they work
(c) Should you go with a consultant?

    (d) Specifications, Request for Information (RFI), Request for Proposal (RFP)

    (e) Bidding process

    (f) Selection of the automated library system

    (g) Benchmarking

    (h) Contract negotiations

    (i) Installation

    (j) Training

    (k) System activation

Chapter 4: **CORE MODULES** details the critical components of four of the five basic automated library systems modules: Cataloging, Circulation, Acquisitions, and Serials. We have placed greater emphasis on the Online Public/Patron Access Catalog (OPAC) module in Chapter 6 and have devoted Chapter 8 to the alternative CD-ROM PAC or ROMCat.

Chapter 5: **RETROSPECTIVE CONVERSION** explains in detail the process of converting a library's holdings into computer records. It includes (a) MARC II format, (b) MICROcomputer Library Interchange Format (MicroLIF), (c) standards for uploading MARC records into microcomputers, (e) the RECON planning process (f) options for converting records, (g) procedures followed by vendors, (h) points to discuss with them, (i) specific vendor requirements, and (j) cost implications.

Chapter 6: **THE ONLINE PUBLIC ACCESS CATALOG (OPAC)** concentrates solely on the OPAC. It includes a brief discussion of early OPAC studies and development, advantages and disadvantages of OPAC's, and factors to consider in designing the OPAC for the patron. Questions to ask the vendor and those to ask user groups are detailed; problems that patrons have encountered are discussed; and concepts for training and clear documentation are emphasized. Additionally, sections are devoted to the use of the OPAC as a multidimensional tool, to its impact on colleges and universities, and to ergonomics and cost considerations.

Chapter 7: **MICROCOMPUTER-BASED AUTOMATED LIBRARY SYSTEMS: A GROWING FIELD** covers the pros and cons of automated library systems running on microcomputers. It briefly discusses the technological advances which made the microcomputer a vehicle for integrating automated library systems in small libraries; outlines tips and traps when purchasing a micro-based system; succinctly reiterates planning guidelines; and highlights features. A list of microcomputer automated library system vendors is provided.

Chapter 8: **CD-ROM-BASED AUTOMATED LIBRARY SYSTEMS: A FIELD IN LIMBO** focuses on CD-ROM PACs or ROMCats. It includes a brief historical overview of the emergence of CD-ROM PACs or ROMCats, highlights vendors in the field; discusses the role of standards, and outlines system requirements and characteristics. Additionally, it discusses librarians' perspectives, identifies advantages and disadvantages of CD-ROM PACs as a storage medium, reviews system selection and preparation guidelines/possibilities, and presents synopses of what others have done in the field.

Chapter 9: **TRENDS WHICH WILL CONTINUE INTO THE FUTURE** summarizes the directions in which we feel automated library systems are heading and the impact they will have on libraries and librarians. It brings together the concepts outlined in previous chapters, categorizes areas of importance that will shape the future, and includes new trends on the horizon. We, as librarians, must have an unlimited ability to adapt with change and advancement. There is no end to the ability to link information, wherever it may be, and to present it to the patron.

A summary of key points is provided at the end of Chapters 2-8. Each chapter includes suggestions for further reading as appropriate. Appendices are provided which include lists of vendors and checklists which are referred to in relevant chapters. The book concludes with a glossary of key terms and an index which we hope will serve as additional aids to the reader.

Acknowledgments

Our sincere thanks to our students in the Master of Library and Information Science program at San Jose State University. They have been evaluators in the classes that we have co-taught. Without them, we would not have been able to test the effectiveness of our lectures or refine the text in this teaching manual to fit their needs. This book is written for them, the budding librarians, systems analysts, and automation experts of the future.

Appreciation also goes to the automated library systems vendors who provided us with ongoing materials and kept us up-to-date as we wrote and as the field changed dramatically.

Special credit goes to Peggy Gaugy who designed the basic illustrations which enhance the understanding of the manual considerably.

Automated Library Systems: An Overview

This chapter will concisely define:

1. what automated library systems (ALS) are, and

2. the terms and jargon associated with those systems. (Bolded words found in this chapter are alphabetically defined, beginning on the next page.)

A library can be regarded as being made up of functions such as acquisitions, serials control, cataloging, circulation, and the online public (or patron) access catalog (OPAC). When a computer system is used to operate these functions, the term Automated Library System (ALS) is used. An ALS consists of **hardware** (the computer equipment) and **software** (the programs which run on the hardware). There is general agreement on the main software components which make up an ALS, i.e., acquisitions, serials control, cataloging, circulation, and an online public (or patron) access catalog. But each company, that sells an ALS claims that its software has "something" that enhances it and sets it apart from the others. This is why the software is the most important component in an ALS.

Initially, librarians were in the forefront of major research and development efforts involving automated library systems. Today, commercial systems dominate. Automated library systems are sold, for the most part, by companies that try to show a profit at the end of the year. In a word, the automated library system field is a "marketplace," where vendors are in competition with each other. The move from a librarian-dominated industry to a vendor-dominated industry and the significance of that move for librarians is discussed in Chapter 2.

It is extremely important for librarians to be able to converse with the vendors. If a librarian does not understand the terms used by a vendor, then he or she should instantly stop that vendor and ask for an explanation. There are, however, some commonly used terms in the field of automated library systems. A librarian who understands these terms can interact better with vendors. These terms will be discussed in the remainder of this chapter and referred to throughout the text.

Definitions

Data Migration

Data migration is moving the library's data (e.g., MARC records, patron records, vendor records) from one system to another system.

Downtime

Downtime can be defined in a wide or a narrow sense. In a wide sense, it is defined as periods when the system should be working and it is not. In a narrow sense, it refers to the periods when the CPU is down.

Fault Tolerant

Fault tolerant is increasing the dependability of a computer system by building in extra hardware, software, and instructions. As a result, if one part of the system malfunctions, the whole system will not fail. The problem will be localized.

Gateway

A gateway is a piece of software which allows exchange of information between dissimilar systems. The user can move from one system to another without knowing any of the communications specifics to do so.

Hardware

See Hardware Platform.

Hardware Independent

Hardware independent is applied to software which is not dependent on any particular make of computer. *See also* Operating System.

Hardware Platform

The hardware platform is the hardware or computer equipment upon which the software runs. Some automated library systems vendors supply only software. Others supply both software and the hardware platform. If the vendor does not supply the hardware platform, the library will have to purchase the equipment separately. Until recently, vendors had a specific hardware platform that their software ran on. Now the key feature is **portability**, which is sometimes called transportability. The term means the ability to run software on more than one hardware platform. Most vendors list several different makes of computers upon which their software will run. Some vendors claim to be **hardware independent**, which means that their software will run on any hardware platform. This allows a library to have a choice of hardware platforms. It also protects the library if a hardware vendor fails; and it allows for growth if the library's needs outgrow the original hardware vendor's capacity to meet those needs. (The **operating system** in use plays a significant role see **Operating System** on pages 7-8.)

When buying the hardware platform perhaps a key question to consider is: Mainframe, "mini," or micro?[1] A mainframe computer is a large-scale computer normally supplied complete with peripherals, such as terminals, printers, light pens, etc. Examples of mainframe computer manufacturers are Convergent (Unisys), Control Data, Honeywell, IBM, Nixdorf, and Sequoia. Mainframe computers tend to have what is called a "closed architecture." They are compatible only with hardware and software from one or two vendors. A minicomputer or "mini" is a medium-scale computer usually operated with interactive, dumb terminals. Examples of "mini" manufacturers are DEC, Fujitsu, Hewlett-Packard, Honeywell, McDonnell Douglas, MIPS 2000, NCR Tower, Prime, Sequent, Sun, Tandem, Ultimate, and Wyse. Minicomputers normally have an open architecture, which means that they are compatible with hardware and software from many vendors. A microcomputer or "micro" is a small-scale computer (such as the IBM PC, XT, AT, IBM PS/2 series, any of the hundreds of IBM compatibles or clones on the market, Apple Macintosh, etc.). The distinction between minis and micros -- and even between mainframes and minis -- is becoming blurred due to several trends over the last few years which are likely to continue. The three most important trends are:

a. *Miniaturization and increased speed.* Computers are becoming smaller in physical size, but faster in their capacity to process information. This

---

1. See Fig. 1 (configurations) at the end of the chapter.

is because of developments in "chip" technology. The heart of the computer is the CPU or central processing unit (often called a microprocessor). The CPU is a silicon chip, with many electrical conduits and switches etched onto it. The CPU can perform extremely fast electronic operations, which are typically counted in nanoseconds (a nanosecond is a billionth of a second).

    b. *Increased memory capacity.* Computer memory is called RAM, or random access memory. It is measured in kilobytes or megabytes. A byte is equivalent to a character, so a kilobyte is approximately 1,000 characters. A megabyte is approximately 1 million characters. A micro can typically hold in its memory several million characters.

    c. *Increased capacity to store information.* A computer's memory, or RAM (random access memory), is volatile. This means that everything in it is wiped clean when the power supply is withdrawn.[2] Thus, computers need permanent storage devices. The storage capacity of computers, including microcomputers, is doubling every two years. Examples of permanent storage devices are floppy disks, hard disks, Bernoulli boxes, magnetic tapes, and recently erasable optical discs. Erasable optical discs (which use laser technology) can store gigabytes of information (a gigabyte is one thousand megabytes).

    Most libraries have either a mini or a microcomputer as their hardware platform, with only very large libraries needing a mainframe. The deciding factors include:

- the number of terminals which have to be run from the hardware platform;

- the number of simultaneous tasks that need to be carried out;

- the amount of memory or RAM (random access memory) needed;

- the amount of storage space needed;[3]

- the operational requirements of the software and the operating system;

- speed.

---

2. Research and development is currently underway which will change this.

3. Estimating database size is discussed in Chapter 5.

Integration or Integrated

In an integrated system, all of the functions (such as acquisitions, serials control, cataloging, circulation, and the online public access catalog [OPAC]) use a single database made up of a collection of files, such as bibliographic files, item files, authority files, vendor files, fiscal files, patron files, etc.[4] All of the functions are fully interactive with each other and are kept automatically in synchronization. This means that any process that can be initiated from one terminal can have that process transferred throughout the entire system by a single command. Scenario: A librarian is sitting at the cataloging terminal and finds a record for a book he or she wants to order. By inputting a simple command at the cataloging terminal, the record is automatically transferred to the acquisition system, an order is generated, the fund is encumbered, and an on-order record is transferred to the circulation system. This is a one-stop processing with no repetition of keying. And, if a book is checked out at circulation, this is simultaneously reflected in the public access catalog.

All of the files in an integrated system are interconnected. For example, the bibliographic files interact with the fiscal files, both of which will then interact with the book vendor files. An integrated system also interfaces with or talks to all other automated systems in use by the library. This includes cataloging utilities like OCLC or RLIN, jobbers, and any accounting systems used by the parent agency of the library.

Locally Developed System

A locally developed system is in use when a library designs, programs, installs, and tests a system locally, from scratch. The system meets the exact needs of the library, and the library can make whatever changes it wants. This, however, can be an extremely expensive route to follow, and there are some dangers:

- The design will be constantly evolving over the course of the project, which can play havoc with deadlines.

---

4. See Fig. 2 at the end of the chapter.

- Considerable programming expertise is required, despite the availability of object oriented systems and other programming tools of the 1990s.[5]

- Two important points to remember are: (1) the first version of any software usually has a lot of "bugs" or errors -- doublecheck everything; and (2) programming the system is very time consuming. As a rule of thumb, multiply the amount of time estimated to program the software by 2.

Mainframe

See Hardware Platform.

Microcomputer

See Hardware Platform.

Migration

Migration is generally applied to a second system installation. This occurs when a library moves from an already installed and working automated library system to a new automated library system. It is also used when a library moves to a new **hardware platform** in order to make its automated library system function more efficiently.

Minicomputer

See Hardware Platform.

---

5. Object oriented systems: Instead of working with bits and bytes of machine language, programmers can manipulate objects that fit the application they are designing (or example, forms for an order procedure). Once a comprehensive group of objects is created, programmers can use them over and over again to assemble applications.

Modular or Modules

Modules are the individual software components which make up an ALS. They can be added or deleted relatively easily to permit a variety of configurations. This modular design means that a library may purchase basic software modules such as acquisitions, serials control, cataloging, circulation, and online public access catalog (OPAC), or just one or two modules, and add the others at a later date. The modules which are set up will function efficiently and will work in an **integrated** fashion with other modules as they are included. The modular design also offers protection. If one module fails, it will shut itself down without shutting down the other modules or the whole system.

Open System

An open system links hardware and **software modules** from separate vendors into a single integrated system by using an interfacing system. This offers selectivity to libraries as they decide on an automated package. One factor to remember, however, is that the library will have to deal with more than one vendor in an open system. The problems that can arise are: (1) with maintenance contracts (instead of just one maintenance contact, the library will have to deal with several contracts), and (2) with the question of responsibility. If a module crashes or fails, it is difficult to determine which vendor is responsible: a) Is it the vendor from whom the module was purchased, or b) Did the module crash due to a flaw in a module (from a different vendor) with which it was interfaced or connected?

Operating System

The operating system is a piece of software which supervises the running of other software and controls the hardware platform. It provides an environment within which other programs can do useful work. A computer must have an operating system. Until recently, most operating systems have been able to operate on only one type of equipment. There has, however, been a move toward operating systems becoming hardware independent. A library will have true portability if its software and operating system are hardware independent. Among the operating systems found in automated library systems, UNIX (many versions) and PICK are the most hardware independent. Other operating systems commonly found are:

- MS-DOS, PC-DOS, OS/2, MacOS (Macintosh Operating System) -- used on microcomputers;
- VMS -- used on DEC VAX minicomputers;
- ULTRIX -- DEC version of UNIX;
- AIX -- IBM version of UNIX;
- MVS, VM, VSE -- used on IBM mini and mainframe computers;
- MPE, MPE\XL -- used by Hewlett-Packard.

Parallel Processing

Parallel processing is using multiple CPUs (central processing units) to share the operating system, the memory, and the disk storage of the hardware platform. Each CPU operates independently, thus allowing several tasks to run simultaneously. When a library needs to upgrade its hardware platform, it merely adds a new CPU. Parallel processing increases reliability. If one CPU shuts down, the others can temporarily pick up its workload. Parallel processing also increases speed and is a cost-effective way for a library to grow. At least one automated library systems vendor -- CLSI -- has been experimenting with, and using, parallel processing.

Portability

Portability, or transportability, is the capacity to run software on more than one hardware platform. (*See also* Hardware Platform and Operating System.)

Response Time

Response time is the time that elapses between the user pressing the <ENTER> or <RETURN> key (after entering a request) and a response appearing on the screen.

Shared System

A shared system is one in which a group of libraries (perhaps a library consortium or libraries in a geographical area) acquires one automated library system, and all the member libraries use it through a data communications network.

Software

Software is the term applied to the computer programs which run on the computer equipment or hardware platform. In the case of automated library systems, the computer programs are designed to handle acquisitions, serials, cataloging, circulation, and the online public access catalog (OPAC). (*See also* Modular or Modules.)

Transparent

Transparent means "hidden" from the user. Some public access catalogs allow the patron to search for library holdings on compact discs. The searcher transparently (without knowing it) accesses updated records from the microcomputer hard disk in conjunction with the master list on CD-ROM.

Transportability

See Portability.

Turnkey

A turnkey system is an automated library system which has been designed, programmed, and tested by a vendor and then offered for sale to libraries, ready to be installed and operated. In theory, when the system is delivered and installed, all that is required is to plug it in and turn it on. It can be thought of as a packaged or off-the-shelf system. The "package" will typically include the hardware platform, software, installation, training, and maintenance. A library may buy all the software modules or just one or two modules. The turnkey system offers the benefits of integration. The number of modules purchased will determine how fully integrated the turnkey system is. If all five modules are purchased, the library will have a fully integrated turnkey automated library system. If only one or two modules are purchased, the turnkey automated library system will be integrated to a lesser degree as several functions will be missing. These functions can, of course, be added at a later date by the purchase of software modules. Most of the automated library systems sold by vendors are turnkey systems. The advantages to a turnkey system are: (1) speed -- it is often possible to install a turnkey system in less than a year; (2) software is "debugged" or error free; otherwise, it is the responsibility of the vendor to fix the errors; and (3) it is not *necessary* to have a systems specialist on the staff.

A librarian with some automation background or training can run the system. The main disadvantage to a turnkey system is that it is designed for the "average" or "typical" library. There may be undesirable features which a library will have to accept, or there may be features missing which a library wants. A vendor will try to accommodate a client, to a degree, but will not consider major changes to the software just to accommodate a client. In short, a library will have to compromise individual needs to a packaged system. Automated library system vendors have established user groups and will often implement changes that have been suggested by the user group in a future revision of the software. The vendor feels that such changes appeal to many libraries. It is thus cost-effective to incorporate the changes into the product.

The Four Fundamental Components of a Computer System

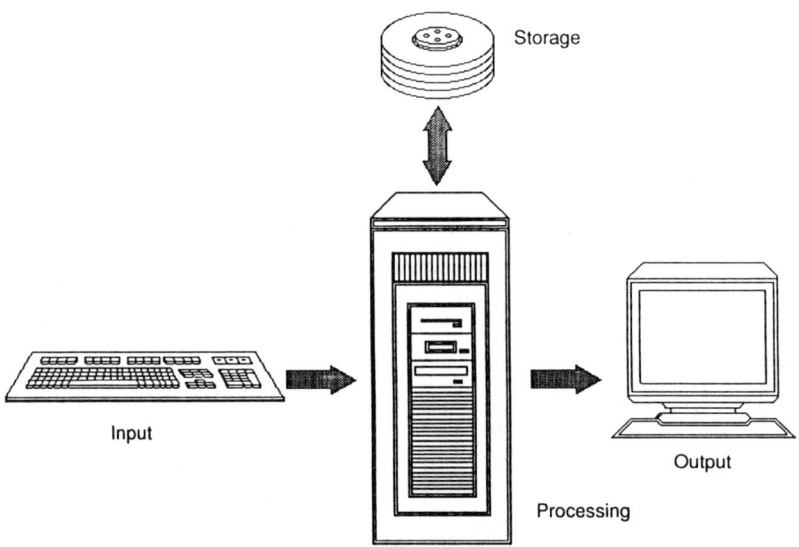

Figure 1a.

Fundamental Components of a Microcomputer System

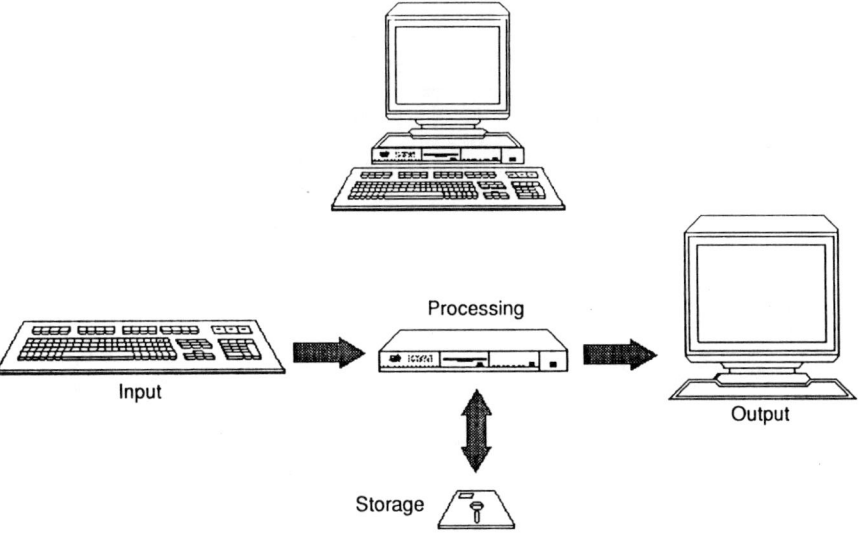

Figure 1b.

A Minicomputer System

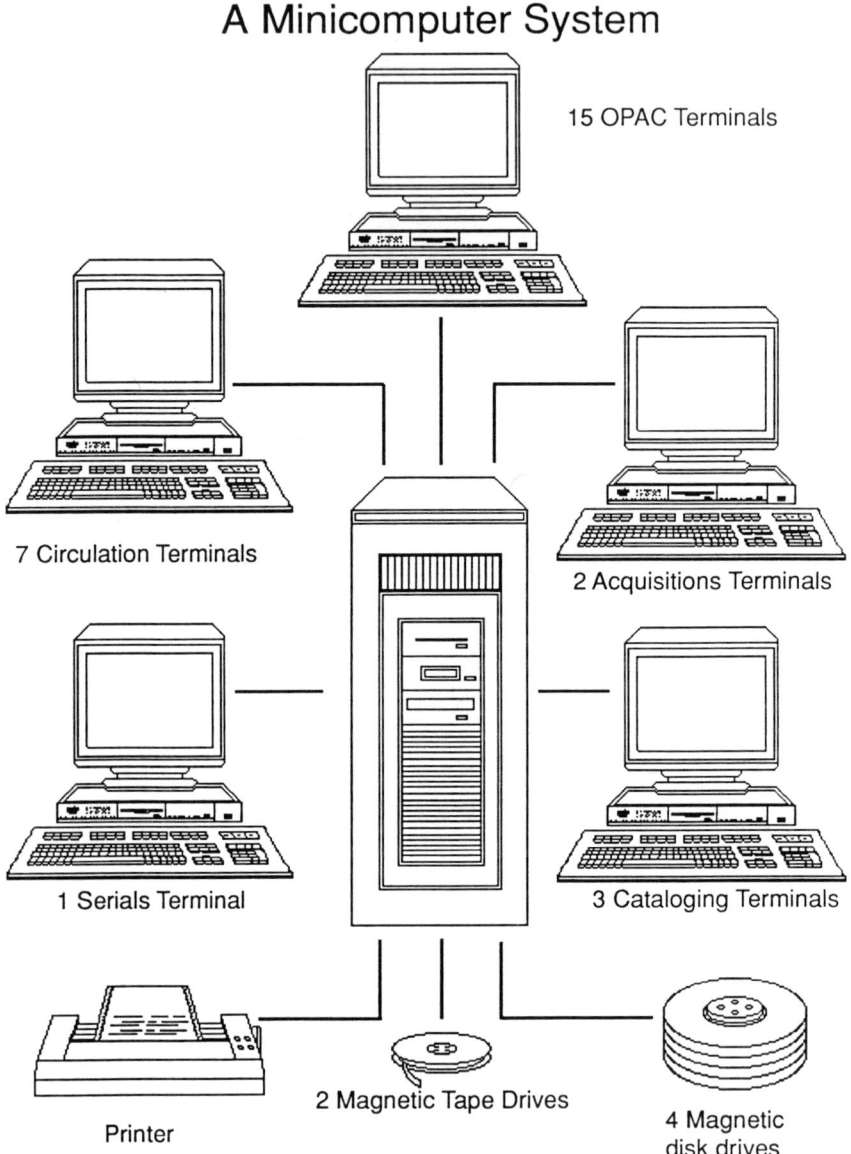

15 OPAC Terminals

7 Circulation Terminals

2 Acquisitions Terminals

1 Serials Terminal

3 Cataloging Terminals

Printer

2 Magnetic Tape Drives

4 Magnetic disk drives

Figure 1c.

A Mainframe Computer System

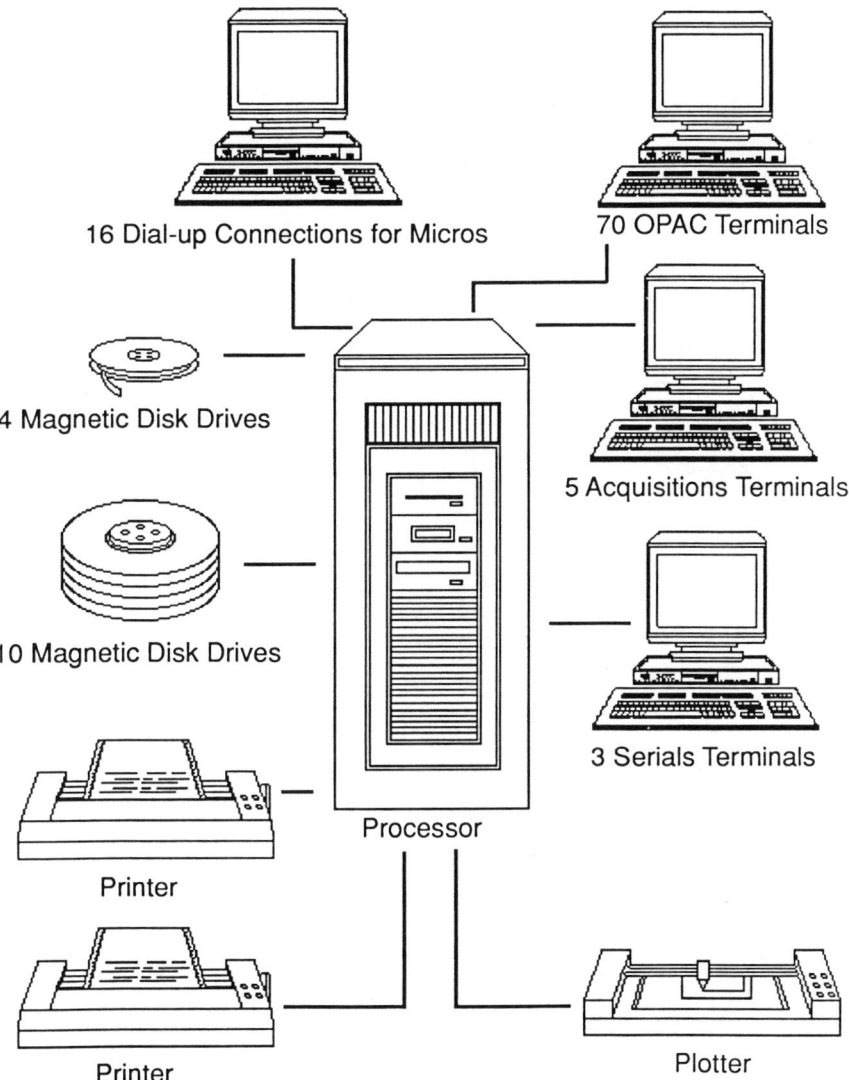

16 Dial-up Connections for Micros

70 OPAC Terminals

4 Magnetic Disk Drives

5 Acquisitions Terminals

10 Magnetic Disk Drives

3 Serials Terminals

Printer

Processor

Printer

Plotter

Figure 1d.

Integration

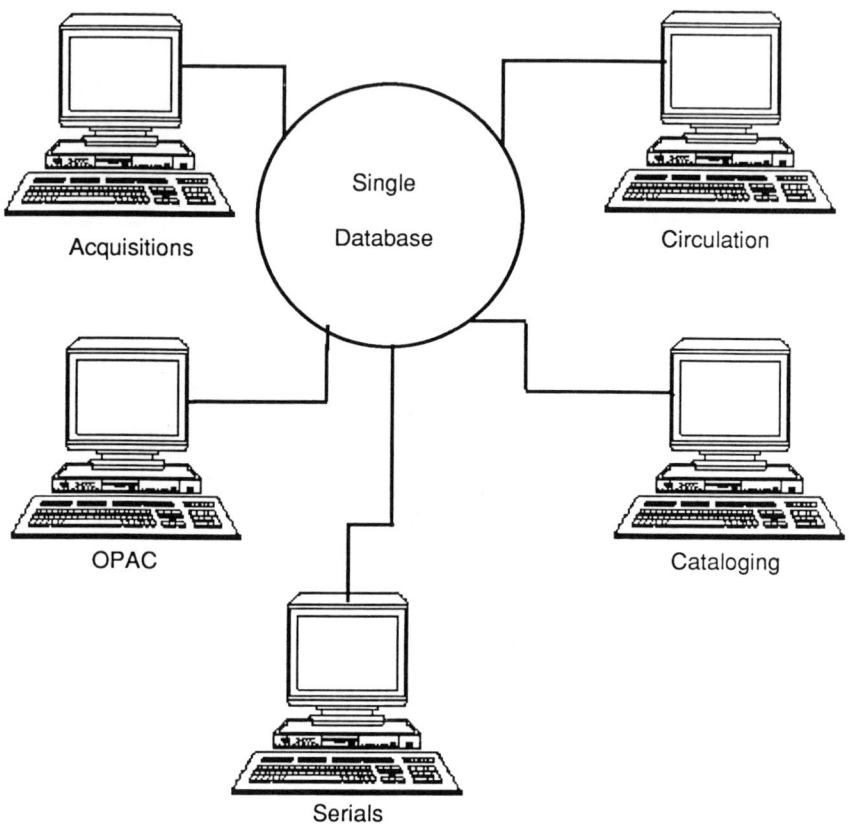

The **single database** is typically made up of bibliographic files, item files, authority files, patron files, vendor files, fiscal files, etc.

Figure 2.

Sources for Further Reading

Boss, Richard W., and Mary H. Casey. 1991. Operating Systems for Automated Library Systems. *Library Technology Reports*, 27, 2(March-April): 121-210.

Key Players/Leaders in the Field: Past and Present

Until the 1970s, librarians were in the forefront of major research and development efforts involving automated library systems. Since the 1970s, commercial solutions have dominated the field. This chapter will briefly outline historical trends, discuss the importance of the marketplace, highlight the primary vendors, and list sources for further reading.

Historical Trends

The theoretical concept of a machine which (1) could store books and articles and (2) permit a user multiple access points to the stored information originated with Vannevar Bush. Bush directed the U.S. Office of Scientific Research and Development during World War II. He predicted that science would develop a new approach to organizing information. Writing in the *Atlantic Monthly* in July 1945, he described a "memex" (or memory extender) which he saw as being a mechanized library. A memex, he wrote,

> is a device in which are stored books, records, communications and which is mechanized so that it may be consulted with exceeding speed and flexibility. On the top are translucent screens. There is a keyboard and a set of buttons and levers (Bush 1945, 102).

In 1945, the technology did not exist which could make the memex a reality. It still does not exist to make all phases of the memex a reality. But, in the 20 years following the publication of Bush's article, great advances were made. In 1946, John Mauchly and J. Presper Eckert, working at the University of Pennsylvania, finished ENIAC I (Electronic Numerical Integrator and Calculator). The machine was designed to compute the trajectory of artillery shells during World War II, but the war ended before the system could be put to use for this purpose. ENIAC was instead used for running feasibility studies for the development of the hydrogen bomb. It weighed 30 thousand tons, was two stories high, and contained 18,000 vacuum tubes.

In the same year, John Von Neuman built the logical (as opposed to the physical) framework for a programmable machine. He devised a central processor, a memory, and input and output devices, all of which were able to store sets of instructions and operate in a step-by-step manner. Also in 1946, the EDVAC computer was built at the University of Manchester in England. EDVAC had the added advantage of being able to store two programs in one computer and switch between the different sets of instructions.

In 1947, a major breakthrough in technology occurred. Bell Labs invented the transistor which allowed large amounts of information to be handled by small, inexpensive devices that eventually replaced vacuum tubes. This led to a decrease in the size of a computer, with a corresponding increase in speed and capacity--a trend that has continued up to this day.

In 1951, UNIVAC I (Universal Automatic Computer) became the first commercial computer on the market using transistors. It could handle a complete set of alphanumeric instructions (letters and numbers) and worked from 1951 until 1963 in the U.S. Bureau of the Census.

Then in 1960, a man named J.C.R. Licklider formulated a concept which became known as "interactive computing" and published it in the paper "Man-Computer Symbiosis" (Licklider 1960). Interactive computing implies a continuous dialog between the user and the system, as opposed to batch processing where data is accumulated over a period of time and then submitted to the computer for processing.

In 1961, the integrated circuit (IC) was born. Robert Noyce of Intel and Jack Kirby of Texas Instruments, working independently, successfully integrated all the components of an electronic circuit onto a single flake of silicon. That meant that thousands of transistors could be replaced by a single silicon chip. At the same time, disk and tape storage devices were developed which gave computers the speed and storage needed for online interactive processing and telecommunications. By the end of the 1970s, VLSI (very large scale integration) was firmly in place, i.e., the ability to place many thousands of circuits onto a single small chip.

Of equal importance was the development of programming languages and software. Although the earliest programming languages were primarily concerned with handling numbers, librarians needed programming languages that could handle characters and text. Several developments took place. In 1957, COMIT was developed at MIT. It could do linguistic computations and handle natural language. COMIT was the first programming language which provided an effective technique for searching for a particular string of information. This was followed by SNOBOL in 1963 which was developed by Bell Labs and could also manipulate strings (or groups of characters). Other text-based programming languages followed, i.e., COBOL (1959), BASIC (1964), PL/1 (1965), PASCAL (1968), C (1978), and ultimately fourth generation programming languages (4GL). These languages had their own tools, such as built-in forms and a database manager. They allowed users to build applications without resorting to a computer language. Technology had advanced to the point where it was possible to build library applications, using bibliographic data. Librarians began to consider seriously what the new technology could do for them--and what problems they had to overcome.

The first major concern which librarians had to address was that they wanted the computer to read and interpret the data in the catalog record. A library's holdings had thus to be put into the computer as a machine-readable file.[1] There were two problems: (1) How could the computer distinguish the parts of the record (the description, the main entry, the subject headings, the call number?); and (2) How would the computer determine where one field ended and another began when the amount of information in a particular field often varied from one item to the next? (One book might require a lot of physical description, whereas a second one might need very little.)

The librarians at Florida Atlantic University (Boca Raton) under Edward Heiliger were among the first to come up with a solution (Heiliger 1964). They suggested the use of field tags, which they called "knots," to identify types of variable length information on a machine-readable record. They developed a numerical coding scheme which would always remain constant. For example, the numerical value 10 on the computer input would always be followed by a main entry, 23 by a title, 2 by the edition statement, and so on. The same group of librarians also had the vision of integrating acquisitions, cataloging, serials control, and circulation into one total library system. The plans drawn up at Florida Atlantic University Library were not carried out in part because of poor communication between the librarians and the computer staff and in part because the time and cost required to accomplish everything were grossly underestimated (Axford 1972). However, their ideas lived on.

In the early 1960s, the Library of Congress (LC) decided to convert LC catalog cards to machine-readable form and realized that a new record format

---

1. In computer terminology, a *file* may be defined as a collection of related and usually similarly constructed records that are treated as a unit, i.e., a library catalog. A *record* is the complete set of information relating to a particular item in the file. Each record consists of a number of constituent elements referred to as *fields*.

was needed. Between 1966 and 1968, LC, in cooperation with 20 other libraries, launched a project to test the feasibility of a machine-readable cataloging system (MARC I). This was followed by similar experiments in Great Britain. USMARC became fully operational in 1968 (MARC II). MARC II is simply a way of tagging bibliographic records by using 3-digit numbers to identify fields. Tag 020 always indicates "ISBN," tag 100 always indicates "author," tag 245 always indicates "title," tag 260 always indicates "publication date," and so on. In MARC II, full standard bibliographic descriptions based on AACR2[2] are possible, and each record is capable of containing a vast number of elements: price of items, Library of Congress subject headings, etc. All types of library materials, such as monographs, serials, music, software, etc., can be handled.

In 1974, the MARC II format became the basis of a standard called Z39.2. This standard was revised in 1979 and again in 1985 by NISO (National Information Standards Organization). This standard laid down the way a MARC record had to be structured. It stated that a record had to have four basic parts: leader, record directory, variable control fields, and variable data fields. The leader contains information about the length, type, and bibliographic level of the record. (i.e., Is it a printed book, manuscript, microform, self-contained monograph, part of a series, etc.?) The record directory can be likened to the table of contents of a book. It gives the location of specific variable fields. Each variable length field ends with a field terminator character; and the last field ends with a field terminator character followed by a record terminator character. The development and acceptance of MARC II and Z39.2 meant not only that a computer could read and interpret the data in the catalog record, but also that it was possible to transfer or communicate bibliographic information in machine-readable form between libraries.

A second major concern which librarians addressed was how to benefit from the computer's ability to give multiple access to material stored in it. The potential of the computer encouraged librarians to develop various new indexing

---

2. AACR2 stands for Anglo American Cataloguing Rules (2nd ed., 1978; revised 1988). This code lays down rules which cover main entry, added entries, the bibliographic description of an item, and the form these should take. It answers questions such as:
1. How should the author's name be written?
2. Should there be an entry for more than one author or more than one title?
3. Should there be a series card?
4. How should the statement of responsibility, edition, material-specific details, publication information, and physical description be entered?

techniques. In 1961, H.P. Luhn, using a computer, produced a "keyword in context" or KWIC index to the titles of articles appearing in *Chemical Abstracts*. He selected key words from the titles of documents and then arranged the titles in an alphabetical sequence, by word:

Library AUTOMATION
BOOK Indexing
A Manual of CATALOGING Practice

A KWOC or "Keyword Out of Context" index listed key words separately in a lefthand column with the corresponding titles appearing to the right.

AUTOMATION	Library Automation
BOOK	Book Indexing
CATALOGING	A Manual of Cataloging Practice
COMPUTERS	The Use of Computers in Libraries
INDEXING	Book Indexing
INDEXING	Library Automation
LIBRARIES	Use of Computers in Libraries
LIBRARY	The Library and the Machine
MACHINE	The Library and the Machine

Keyword indexing is not new. It existed in the 19th century when it was referred to as "catchword" indexing. It was, however, tremendously suitable for the computer as it required a minimum of intellectual effort. It was inexpensive; there was no vocabulary lag; and it presented multiple access points. On the other hand, there was no vocabulary control over synonyms, word forms, or homographs and no opportunity for establishing cross-references. Also, KWIC and KWOC indexing only operate satisfactorily when the title of a document is expressive of its subject content. They may even separate related topics. The three items above: *Library Automation, The Use of Computers in Libraries*, and *The Library and the Machine* illustrate this point.

Librarians overcame these problems by:

(1) creating computerized keyword indexes which enriched KWOC indexes by allowing additional keywords.

(2) collocating related works under one heading.

(3) including authors' names as index entries.

(4) facilitating speedy coordination between concepts. This type of indexing is called "double KWIC." The context of titles containing the same keyword are rotated to form an ordered list of subordinate entries under the main term. An asterisk was often used to replace the main term in each context.

> COMPUTER
> CATALOGING by *
> FILING. Rules for *
> LIBRARY Management. The * in
> RULES for * Filing

(5) preserving the context of a subject statement at all entry points. Two well known systems of this type are PRECIS and NEPHIS. PRECIS stands for PREserved Context Index System and was developed by Derek Austin at the British National Bibliography in London. NEPHIS stands for NEsted PHrase Index System and was developed in Canada at the University of Western Ontario. Librarians also realized that it would be possible to put controlled language index terms and authority files on the computer.

Many libraries built on the developments discussed above and designed automated library systems, notably Illinois State Library in Springfield [Circulation] (Hamilton 1968); E. Illinois University in Charleston [Circulation] (Rao and Szerenyi 1971); Midwestern University in Wichita Falls, Texas [Circulation] (Boyer and Frost 1970); Oregon State University Library in Corvallis [Acquisitions] (Auld and Baker 1972); Washington State University Library in Pullman [Acquisitions]; the Redstone Scientific Information Center in Alabama [Acquisitions, Serials, Cataloging, and Circulation] (Bently and Cooney 1974); the Universite Laval Library in Quebec [Serials]; Northwestern University Library in Evanston, Illinois [from which NOTIS--Northwestern Online Total Integrated System--was to come]; UCLA Biomedical Library [which did some advanced work on serials automation] (Fayollat 1972); and MIT [which developed INTREX, also called Project MAC and TIP, one of the first online catalogs].[3]

---

3. See Chapter 6.

The University of Chicago Library was one of the earliest innovative users of MARC, utilizing the MARC record to help with collection development. Each MARC tape obtained from LC was matched against subject profiles defined by the LC class number. The University of Chicago Library also searched on the MARC field 020 (ISBN). In this way, the library could generate lists of items published by each publisher they had blanket order arrangements with (Payne et al. 1977).

Another innovative library was Stanford University Library which developed BALLOTS (Bibliographical Automation of Large Library Operations) for technical services. BALLOTS was to become the foundation for RLIN (the Research Libraries Information Network) run by RLG (the Research Libraries Group formed in 1974 by Columbia University, Harvard, Yale, and the New York Public Library for cooperative collection development). BALLOTS was deliberately designed to integrate more closely the technical processing functions of the library. It was made up of four main files: (1) the most recent 6-12 months of MARC records from LC; (2) an in-process file which contained information on items anywhere in the processing stage; (3) a catalog data file containing an online record for each item fully processed; and (4) a reference file which contained "See" and "See also" references. BALLOTS had validation capabilities for certain types of information such as account codes. It could handle the ordering of a "multipart set" by exploding the record into the required number of distinct records. It also had a wide search retrieval capability and could search on truncated words, keywords, LC subject headings, etc. BALLOTS was so successful that the acquisitions and cataloging departments were consolidated and several staff positions were reduced (Stanford University BALLOTS System 1975).

Ohio State University Library installed a creative online circulation system in the early 1970s. Searching was possible by call number, title key, and a combination author/title key. A user could see which library or libraries owned a copy of the item and whether the item was charged out. Search terminals were available at most of the branch libraries on the campus; users could charge out books from remote locations (Atkinson 1972).

Academic librarians in Ohio, under Frederick G. Kilgour, were responsible for starting a cooperative venture in cataloging which went online in 1971. They realized that, apart from minor local variations, the cataloging data for a given item are essentially similar from library to library. In 1972, non-academic libraries in Ohio were allowed to join the system; in 1973, libraries outside the state joined; and in 1981, the Ohio College Library Center (OCLC) became the Online Computer Library Center (OCLC), offering cataloging and other services to libraries.

In the 1970s, a change began to occur in the development of automated library systems. Control gradually moved away from large university and college libraries (generally funded by "soft" money or by grants from sources such as the Department of Education, NASA, or the National Science Foundation [NSF]) to commercial vendors. In 1971, a commercial company called Computer Library Systems, Inc., offered an automated acquisitions system for sale which was installed in the Cleveland Public Library in December 1971 (Palmer 1973). In 1973, the same company offered an automated circulation system, which it called LIBS100. Gradually, other companies entered the marketplace. The 1980s was a period of growth for vendors selling automated library systems; by the 1990s, close to 50 companies were offering automated library systems for sale to libraries.

What prompted the change? By the 1970s, computer costs had dropped considerably. Comparatively low-cost computers were available which were able to handle several tasks simultaneously. Rapid access storage devices were also available. The improvements in technology continued with computers becoming smaller, faster, capable of remembering and storing more and more information, and costing less and less money. The development of the MARC II format meant that it was possible (1) to convert existing manual records into machine-readable form and (2) to share these records among libraries. Librarians were becoming aware that the computer could take the drudgery out of labor-intensive tasks such as circulation and the adding, deleting, and changing of records in the catalog. This was further brought home with the introduction of AACR2 in 1978, which meant modifying the content of the records and refiling the card catalog.

The development of automated library system software, however, was a complex business, and only a few libraries had had the expertise or the money to become heavily involved in its design. Librarians nevertheless became interested in buying software which had already been programmed and which could run on computers that had suddenly become affordable. The rapidly dropping prices of equipment, the remarkable increase in capabilities, the benefits of having data in machine-readable form, and the cooperation made possible by the use of the computer made the purchase of an automated library system seem attractive to many libraries. It was a cost effective alternative to in-house development. The same factors made commercial development of automated library system software economically viable in the 1970s. With a mass market system, up-front development costs could be distributed among many customers.

Importance of the Marketplace

In the 1990s, automated library systems are sold almost exclusively by commercial vendors. James Rush feels that this is a fact with which many librarians have not yet come to terms (Rush 1988). He argues that librarians' approaches to the automated system marketplace are characterized by:

1.   an inability to accept standardization (despite MARC II and AACR2) and a demand for tailor-made systems which will perpetuate local practices. This is why automated library system software has to be written with options for the librarian to customize the product via parameters or tables.

2.   inertia. Rush argues that librarians are poor decision-makers. The period of time between initial vendor contact and the consummation of a contract is very protracted, often 2-3 years. As a result, marketing and sales costs are very high.

3.   technological innocence. Librarians are unable to deal with and assess vendor products adequately.

4.   weak management from a business perspective. Rush argues that libraries usually do not have well constructed long-range plans and generally do not have adequate conceptions of the economics of automation. As a result, he says, libraries tend to be cheap, rather than economical.

So what is the answer? Librarians must understand that companies selling automated library systems are in the business of selling a product and of making money. Professional librarians are still involved with the design and development of automated library systems, but as employees of commercial vendors (working primarily in sales, training, and writing documentation). These librarians are aware, too, that the company must show a profit--or at least break even--in order for their salaries to be paid.

It is not necessary for librarians to take a combative stance, but librarians should approach the buying of an automated library system as assertive customers. They need to do their homework, ask questions, and insist on having all features of the product explained. Vendors are in a hurry, especially if the end of the financial quarter is approaching; they are also project-oriented, not process-oriented. Librarians must focus on the goal of the library's automation process, namely: How will the proposed technological change benefit patrons and staff and improve service?

All of this has made the librarians' life more difficult and forced them to look outside the profession for help. Librarians have had to acquire bits of other professions in order to be good, assertive consumers of automated library systems. They have had to learn computing, accountancy, financial planning, budgeting, and contract law. Above all, they have had to understand market forces.

The cost of any automated library system will be what the market can bear--and the market is the library. Librarians also need to understand that the market for automated library systems, while growing, is still small. Vendors are in a high-risk business.[4] Librarians need to check vendor viability by reviewing Dun and Bradstreet summaries of SEC (Securities and Exchange Commission) filings for publicly owned companies. This will supply information on debt structure and product line, on depreciation, background, and holdings, and on earnings and interim audits. For private companies, certified audited financial and bonding requirements should be invoked. Rush lists three measures of success which can be applied to automated library systems vendors:

1. profitability (measured as a percentage or as an absolute monetary value);

2. market share (measured as a percentage of total installed base, as a percentage of the total potential market, as a percentage of the total real market, or as a percentage of the total value of systems sold);

3. marketplace perception of the product.

He also recommends that smart librarians check the working capital, inventory, and debt of the vendor with which they are hoping to deal (Rush 1988).

---

4. Only three of the early vendors have survived into the nineties: Computer Library Systems, Inc. (now known as CLSI; previously known as CL Systems); GEAC; and Gaylord Brothers. Carlyle, GEAC, and CLSI all went into Chapter 11, bankruptcy reorganization, but managed to survive and are still in business today.

Primary Vendors

The following will briefly highlight the "key players" in the field of automated library systems as of 1992. All vendors offer the basic modules of cataloging, circulation, acquisitions, serials, and online public access catalogs. Many vendors offer other modules, such as media booking, reserve bookroom, community information, etc. Vendors which deal *only* with microcomputer-based systems or CD-ROM-based systems are not included. They will be discussed in Chapters 7 and 8.

Ameritech Information Systems
4950 Blazer Memorial Parkway
Dublin, OH 43017
(614) 793-5511

Ameritech Information Systems was formed in 1989 and is a subsidiary of Ameritech Corporation, a Chicago-based parent of the Bell Company. The company has acquired (1) the Alice-B software, which was developed by the Tacoma (WA) Public Library; (2) OCLC's LS/2000 Automated Library System; (3) NOTIS, and (4) Dynix. (*See also* NOTIS Systems, Inc., and Dynix) Ameritech also offers microcomputer-based acquisitions and serials control systems (ACQ350 and SC350) which it acquired from OCLC.

CARL Systems, Inc.
3801 E. Florida Ave.
Bldg. D, Suite 300
Denver, CO 80210
(303) 758-3030

The company was formed from the Colorado Alliance of Research Libraries automation development efforts and was previously known as Eyring. The system runs on Tandem computers, using the Guardian operating system. In 1991, CARL took over maintenance and support responsibilities for the UTLAS T/Series 50 systems.

Carlyle Systems, Inc.
2000 Alameda de Las Pulgas
San Mateo, CA 94403
(415) 345-2500

The company came into existence in 1981 and offered an online public access catalog in 1983/84. Carlyle initially used propriety hardware but its modules now run under UNIX on a variety of hardware platforms. The system is called Voyager.

CLSI
320 Nevada Street
Newtonville, MA 02165
(800) 365-0085
(617) 965-6310

The company was founded in 1971 and is based in Newton ville, Massachusetts. It is now a subsidiary of the IHS (Information Handling Services) Group. The system is called LIBS 100plus. CLSI originally used its own (proprietary) operating system and Digital PDP11 minicomputers. LIBS 100plus now runs under UNIX and will function on DEC mainframe computers, Sequent[5] and Altos minicomputers, Altos, and Wyse microcomputers and Wyse terminals. On January 12, 1991, CLSI signed an agreement with Innovative Interfaces whereby CLSI now offers the Innovacq serials control and acquisitions systems. CLSI entered Europe in 1981 and has offices in London, Paris, and Amsterdam and has distributors in Australia and Finland.

Comstow Information Services
249 Ayer Road
P.O. Box 277
Harvard, MA 01451-0277
(508) 772-2001

The system is called BiblioTech and came on the market in 1981. It runs on DEC VAX minicomputers, using the VMS operating system. A version of the software, which runs under the UNIX operating system, has recently been developed. Along with the basic modules, there is a thesaurus-control module. The company focuses mainly on corporate and government libraries.

---

5. Sequent has been a pioneer in the use of parallel processing. See definitions in Chapter 1.

Data Research Associates (DRA)
1276 North Warson Road
P.O. Box 8495
St. Louis, MO 63132-1806
(800) 325-0888

The company was founded in 1976 and is based in St. Louis, Missouri. The system is called ATLAS (A Total Library Automation System). It runs on DEC-VAX computers, using the VMS operating system. DRA is very committed to the DEC platform and plans to use the next generation of DEC machines built around the "alpha" chip. The system will also run on HP and IBM computers.

Data Trek Inc.
5838 Edison Place
Carlsbad, CA 92008
(800) 876-5484
(619) 431-8400

The company was founded in 1981 and is based in Carlsbad, California. The original system was called CARD DATALOG and is still available as the Manager Series. The company also markets the Professional Series ULS (ULTIMATE LIBRARY SYSTEM). The Data Trek systems run on VAX minicomputers, using the VMS operating system, on IBM and IBM compatible microcomputers, using DOS, and on Macintosh computers. The company provides English, French, and Spanish versions of the ULS for its international customers.

DATALIB
Centel Federal Services Corporation
11400 Commerce Park Drive
Reston, VA 22091
(800) 843-4850 Ext. 7005

The company is based in Reston, Virginia. It came into exis tence in 1984. The software runs on DEC VAX computers, using the VMS operating system. It will also run under the UNIX operating system.

Dynix
151 East 1700 South
Provo, UT 84601
(800) 288-8020
(801) 375-2770

        The company was founded in 1983 and is based in Provo,
Utah. It has offices in the United Kingdom, Ireland, Canada, Australia,
and New Zealand. In February 1992, Dynix was acquired by the
Ameritech Corporation. The Dynix system uses the PICK operating
system and runs on a variety of hardware platforms, including the
Ultimate range of minicomputers,[6] Tandem MIPS, IBM, Hewlett-
Packard, Prime, Honeywell, McDonnell Douglas, and Wyse. Dynix is
reaching out to smaller libraries and especially to schools with its
SCHOLAR system and to corporate libraries with MARQUIS.

Gaylord Information Systems
P.O. Box 4901
Syracuse, NY 13221-4901
(800) 962-9580
(315) 457-5070

        The company was founded in 1975 and is based in Syracuse,
New York. It has several circulation-only products. In 1989, it
introduced GALAXY. The system runs on DEC minicomputers and
IBM microcomputers, using the VMS and DOS operating systems.

In addition, Gaylord has linked itself with Campus America to offer the
POISE Library Information System. POISE LIS is an integrated library
system which is based on Galaxy software. It accesses the POISE
Administrative System which includes applications such as admissions,
financial aid, registration/academic history, tele-registration, degree
audit/academic advisement, student billing, receivables, fiscal
management, fixed assets, payroll, and development/alumni.

---

6. Ultimate has minority shares in Dynix.

GEAC
Suite 300, 11 Allstate Parkway
Markham, Ontario, Canada L3R 1B3
(416) 475-0525

GEAC is a Canadian company founded in 1973 and based in Markham, Ontario. The original system was developed in conjunction with the Universities of Guelph and Waterloo in Canada. GEAC has offices in the United Kingdom, Ireland, Holland, France, Germany, Sweden, Australia, and the United States. The company offers the GEAC Library Information System which runs on its own mainframe computers (the GEAC 8000, 9000, and 29302), using its own proprietary operating system.

In 1988, GEAC acquired Advanced Libraries and Information, Inc. of Hawaii. After making some changes to the software, GEAC introduced ADVANCE which runs on a variety of hardware platforms, including CITOH, DEC, Fujitsu, Prime, Honeywell, and Sequoia and uses the PICK operating system.

ILS (International Library Systems)
320-2600 Granville Street
Vancouver, BC Canada V6H 3V3
(604) 734-8882

The company was formed in 1989 by the former employees of the Sydney Development Corporation's library automation division and is incorporated under the Canada Business Corporation Act. ILS supports the Sydney Library System (in existence since 1981) and is in the process of revising all of the software modules. It runs on IBM PCs and DEC VAX minicomputers.

IME Systems, Inc.
990 Washington Street
Dedham, MA 02026
(617) 320-0303

IME was formed in 1984. The software is called Information Navigator and runs on all sizes of computers under both UNIX and MS-DOS operating systems.

Information Dimensions, Inc.
5080 Tuttle Crossing Blvd.
Dublin, OH 43017-1396
(800) 328-2648
(614) 761-7446

The company was founded in 1983. It is a subsidiary of Battelle and is based in Dublin, Ohio. The system is called BASIS Plus and is a document management and retrieval system. The library management part was originally called Techlib STACS which has been updated to Techlib PLUS. It runs on IBM and Control Data mainframes and Wang VS and DEC VAX minicomputers or super-micros. The operating systems which can be used are MVS, Wang VS, VMS, VM, ULTRIX, CD NOS/VE, VM-IBM/CMS and recently, UNIX.

Inlex
One Lower Ragsdale Dr.
Bldg. #1, Ste. 100
P.O. Box 1349
Monterey, CA 93940
(800) 553-1202
(408) 646-8600

The company was founded in 1983 and is based in Monterey, California. The system is called Inlex 3000. Inlex runs on Hewlett-Packard minicomputers, using the HP MPE or MPE/XL operating systems. INLEX recently acquired marketing and sales rights to The Assistant from Library Automation Products, for all of the world except Asia. The Assistant is an automated library system for smaller libraries, running on IBM PC and compatible machines.

Innovative Interfaces
2344 Sixth Street
Berkeley, CA 94710
(800) 444-2344
(510) 644-3600

The company was founded in 1979 and is based in Berkeley, California. It developed a so-called "black box" in 1978 which enabled

OCLC and CLSI to work together. Innovacq was introduced in 1981, offering Acquisitions, followed by Serials Control in 1983. Innopac was introduced in 1985 offering Circulation, Cataloging, Online Public Access Catalog, and direct connect to Innovacq for Acquisitions and Serials Control. It runs on a variety of hardware platforms, including DEC and UNISYS/Convergent computers. The operating system is UNIX. On January 12, 1991, Innovative Interfaces signed an agreement with CLSI whereby CLSI now offers the Innovacq Acquisitions and Serials Control systems.

IBM (International Business Machines)
Academic Information Systems/Library Marketing
472 Wheeler Farms Road, Mail Stop 33
Milford, CT 06460
(203) 783-7350

The system is called DOBIS/LIBIS and appeared on the market in 1978. It runs only on IBM mainframe and minicomputers, using MVS and VSE operating systems. The system was developed in conjunction with the Universities of Dortmund and Leuven in Holland.

Multicore Library Services
4924 Reed Road, Bldg. A
Columbus, OH 43220
(800) 753-0053

The company was founded in 1985 and is owned by the Sobeco Group in Montreal, Canada. The software, called MultiLIS, was derived from the Universite de Montreal library system. It runs on DEC VAX, NCR Tower, and MIPS minicomputers, using the VMS and UNIX operating systems. MicroLIS is planned for use on microcomputers.

NOTIS Systems, Inc.
1007 Church Street, 2nd Floor
Evanston, IL 60201-3622
(708) 866-0150

The NOTIS system comes out of Northwestern University. The company became for-profit in 1987 and is based in Evanston, Illinois.

The product is called Library Management System. In the summer of 1990, NOTIS released KeyNOTIS, primarily for smaller libraries. The advantage of KeyNOTIS is that it combines all of the options of the Library Management System with a programmer-less environment. KeyNOTIS can be operated completely within the library by library personnel. It runs only on IBM mainframe computers. The Library Management System runs on IBM mainframes and Nixdorf, Magnuson, and Motorola computers. In 1991, NOTIS was acquired by Ameritech.

PALS
UNISYS Corporation
One Unisys Place 4B61
Detroit, MI 48202
(313) 972-7441

The company was founded in 1984. PALS is based on the Mankato State University (MN) library system. The software works with the UNISYS 1100/2200 mainframe computers, using the OS1100 operating system.

SIRSI Corporation
110 Walker Avenue
Huntsville, AL 35801
(205) 536-5884

The system is called UNICORN. It runs on mainframe, minicomputers, and microcomputers, using the UNIX operating system.

VTLS, Inc.
1800 Kraft Drive
Blacksburg, VA 24060
(703) 953-3605

VTLS is based on the Virginia Tech Library System. The software runs on Hewlett-Packard and IBM computers, using the MPE/MPE-XL and VM operating systems. Micro-VTLS is also available, running on IBM PC's, using MS-DOS.

Suggested Reading

As we have stated, the automated library systems market is a high-risk one. Companies come and companies go. The following sources should be consulted on a regular basis in order to keep in touch with the key players.

Information Technology and Libraries, 1982-
LITA
American Library Association
50 E. Huron Street
Chicago, IL 60611-2795

Library Hi Tech, 1983-
Pierian Press
Box 1808
Ann Arbor MI 48106

Library Journal, 1876-
Cahners Publishing Company (NY)
Bowker Magazine Group
249 W. 17th Street
New York, NY 10011

The April 1st issue each year includes an analysis of the automated library systems marketplace.

Library Systems Newsletter, 1981-
American Library Association
50 E. Huron Street
Chicago, IL 60611-2795

Library Technology Reports, 1965-
American Library Association
50 E. Huron Street
Chicago, IL 60611-2795

Summary

This chapter has outlined the developments in computer technology which have made possible the automated library systems of today. It has traced the development of the computer from its early beginnings, using vacuum tubes -- through transistors -- to the integrated circuit. The integrated circuit made possible tremendous increases in the processing speed of the computer and at the same time, reduced its physical size and cost. A concurrent development was the increasing sophistication of computer programming languages. Of special significance for librarians was the development of string manipulation languages, which could handle groups of characters.

With the advent of affordable computer technology, librarians began to address their own specific problems -- in particular, how the computer could read and interpret the data in the catalog record. The answer was MARC II, developed by Library of Congress. MARC II has become the standard format for handling records in machine-readable form. Librarians also developed various indexing techniques so that the library could benefit from the computer's ability to give multiple access to material stored in it.

Early automated library systems developed in libraries are discussed; 1971 is highlighted as the year in which a commercial company, Computer Library Systems, Inc., installed a commercially developed automated library acquisitions system in the Cleveland Public Library. This began the gradual move towards a vendor-dominated industry. Currently, the automated library systems marketplace is totally vendor-dominated. Librarians have had to become assertive consumers and keep in touch with market forces. They have had to learn lots of new skills, including computing, accountancy, financial planning, and negotiating.

The chapter lists the primary automated library systems vendors as of 1992. Sources are listed which should be consulted on a regular basis in order to keep in touch with the key players in the field.

References

Atkinson, Hugh C. 1972. The Ohio State On-line Circulation System. In *Proceedings of the 1972 Clinic on Library Applications of Data Processing*, 23. Urbana, IL: University of Illinois Graduate School of Library Science.

Auld, Larry, and Robert Baker. 1972. Lolita: An On-line Book Order and Fund Accounting System. In *Proceedings of the 1972 Clinic on Library Applications of Data Processing*, 29-53. Urbana, IL: University of Illinois Graduate School of Library Science.

Axford, H. William. 1972. Florida Atlantic University. In *Encyclopedia of Library and Information Science*, 547. New York: Marcel Dekker.

Bently, Jane F., and Leo J. Cooney. Summer, 1974. Automation at the Redstone Scientific Information Center -- An Integrated System. *Library Resources and Technical Services* 18(3): 259-267.

Boyer, Calvin J., and Jack Frost. 1970. Online Circulation Control -- Midwestern University Library's System Using an IBM 1401 Computer in a Time Sharing Mode. In *Proceedings of the 1969 Clinic on Library Applications of Data Processing*, 135. Urbana, IL: University of Illinois Graduate School of Library Science.

Bush, Vannevar. July, 1945. As We May Think. *Atlantic Monthly* 176(1): 101-108.

Fayollat, James. Sept.-Oct., 1972. On-line Serials Control System in a Large Biomedical Library. Pt. 1 Description of the System. *Journal of the American Society for Information Science* 23(5): 318-322.

_____. Nov.-Dec., 1972. On-line Serials Control System in a Large Biomedical Library. Pt. 2 Evaluation of Retrieval Features. *Journal of the American Society for Information Science* 23(6): 353-358.

_____. March-April, 1973. On-line Serials Control System in a Large Biomedical Library. Pt. 3 Comparison of On-line and Batch Operations and Cost Analysis. *Journal of the American Society for Information Science* 24(2): 80-86

Hamilton, Robert E. 1968. The Illinois State Library Online Circulation System. *In Proceedings of the 1968 Clinic on Library Applications of Data Processing*, 11-28. Urbana, IL: University of Illinois Graduate School of Library Science.

Heiliger, Edward H. May 25, 1964. Use of a Computer at Florida Atlantic University for Mechanized Catalog Production. In *IBM Library Mechanization Symposium, Endicott, New York, May 25, 1964*, 165-186. White Plains, NY: IBM Data Processing Division.

Licklider, J. C. P. March, 1960. Man-Computer Symbiosis. In a paper presented to the National Academy of Sciences, Washington, D.C.

Palmer, Richard Phillips. 1973. *Case Studies in Library Computer Systems*. New York: R. R. Bowker. 184-185.

Payne, Charles, et al. Jan., 1977. The University of Chicago Library Data Management System. *Library Quarterly* 47(1): 9.

Rao, Paladugu, V., and N. Joseph Szerenyi. June, 1971. Booth Library On-line Circulation Systems (BLOC). *Journal of Library Automation* 4(2): 101.

Rush, James. 1988. The Library Automation Market: Why Do Vendors Fail? *Library Hi Tech* 6(3): 7-33.

Stanford University Ballots System. March, 1975. Project BALLOTS and the Stanford University Libraries. *Journal of Library Automation* 8(1): 41-43.

Sources for Further Reading

Boykin, Joseph F. Winter, 1991. Library Automation 1970-1990: From the Few to the Many. *Library Administration and Management* 5(1): 10-15.

Hildreth, Charles R. 1987. *Library Automation in N. America: A Reassessment of the Impact of New Technologies on Networking*. New York: Saur.

Muro, Ernest A. 1991. *Automation Services for Libraries, A Resource Handbook*. Annandale, NJ: Vendor Relations Press.

_____. 1991. *Automation Services for Libraries, A Resource Handbook of Marketing and Sales*. Annandale, NJ: Vendor Relations Press.

The Planning Process

Implementing a computer-based library system requires careful planning. By the time the library manager is ready to look at specific alternatives, those involved should have set goals and objectives and done a preliminary analysis based on current operations and future needs. They should know exactly why automation is taking place and what it is expected to accomplish. Whether you are planning for your first system, migrating to a new vendor, or upgrading your present system, the steps involved will be the same: analyzing the existing system, providing for future needs, and making projections. Planning for the next system should get underway as soon as the previous system is installed. Don't wait until your current system is at full capacity to plan for the next one. This chapter will clearly identify each of the following planning stages of automating a library and discuss the steps involved:

    a. Justification for automating/migrating

    b. Committee process

    c. Should you go with a consultant?

    d. Specifications

    e. Bidding process

    f. Selection of an automated library system

    g. Benchmarking

    h. Contract negotiations

    i. Installation

    j. Training

    k. System activation

Justification for Automating/Migrating

Most libraries are required to justify the need for automating, upgrading, or moving to a new system to a higher authority. Persuading management to approve an automated library system and come up with the funding is not an easy task. Librarians find it difficult to pin down exact costs of workflow, specified activities, and direct benefits to the patrons. If the library is small, approval may be given outright. Funds are often limited, a preliminary budget is set, and the librarian selects a system that most closely matches the library's needs and financial constraints. In larger libraries, however, justification is the critical first step in gaining approval for the project. It helps if you have done it before. Documentation must be presented to administrators which identifies the problems in the current system and justifies implementing an automated system.

A project leader or manager is usually designated to head the project and write the justification. This may be a librarian who doubles as the project manager or a responsible and informed member of the work force who is relieved from current duties to assume a new role for the duration of the project. A cross-section of recent library automation studies indicate that "Project leadership should rest in a single individual. . . . Above all, the person needs to have legitimacy within the organization and to be effective as a planner and problem solver but also skillful in overseeing the dynamics of the project -- the organizational processes and human interaction," (Drabenstott, 1990, 56). The project manager must be an informed buyer, able to think and write creatively; grasp the fundamentals and understand perplexing terminology; analyze complex situations; work effectively and flexibly with staff, vendors, programmers, and others involved in the development of the system; identify, compare, and evaluate the advantages and disadvantages of automated systems; establish timeframes and meet deadlines; coordinate system installation and training; and keep administrators advised of the project's problems and progress.

The project manager can develop a rationale for automating by assessing current operations and by examining a number of different perspectives:

Assessing Current Operations

By the time a library has decided to automate, it has usually done so because of existing conditions. In order to justify the need for an automated system or an upgrade, the project manager must analyze current operations without bias, pinpoint problems caused by the present system, and evaluate as many results as possible. At the same time he or she must explore ways in which automation may lead to improvement. It is often helpful to interview staff in order to help identify specific problem areas and to formulate a list of desired features. Dennis Reynolds suggests five general areas to be considered: time, money, control, relationship, and service. He states, "An analysis of current operations should determine for each task or set of tasks involved:

- How much staff time is being spent on it;

- How much money it is costing (including staff);

- How much control is being exercised over the items or records handled;

- How it relates to other tasks;

- How it translates into level of service for the library user" (Reynolds 1985, 236-237).

Examining Perspectives

Reynolds also emphasizes that "it is important in establishing a basis for planning that a library sort out and articulate the relative importance of each reason for which it is automating." He pinpoints the following areas (Reynolds 1985, 208).

Cost and Cost Effectiveness. The cost of automating a library varies widely and often entails substantial financial outlay. Throughout the 1960s and 1970s, funding was frequently obtained through grants, endowments, or financial outlays provided by a parent body or benefactor. In the 1980s, allocation of funds was more closely scrutinized and became more competitive. Interestingly enough, however, libraries automated on a larger scale than ever before, primarily because the costs of automation did not increase as fast as the cost of other goods and services. The commercial market expanded; competition increased; microcomputer-based computer applications and options developed;[1] and the cost of automation was within the reach of even the smallest library.

---

1. The development of microcomputer-based systems is discussed in detail in Chapter 7.

Librarians try to justify automation on the grounds that operating costs will immediately be lowered. For example, an automated system almost always improves processing efficiency over a manual system. A library collection may be growing rapidly, and patron use may be increasing at a steady pace. Increased efficiency is realized when the same tasks are performed with fewer staff or in less time than was possible under the manual system. An automated system will decrease the rate at which it is necessary to add staff and better contain the rate of increase in per-unit operating cost over time. It therefore becomes cost effective to automate. It should be noted that on the whole, financial savings depend on the specific situation or circumstance and are often not as sweeping as anticipated.[2]

Improved Administration and Management. Librarians seldom cite improved administration and management alone as a convincing argument for purchasing an automated system, but an automated system can be used effectively for budgeting, collection analysis and development, and staff scheduling. Statistical control is easier. The potential for improved management can be a persuasive supplementary selling point.

Visible Effects of Manual Breakdown. Sometimes the chief reason for automating is that the existing manual system is no longer able to deal effectively with the heavy workload. Examples include visible backlogs in cataloging, lack of accurate or timely fund-account reports in acquisitions, disorganized circulation files, inconsistent card catalogs, and overdue books. Visible effects of manual breakdown are a persuasive selling point. Librarians find themselves drawing heavily on this justification.

Improved Service. Improved service to the user is one of the most concrete benefits to be gained. In acquisitions, automation often leads to acquiring and processing materials faster and getting them onto the shelf more quickly than under the previous manual system. With circulation systems, improvement in inventory control leads to better service. Searches through the online public access catalog often allow users to access up-to-date data, compiled

---

2. There are numerous costing techniques. Cost benefit analysis is used by libraries most frequently because it compares inputs (costs) and outputs (benefits) in monetary terms. See Cortez, Edwin M., and Edward J. Kazlauskas. *Managing Information Systems and Technologies.* New York, NY: Neal-Schuman, 1986.

with greater flexibility in a fraction of the time it would have taken to conduct an equivalent search manually. Online catalog systems provide similar benefits for staff. The most difficult obstacle to overcome lies in assigning a dollar amount to benefits derived. There are no steadfast answers in determining at what point enhanced service is worth the added investment.

Sharing Resources. Sharing resources has become a viable strategy used to alleviate the need to collect and house all documents that might be requested by clientele. Automated systems can facilitate the sharing of resources by making communications and dissemination of information faster, more efficient, and less expensive than manual channels. Governing bodies, who see resource sharing as an activity by which the library will serve an even broader community and drain its resources, must be convinced by the positive argument that the library will be able to draw on a much broader pool of resources while reducing the need for expansion.

General Acceptance. The use of computers has become prevalent throughout society. They are a generally accepted component of the business and home environments. Governing bodies are much more favorable to the basic concept of computerization, and the challenge of convincing them that the library needs expensive and complex technology to support staff and patrons is not as difficult as it once was.

Given the climate of acceptance, the astute project manager can present a case convincingly. The lowering costs of hardware, the diversity of the equipment, and the number of available options continue to make automating attractive.

Throughout the 1980s and early 90s, automation has been tried, tested, and accepted in libraries. A library without automation has lost its calling. It cannot compete. Patrons expect instant feedback; they are familiar with computers which provide fast and accurate communication that link the user to his request and complete the cycle; their expectations are fulfilled, and they leave, satisfied customers. A favorable setting and a new level of awareness were established in the 1980s allowing us, as librarians, to justify automation in an unprecedented way.

Vendor Dissatisfaction. In addition to the above perspectives cited by Reynolds, libraries are contemplating upgrading or migrating to a new system may cite dissatisfaction with their current vendor as a reason to convert. For example, libraries that have had severe problems with their present systems have cited low confidence levels regarding the contents of their system files, particularly the transaction files. It is very important not to leave your current vendor angry so that your system is operational until you have made the transition. Be very careful to take all the right steps and document them so that your current vendor will cooperate and not interfere with the conversion. This takes a good deal of tact and forethought.[3]

Potential Problem Areas to Address

Problems that are identified should be translated into clear statements that can be used to justify automation. Common examples include:

Problem 1: Library material is overdue. Overdue materials are not easily identified by manual methods or outdated systems. Consequently, patrons are not notified on a timely basis and requests are not honored. Argument: An automated circulation system would locate titles in the library collection and issue overdue, recall, and hold notices.

Problem 2: Periodical issues are past due; sporadic missing issues are prevalent. Argument: An automated serials acquisitions check-in feature would allow the staff to instantly assess the outstanding issues and generate claim or cancellation notices as well as link information to jobbers.

Problem 3: There is a permanent backlog in cataloging. Staff are unable to cope with an increasing load. They are able to process only 75 percent of the annual acquisitions. Argument: An automated catalog would streamline operations; give the cataloger access to machine readable catalog records; and standardize the library's bibliographic records to bring them in line with other libraries.

Problem 4: Patrons are dissatisfied with the antiquated card catalog system. It doesn't provide consistent subject access points, and they are going to automated libraries to access needed research material. Argument: An online public access catalog could provide consistent, multiple access points and increase speed of retrieval and efficiency. Dial-in access from remote areas could be made available, if needed.

---

3. For those libraries that are migrating data, see Chapter 5 (Retrospective Conversion).

Problem 5: The current system cannot generate statistics needed by the library's governing board without hiring more staff or eliminating necessary library services. Argument: Automated Library Systems have a report feature which can access information from various modules, such as acquisitions, catalog, circulation, or serials, and compile it into a statistical report quickly and efficiently without having to increase staff or staff time.

Problem 6: The transaction and delinquency files of the current automated system are antiquated and do not display all of the fields necessary to keep patrons current and staff aware of problems. Also the circulation system is becoming overloaded and frequently goes down. Argument: An upgraded circulation system would allow for more storage. Newer automated systems provide more features and will allow for staff input regarding the display of required fields.

Supporting Data

Statistical and budgetary information should be submitted, along with an assessment of the features required and desired in the selection of a new system. Supporting data must be included so that administrators can relate current needs and costs to those projected under an automated system. For example:

- Budget by area: What is the cost of cataloging a book? What is the cost of checking out a book?

- Look at staff duties: What are the repetitive, high volume, high use areas (i.e., check-in, check-out; production of overdue notices)?

- Complete a forms analysis: What forms do staff fill out regularly? How much time and cost are involved in each transaction?

- Show that computers make more efficient use of staff time:

  Everyone with a computer is able to share the most up-to-date information on the status of library material.

  Telephone interdepartmental inquiries are reduced. Staff do not have to physically walk from department to department in search of information.

- Delineate ways in which automated library systems benefit patrons:

  They provide faster access and remote dial-up access to the collection; more access points to the collection; and more information about the collection.

- Show that automation will provide more meaningful statistical information: for example, circulation data helps with collection development.

Committee Process

Although the Project Manager retains the ultimate responsibility for making informed decisions in planning and implementing the automated system, it is essential to include the staff in various phases of the automation project. If you are migrating to a new system or upgrading your present system, it is advantageous to use the expertise of staff who helped implement the previous system. Both Heitshu (University of Arizona) and Pollard (University of Alaska, Fairbanks) note that in implementing their automated library systems, more informed decisions could have been made if those who were to use the system had had greater involvement in the design and implementation (Drabenstott, 1989, 56-57). The ultimate success of the new system depends upon the support and interest given by the people who manage and operate it. They will be much more prone to accept it if they are personally involved in its development and can see tangible benefits to themselves and to the library.

Heitshu argues that the project structure needs to be broadly based in order to facilitate decision-making and encourage organizational change (Heitshu 1989, 64). The project steering committee, for example, might be composed of key library staff from the sections to be automated as well as representatives from other departments or units involved in the automation (Corbin 1985, 48). Committees provide the foundation for a well-prepared automation plan and allow the project manager to enter into well informed, carefully considered negotiations and contractual commitments with the vendor. Their groundwork helps administrators meet potential crises more adeptly and respond to unforeseen events so that they can adjust expectation levels accordingly. Their continuing involvement facilitates the maintenance of both administrative and technical control over the project and provides a means of infusing or integrating the project into the organization.

The duties and responsibilities of each committee should be clearly defined. A project goal should be outlined; and a calendar of events, including timeframes, should be projected. (A PERT chart or Gantt chart may be used.[4]) As a rule of thumb, the larger the library, the broader the participation and the larger the number of committees formed. The following will give the reader a bird's eye view of the full scope of the committee process. It will present a selection of concrete examples of typical committees and their duties in the small library and in the larger library.

The Small Library -- Advisory, Automation, or Steering Committee

It is now economically feasible for many small or special libraries to install automated systems.[5] Some are just beginning to automate, and others are in the process of adding modules to pre-existing systems. Though their staff is typically limited, a central committee is generally formed in order to broaden the scope of input and interrelate expertise. Smaller libraries appoint an advisory task force which consists of librarians and staff who work on the specific subsystems to be automated, such as acquisitions/serials control, cataloging, or circulation. Committee members are expected to have an understanding of the organization and its operations. In particular, persons with inquisitive and analytical minds or those with specific qualifications (such as computer backgrounds or systems analyst skills) are sought to:

---

4. The Program Evaluation and Review Technique (PERT) chart allows easy identification of events requiring varying amounts of elapsed time. Events are listed chronologically in specific timeframes (i.e., Preparing System Specifications 6-05-91/6-19-91) and enclosed in boxes. Boxes are linked together by a series of dots. They look very much like cars in a train which contain valuable information. One can see at a glance whether events co-occur, are independent, or are dependent on one another.

The Gantt chart also displays critical paths graphically. Daily, weekly, or monthly timeframes are generally used as column headings. Tasks are listed down the left side of the page. For each task, the beginning and the end of the projected time period are marked with "x," and a timeline is drawn between them. The horizontal line graphically displays events which overlap in time.

5. For a discussion of microcomputer-based automated library systems, see Chapter 7.

- establish project priorities, goals, and objectives;

- analyze existing operations;

- identify requirements and specifications for the automated system;

- select a consultant, if needed;

- evaluate hardware and software;

- determine needs for retrospective conversion;

- provide diagrams of workspace and furniture layouts;

- offer general advice and guidance during the installation process;

- provide written documentation, including alternatives, as well as support for the project in general;

- develop an orientation program to familiarize all library staff with the automation process;

- recommend training for those who will manage and operate the new system;

- deal with ongoing problems as they occur.

The Larger Library

Larger libraries are often departmentalized and can be easily divided into a number of smaller committees. An advisory committee, such as the one described above, is often formed in the preliminary stages of automation. In larger libraries, it consists of specialists from various departments and has a front-line, ongoing commitment to both the Project Manager and the project as a whole. It makes both oral and written recommendations to the Project Manager, based on reports from lower-level committees. We will call it a primary or first-level committee.

From the advisory or first-level committee, members with particular expertise may be selected to head a number of smaller secondary or second-level committees. These unique committees vary according to the size of the library and the size of the automation project. They report to the advisory committee through their first-level committee head(s). Typical second-level committees and their duties are listed below.

Second-Level Committees

System Requirements Committee. The System Requirements Committee has the responsibility of gaining input from the work force and developing a list of requirements desired by the new system, based on staff workload, workflow, operating needs, staff reports, and suggestions. They may obtain information either directly or indirectly from subcommittees such as those formed in the areas of acquisitions/serials control, cataloging (retrospective or database conversion), circulation, and online public access catalogs.[6] Typical duties of the System Requirements Committee are listed below:

- Identify the categories of requirements to be written;

- Compile a list of requirements in each category;

- Determine task-oriented work areas, and complete workflow studies in each area;

- Obtain third-level reports from individual module committees: acquisitions/serials control, retrospective conversion, circulation, and online public access catalog;

- Study sample lists of requirements collected from other libraries;

- Incorporate all of the above, compare ideas, and hold weekly meetings to review progress;

---

6. The duties of these third-level module committees will be delineated at the end of this section on second-level committees. For further information, please see Chapter 4 which discusses the five core modules, Chapter 5 which discusses the process of converting a library's holdings into computer records, and Chapter 6 which concentrates solely on the online public access catalog.

- Draft a set of requirements for aspects of the automated system to be acquired.

RFP Drafting Committee. The RFP Drafting Committee consists of some of the members of the advisory committee. If an automation consultant is recommended, he or she may provide general assistance and guidance during the bid and review process. Persons with a knowledge of computer hardware and software programs are included. The final document should be edited for clarity, consistency, and style before it is sent for approval. Typical duties of the RFP Drafting Committee are listed below:

- Obtain the set of requirements drafted by the System Requirements Committee.

- Request third-level reports from the Acquisitions/Serials Control, Retrospective Conversion, Circulation, and Online Public Access Catalog Committees;

- Gather sample RFPs from other libraries;

- Prepare a draft in each category of specifications for discussion and study;

- Revise drafts to incorporate comments and suggestions;

- Consolidate drafts into a single document;

- Obtain approval for submission to vendors;

- Identify vendors and mail copies of the approved RFP.

Systems Selection Committee. The Systems Selection Committee consists of the Project Manager and some of the members of the advisory committee, with the Project Manager generally acting as Chair of the group. This group analyzes results and selects the automated system after the bids have been received. Members of the Systems Requirement Committee and RFP Drafting Committee may also sit on this committee. Typical duties of the Systems Selection Committee are listed below:

- Establish rules for selecting the best response to the RFP;

- Review and evaluate bids from vendors, paying particular attention to:

   Hardware
   Software
   Upgrades
   Expansion Capability
   Compatibility with other systems within the library
   Networking capabilities with outside systems
   Response time
   Documentation
   Training
   Financial stability of the vendor
   Overall cost
   Training and support;

- Compare RFP responses with library requirements and desires;

- Attend system demonstrations;

- Interview vendor clients, and make site visits to see firsthand how the system operates;

- Prepare a detailed evaluation report, comparing vendor responses;

- Select the automation system that best meets the overall needs of the library;

- Negotiate costs and terms with the selected vendor;

- Sign purchase and maintenance contracts.

Retrospective Conversion Committee. The Retrospective Conversion Committee should include professional and paraprofessional members of the catalog staff. It is responsible for overseeing the conversion of bibliographic records from their present form to full machine readable records (MARC II format). The committee will be instrumental in selecting a vendor for the database conversion process. Typical duties of the Retrospective Conversion Committee are listed below:

- Examine job descriptions and workflow;

- Research database creation and maintenance;

- Identify records to be created or converted;

- Investigate retrospective conversion vendors in terms of: currency, completeness, accuracy, consistency, derivation, and length of records; the structure used for matching records; authority control methods in use;

- Examine field size and flexibility of structure;

- Estimate database size;

- Examine index creation;

- Prepare existing records for conversion;

- Establish a schedule for loading the new MARC tapes into the database;

- Evaluate accuracy of conversion by checking random records.

Training Committee. The Training Committee should include a broad base of clerical, paraprofessional, and professional staff. Training is more effective if it is based on job-related use and knowledge and is provided to every member of the work force. Upon completion of designated training workshops, each staff member should be familiar with basic automation terminology, fundamental concepts, and general applications within the scope of work-related duties. Typical duties of the Training Committee are listed below:

- Review the vendor training process;

- Select appropriate staff to attend vendor training sessions and, in turn, to train remaining staff. Staff should be selected for their leadership qualities, credibility, ability to highlight key concepts, and expertise in clearly and logically translating complex information to other staff in a simple and understandable manner;

- Subdivide remaining staff into appropriate groups, and organize task-oriented training sessions as needed;

- Design complementary training materials;

- Present workshops;

- Provide clear instructions and procedure guides to explain how to interrelate and operate each device, correct problems, and check equipment;

- Provide time for staff to practice away from public access areas;

- Provide ongoing, updated training as new software releases occur and as procedures change.

Third-Level Subcommittees

Module Committees. Module committees are comprised of professional librarians and technical staff within each area of expertise: acquisitions/serials control, catalog, circulation, and online public access catalog. Involvement is educational as staff from all levels are asked for personal input. As automation plans develop, workflow is seen as interconnected and coordinated. As a result, the entire work force is kept informed on the progress of implementing the automated system.

Acquisitions/Serials Control Committee
Sample Duties:

- Examine job descriptions and workflow.

- Prepare statistical reports on number of purchase orders, renewals, standing orders, monographs and serials received, claims, cancellations, item records, binding records, fund accounting records, and vendor/jobber records.

- Look at specific features, such as the generation of routing lists and the creation of problem alert lists (i.e., cessations, suspensions, and title changes).

- Investigate the need for repeatable fields in the serials check-in area. For example, it may be important to have a feature which will provide historic records of receipts or one which will automate statistical reports.

- Evaluate the need for functional requirements, such as electronic links or interfaces to vendors and jobbers or other libraries.

- Project future needs.

Catalog Committee
Sample Duties:

- Examine job descriptions and workflow.

- Work in conjunction with the Retrospective Conversion Committee to establish a timetable for phasing in the new system and phasing out the old.

- Investigate electronic links or interfaces to bibliographic utilities providing catalog records (i.e., OCLC or RLIN);

- Determine how bar codes and pocket/spine labels are generated on various automated systems.

- Look at the procedures used for backing up catalog records.

- Project future needs.

Circulation Committee
Sample Duties:

- Examine job descriptions and workflow.

- Prepare statistical reports on number of books and other library materials circulated inhouse, interlibrary loans, fines, renewals, holds, recalls, overdues, reserves, bibliographic records of circulated titles as well as titles to be circulated, and borrower records.

- Investigate loan period options available in various systems.

- Project future needs.

Online Public Access Catalog Committee
Sample Duties:

- Examine job descriptions and workflow.

- Investigate number of terminals needed for staff and patrons.

- Look at screen design, ease of use, and patron comfort.

- Determine access points for the patron.

- Examine clarity of search methods, and compare results.

- Discuss the possibilities of providing offsite dial-up access for patrons.

- Design a patron orientation program.

- Prepare reports on the above.

Numerous other committees may be formed, as needed, depending upon the size of the library or libraries involved in automation. For those libraries that are allocating additional space or moving to a new location, a Site Selection Committee would be appropriate. Libraries may elect to have only one all-encompassing, advisory committee or a full range of 40 committees or more.

First Level Committee

Steering or Advisory

Second Level Committees

System Require-ments	RFP Drafting	Systems Selection	Retro-spective Conversion	Training

Third Level Committees

Module Committees

Cataloging	Circulation	Acq/Serials	OPAC

Figure 3.

Should You Go with a Consultant?

A consultant is hired to assist with the formalities of the library automation project. This is done generally when the library staff does not have the specialized background, skills, time, or support needed to document a set of specifications, or to examine, compare, and evaluate the myriad system features available from different vendors. Larger libraries, which interact with multi-institutional networks, sometimes feel that an experienced consultant is well worth the fee. Smaller libraries, however, can seldom justify the investment.

It has become a general trend in the 1980s and 1990s for librarians to become involved in the politics and dynamics of automation. They are learning body language and "buzz" words and are better able to retain responsibility and make informed decisions. Many have already had experience installing systems and find themselves better prepared to migrate to new systems or upgrade their present systems. Recent studies indicate that librarians are hiring consultants more and more in an advisory capacity. For example, the College of Charleston, a state-supported institution of higher learning located in South Carolina, was involved in a campus-wide planning process. Designated staff coordinated demonstrations, investigated systems developments, performed a systems analysis, developed Gantt charts (time lines for various activities), prepared a Request for Information (RFI), and detailed specifications in a Request for Proposal (RFP) before negotiating the final contract themselves. Only after drafting the RFP, using their own expertise, did they hire a consultant to review their work. The consultant made a few minor recommendations, and the experience was both cost effective and reassuring.

In single-institution projects, the consultant usually focuses on the "preparation of bid documents, evaluation of responses, and negotiation of contracts. . . . In many locations, local user groups also sponsor programs or provide informal assistance that can be helpful to the library in evaluating and selecting equipment or services" (Reynolds 1985, 230-231).

The project manager and advisory committee should examine, compare, and evaluate proposals received from prospective consultants. Additional or clarifying information may be requested if necessary; and inquiries should be made to other libraries who have used the consultant's services. As a legal precaution, a contract is drawn up and signed by both the project manager and the consultant who is selected. Specific duties to be performed are at the discretion of the library. In general, the consultant may:

- conduct feasibility studies of automated acquisitions/ serials control, cataloging (retrospective conversion), circulation systems, and online public access catalog;

- assist in establishing requirements for the integrated system;

- design specifications for the RFP;

- assist in the evaluation of alternative automated systems;

- provide advice in the selection of the new system;

- assist in the dynamics of site preparation and installation of the automated system;

- assist in the negotiation of a contract with the successful vendor;

- provide consultation and advice throughout the project.

Specifications

Members of the RFP Drafting Committee are asked to compile a list of specifications which outline both mandatory (absolute) and desirable (requested, but not mandatory) requirements for the new system. This list should be as precise and as detailed as possible in order to provide potential vendors with the specific needs and requirements of the library. Two basic documents are used most frequently by librarians to solicit information from vendors. The first is a brief request for information (RFI) sent to vendors about their automated systems. The second is a more formal request for a proposal (RFP) sent to selected vendors to solicit price quotations for actual bid.

Request for Information (RFI)

A Request for Information is an informal document which may be written on headed library stationery. It is sent to a variety of possible vendors initially to find out just exactly what modules make up their automated system, how they interface or interconnect, the functions they perform, and a general cost structure. Vendors usually send out a packet of information for evaluation along with a cover letter. Librarians, in turn, evaluate the information and judge the degree to which the automated system meets the needs of the library. Vendors that provide the best possible match are selected as potential candidates. A very detailed document, called a Request For Proposal (RFP), is then formally written by the RFP Drafting Committee and submitted to designated vendors for bid.

Request for Proposal (RFP)

The Request for Proposal is a very complex and time consuming document to write. Librarians have become very informed buyers who meticulously write detailed documents to cover every legal loophole. The RFP includes specific instructions to the bidders, requiring them to seek clarification of any item that is not clear and to check all responses for accuracy before submitting a proposal. The document lists very precisely all of the specifications required by the library that the vendor must try to match, and all criteria for evaluation are enumerated. The name and address of the library where the bids are to be sent is clearly stated on the face of the proposal. Competitive, sealed bids are to be received by the time and date noted in the proposal.

Historical Background. In the late 1970s, librarians knew very little about automation. Vendors were able to take advantage of that lack of knowledge and reap heavy profits by selling them systems that were still in the production stage or didn't fulfill expectations. Contracts were written by the vendors and for the vendors, not for the librarians. As one vendor put it, "Selling automated systems to librarians in the 1970s was like Sherman's march through Georgia." It was that easy to take money from librarians.

However, times have changed. Librarians are no longer naive buyers. They frequently submit detailed RFPs which vendors must peruse, item by item. This procedure has become so tedious and time consuming that vendors have had to hire more staff or pay present employees overtime in order to respond to the RFPs in a timely fashion. Vendors are now arguing that by submitting such lengthy RFPs, librarians are defeating their purpose by indirectly increasing the cost of the automated system.

Pros and Cons: There has been some discussion about the value of RFPs. They are costly for the library to prepare and costly for the vendor to respond to in multiple copies. Vendors point out that these costs are ultimately passed back to the library. There are advantages and disadvantages to writing an RFP (competitive procurement) and to not writing one (non-competitive procurement). Many libraries remain committed to the idea of competitive procurement and the RFP. It lets them convert their specific needs into detailed written form.

Competitive Procurement

Advantages
Precise specifications
Potential lower cost
Negotiation
Best solution proposal

Disadvantages
Takes longer to procure
Must evaluate less acceptable solutions

Non-Competitive Procurement

Advantages
Quicker to procure
Technology is current
Less need to be precise
Lower up-front cost

Disadvantages
Not matched to requirements
No negotiation

Writing the RFP Document. Writing the RFP is a vital part of the planning process. The RFP provides vendors with a formal proposal and gives them a perspective on how to satisfy the needs of the library. It is written specifically to identify what is acceptable and what is not acceptable in the proposed automated system. Librarians use it both as an evaluation tool to compare each vendor's ability to meet the needs of the library and as a basis for negotiating a contract with the chosen vendor. It is useful to examine RFPs written by other libraries and/or previous ones used by your own library. While there are indeed differences in requirements among libraries, RFPs often contain sections that can be cloned.

A cover letter should be required of all vendors submitting competitive bids. Usually, the vendors are asked to include documentation attesting to their qualifications, experience, and financial stability. Their statements address the scope of business operations, size, personnel, and number of years in business and provide names, addresses, and telephone numbers of key officers and current customers to contact. Vendors should identify the basic configuration being used by each client, the size of the files, and the volume of activity being handled. This provides a valuable source of information concerning quality of service rendered. The library should also run a credit check on audited financial statements for the past five years. These are very important considerations in the proposal process. The library does not want to get stuck with a vendor that is about to go out of business or one that cannot back up the product purchased! Most librarians find it advantageous to analyze library needs in terms of functional specifications and system specifications.

Major functional specifications include:
cataloging, circulation, acquisitions, serials control, online public access catalog, and reports/statistics.

Other functional specifications to be considered are:
interlibrary loans, binding, inventory control, item tracking, booking, journal citation access, information and retrieval files, other bibliographic databases, data files, and electronic mail.

When you have decided what functional specifications will match the needs of your library, it is beneficial to provide a separate section in the RFP to describe the library's requirements and expectations for each component. This clarifies for the vendor exactly what features are important to you. For each component specified, three general areas should be addressed:

1. Purpose: List the tasks that you want the component to fulfill.

2. Input: Describe the type of data which will be input into that component.

3. Output: Explain what your library expects that component to be able to produce.

For example, the purpose of the serials component is:
to check in serials publications;
to generate claims for missing issues;
to produce special correspondence to vendors;
to renew subscriptions;
to maintain holdings records for serials, standing orders, series subscriptions, newspapers, and microforms;
to maintain routing lists;
to facilitate resource sharing;
to produce holding lists.
(as stated by: Northland Pioneer College 1988, 17)

Input -- Data that will be put into the system include:

Title	ISSN
Linking title(s)	Next expected receipt date
Subtitle	Format
Place of publication	Index data
Publisher	Language
Vendor	Routing
Beginning date	Location
Holdings statements for	Bindery Information
volume, number, issue,	Fund accounting
month, day, year	Call number
Frequency	Notes.

(Northland Pioneer College 1988, 17)

Output -- the following documents and reports are desired as part of the serials component:

Claim notices	Labels
Local holdings lists	Bar code labels
Input to regional holdings	Vendor performance lists
lists	Locations lists
Routing lists	Standing order lists
Problem alert lists	Newspaper lists
(cessation, suspensions,	Missing issues
title changes)	Statistics (title, volumes,
Periodical lists	reels, fiche) per
Microform lists	locations; added per year
Vendor correspondence	and grand totals.

(Northland Pioneer College 1988, 17)

System specifications to be evaluated include:
system capacity, availability, reliability,
response time, downtime, compatibility,
connectivity, and portability/transportability[7]

The list of items for inclusion can become quite extensive. The RFP also typically includes policies and procedures relating to performance bonds, terms of payment, hardware and software maintenance, site preparation, delivery

---

7. For a discussion of these terms, see Chapter 1.

and scheduling guidelines, installation, and training procedures. Vendors are usually required to submit a complete delineation of costs, both immediate and ongoing (i.e., maintenance, additional equipment, and supplies), so that librarians know what they are paying for and can compare costs among competitive bids.

The library's needs should be stated realistically, clearly, and succinctly in the RFP and should not be based on the capabilities of any one system. In formulating your library's requirements, try to be realistic in terms of what is available and what the library can afford. As a rule of thumb, do not dictate; do not leave anything out; and use clear terminology.[8]

The content of the RFP may vary according to the library's needs, but relevant examples of the basic categories are listed below. They include the following groupings:

- Information/instructions for the bidders, i.e., schedule of distribution of the RFPs to include deadlines for responses; dates/criteria for evaluation of responses, contract negotiation, awards, and installation of hardware and software; procedures for providing addendums, withdrawal of proposals, appeals, and vendor conferences; and names and addresses of key people to contact within the library.[9]

- Background information on the library environment, i.e., mission, goals, objectives, description of the organizational structure and current operations.

- A detailed explanation of the library's environment within which the system specifications are to work, i.e, existing hardware and software in each department or section, estimated number of records the library has and the format used (full MARC records/local variations), estimated growth (projection of the number of book acquisitions per year), estimated number of terminals needed.

- A list of functional and system specifications required by the library, grouped into separate categories of "mandatory" and "desired" and clearly labeled. (In connection with "mandatory" requirements, the

---

8. For a sample RFP for an integrated library system, see Corbin 1985, Appendix D:204-247 and Boss 1990.

9. For further information, see Cortez 1987, 44-53.

word "must" and the phrase "It is required that . . . " are used; in connection with "desired" requirements, the word "should" and the phrase "It is desirable . . . " are used.)

- A timeline, spelled out, i.e., "The system must be up and running within a year because money will be pulled," or "The system may not be installed between May 1 and May 15 because it will disrupt students taking exams."

- Parameters for testing the system, i.e. acceptance tests (evaluation tests) or parallel tests (old system and new system running together for a specified period of time: 30-60 days)

- Financial framework; a rough idea of the amount of money the library is able to pay, i.e., "Cost of the system proposed must be in the range of . . . "

- A list of uniform questions directed at all bidders. For example:

    How often does the automated system upgrade, and what are the costs involved?

    How compatible is the new system with other systems, such as OCLC/RLIN?

    What are the expansion capabilities of the system?

    What training procedures are available, and what is the cost?

    What kind of ongoing system maintenance and support is available after the modules are up and running?

    We have a large Spanish collection and require some system control. Does the system allow for multilingual flexibility in designing OPAC screens, and if so, how much input do librarians have?;

PLANNING AND THE RFP PROCESS

- Needs Assessment
- RFP Process
- RFP Document
- Specifications
- Technical Proposal Evaluation
- Cost Proposal Evaluation
- Negotiation
- Reviews and Approvals
- Award

Figure 4.

RFP DOCUMENT

- Library Procurement: Conditions and Objectives
- Information for Vendors
- Request for Vendor Documentation
- Systems and Functional Specifications:
      Mandatory and Desirable
- Timeline Spelled Out
- Financial Framework
- Parameters for Testing
- Evaluation and Selection Process
- Site Preparation
- Implementation
- Provisions for Training and Support
- Questions for All Bidders

Figure 5.

SPECIFICATIONS

Background

- Description of the Library
- Description of the Current System
- Overview of the System Being Procured

System Specs

- Capacity
- Availability
- Reliability
- Response Time
- Downtime
- Compatibility
- Connectivity
- Portability / Transportability

Functional Specs

- Cataloging
- Circulation
- Acquisitions
- Serials Control
- Online Public Access Catalog (OPAC)
- Reports / Statistics

Implementation Plan

- Conversion
- Installation / Delivery
- Acceptance Tests
- Training
- Longterm Hardware and Software Management:
  Support
  Response Time
  Reliability

Figure 6.

Bidding Process

To ensure a fair bid process the RFP should include a schedule of the following events:

- Distribution of RFP;

- Bidder's Conference (to clarify questions);

- Deadline for receipt of vendor proposals;

- Opening of bids;

- Proposal evaluation;

Contract negotiation (Cortez 1987, 46).

Vendors will respond to the RFP within a specified time period (usually six to eight weeks) by submitting a detailed list and account of the system that they can supply to meet the requirements of the library. Some will meet specific needs; and others will not match the capabilities required/desired. When a vendor submits a bid, the proposal is valid for a predetermined number of days, i.e., 120 days from the opening of bids. If your RFP is written with forethought and organization, you will be able to place responses side-by-side and compare them (vendor capability against vendor capability) as they are received.

Certain protections are built in. Those vendors that choose to respond are compelled to reply to all requirements and specifications in clear, unambiguous language. If the library has defined certain terminology to be used, bidders must adhere to stated terms and definitions so that proposals can be reviewed and compared by the library in an unbiased manner. The library usually retains the right to accept or reject a proposal. Nonacceptance of a proposal simply means that other bids were more in line with the library's needs. Specific penalties for early withdrawal of a proposal are spelled out in the RFP. These stipulations usually prevent vendors from withdrawing the proposal during the evaluation or negotiation stage, thus wasting valuable time and library resources. It should be noted that the RFP is a "negotiated" bid process. The library is not required to accept the lowest bid but rather negotiates with the vendor for the best return.

Selection of an Automated Library System

Librarians must not be hoodwinked into buying an automated library system with glitch and glamour that they don't need and will never use. A big trick used by vendors is to get you to look at things you haven't asked for or even considered. Librarians must be intelligent buyers. Remember, the price of the product is what the market will bear. Don't always look for logic. Software licenses, for example, are based or priced according to the size of the library and on how much librarians know what they are doing. Think of each transaction as an assertive customer. Take the time you need to evaluate bids. Look closely at your library's needs and compare them to the proposal at hand. Be sure to read all of the small print, and be selective when comparing alternative automated systems.

Whether you are implementing your first system, migrating to a new system, or upgrading your present system, be sure to examine each functional, technical, and performance response and match them against those required in the RFP. Ask vendors to repeat any portions of text or supporting documents that are unclear. Write to suppliers, and request a formal, written reply. Attend demonstrations. Talk to other users who have a vested interest. As you compare the features offered by vendors with specified requirements listed in the RFP, pay particular attention to the mandatory ones. Ask questions about and analyze the following categories of importance:

- Functional and system specifications: Is the proposal itself complete and comprehensive? How closely does it match the library's requirements? Does it address all of the mandatory requirements of the library?

- Software: Does the library lease or own the software? Is the library protected if the vendor goes bankrupt? Will the software, (including the operating system) work with other hardware platforms? Is a software maintenance contract provided; and if so, what is the cost?

- Hardware: Does the vendor manufacture, guarantee or service the hardware? What is the cost of the maintenance contract?

- Compatibility with other systems: Will the new system "talk" with other systems in use in the library, i.e., OCLC?

- Networking: Will the new system communicate with other systems outside the library?

- Response time: What is the vendor's definition of "response time"? What are the response times for each module? Will the automated system be impacted by linkage to other computers that are added?

- Upgrading: What accommodations are made for upgrading equipment and software? Does the library have to pay for future revisions of software?

- Expansion: What are the growth and limitations of the automated system? How much storage does the hardware have? Is it expandable?

- Training: What is the cost of training? How many trainers will be available to train the staff and what is the time element involved? Is the proposed training period compatible with the library's needs? What is the quality of the service offered? Who is trained? Have others benefitted from it?

- Training documentation: What documentation is provided for training purposes? Are user manuals clearly written and comprehensible?

- Company reliability documentation: What is the financial stability of the vendor? Are audited financial statements included? Are names, addresses, and telephone numbers of key personnel provided?

- Client documentation: Are there other libraries using the proposed automated system? Are names, addresses, and telephone numbers of key personnel provided?

- User groups: Are there user groups to contact to discuss problems and practices?

- Projected Costs: What are the projected costs over a five-to seven-year period, i.e., training, cabling, insurance, modifications, library furniture, supplies, etc.?

Benchmarking

After you have evaluated the proposed systems and have selected the vendor that most adequately matches your library's requirements, you may want to evaluate the actual performance of the system. Upon successful completion of a series of evaluation tests, a library accepts the automated system, and signs a contract. Benchmarking can be defined as demonstrating the capabilities of the automated system as it would operate in your library setting. The preferred method involves having the project manager or team go to the vendor headquarters where a predesigned automated system is set up. The alternative is to have the vendor operate the equipment in your library.

"Benchmarks usually involve the use of various performance indicators such as response time, report preparation time, and total time to catalog X number of items with Y number of terminals operating at predefined speeds" (Matthews 1980). It is very important that the files used in the performance test are as large as those found in the proposed system and that the data processed during the test is representative of the data with which the system will eventually work. Benchmarking should simulate as closely as possible actual conditions under which functions will be performed. Each function should be executed separately and evaluated against the specific requirements established in the library's list of specifications.

The vendor should demonstrate for you that the system is able to perform required tasks for a specified period of time without failure. For example, a reliability standard for a circulation system might involve a 98 percent level of effectiveness for a period of 60 consecutive work days. If the system were "down" for more than 1.2 days out of 60 days or an average of 7.2 days per year, the circulation staff would not be able to adequately charge and discharge books.

It is common for the RFP or Systems Selection Committee to draw up a "Memorandum of Agreement" to include penalties. Standard language used in the document might be "On the basis of the RFP, the system will be up and running by," or "The automated library system will do what it is supposed to do or. . . . " If the vendor is unable to meet a prespecified level of effectiveness, the library may deselect that vendor.

Benchmarks are expensive to prepare and conduct. However, if the project team has not had the opportunity to observe operative vendor systems in other libraries or wants additional verification that the system will do what it is supposed to do, benchmarking is the answer.

After all of the components of the automated system have been successfully benchmarked, the contract is signed, the new system is installed, and the staff is trained. Once the system is fully activated, acceptance tests are completed on site to evaluate performance.

Contract Negotiations

The contract itself is a complicated document usually drafted by the library's legal representative in conjunction with the project management staff. It protects the interests of the library and ensures that the automated system performs as described in the vendor's proposal. It succinctly delineates the ways in which the vendor must provide the support necessary to implement and successfully maintain all of the functional and system specifications and includes provisions for documentation and training. The contract should clearly state the procedures and schedule to be followed in paying for the system, and payment should be contingent on system implementation and acceptance, not on calendar dates.

If you are migrating or upgrading, examine previous contracts for loopholes or omissions.[10] Most vendors will offer you a standard contract, but you should be aware that these documents are written to protect the vendor's interests, not the library's. The importance of a well drafted contract cannot be overstated. Your contract should be precisely articulated to include terms, conditions, and penalty clauses in order to avoid future conflicts and liability.[11]

Installation

Within 90 days after the contract has been signed, you are ready to begin the process of installing, activating, evaluating, and accepting the new system. Before installation can take place, the site must be prepared. Site preparation

---

10. The issue of proprietary software can be a very serious one. Your current vendor will be very concerned with the way in which you obtain data from the system and move it to a new system. Be careful to discuss this with your new vendor and document everything in your contract so that you will not be vulnerable to a lawsuit. Cooperation, diplomacy, and forethought are assets. There have been several instances where previous vendors have become quite angry and lawsuits have been threatened.

11. For further information on writing and negotiating the contract, see Cortez 1987, 81-102.

should be contingent on specifications supplied by the vendor which indicate layout guidelines for the new equipment. These specifications should be followed precisely because warranties can be voided if proper installation procedures are not complied with. Typical specifications include:

- Hardware installation specifications, i.e., dimensions, space clearance, weight, power requirements (dedicated outlets, length of cable, surge protectors, etc.);

- Electrical power specifications, i.e., amps, volts, wattage, number and type of receptacles; power supply generators, surge protectors;

- Temperature specifications, i.e., 60-70 degrees Fahrenheit with adequate air flow;

- Humidity specifications, i.e., 40-60 percent;

- Ceiling, floor, and partition specifications, i.e., insulation and space for electrical lines and cables;

- Storage facilities specifications, i.e., shelving or storage cabinets for disks, tapes, cartridges, paper, cleaning supplies, spare parts, backup hardware;

- Lighting specifications, i.e., positioning of lighting; fluorescent lighting to reduce glare on computer screens;

- Cabling specifications, i.e., type of cabling necessary to transmit data; cable length requirements; cable paths (up walls, under floors, or in ceilings);

- Floor specifications, i.e., raised flooring to conceal power cables or to distribute weight of equipment; type of floor covering which best minimizes static electricity and noise;

- Safety and fire specifications, i.e., smoke detectors, fire extinguishers, fire retardant materials;

- Security specifications, i.e., equipment locks, safe locations for monitoring of equipment.

A major implementation task is to achieve environmental conditions that are suitable for both personnel and the new system. For example, extremes in temperature and humidity adversely affect the performance of personnel and can also cause the equipment to malfunction. Magnetic disks, used for online storage, and magnetic tapes, used for backup, must operate in a relatively dust-free environment. It may be necessary to provide a partitioned area to accommodate the processor, magnetic tape units, and even printers, if noise is a problem. Inadequate lighting can cause visual discomfort, headaches, fatigue, and depression. High levels of illumination reflect glare on the monitor, the keyboard, and the desktop and distort the reading of documents. Fluorescent lamps have been found to simulate daylight most closely and are suggested. For all of the above factors, vendors should be consulted for advice.

In addition, you will want to look at different ways of arranging furniture around the new equipment. Try to design a layout that is pleasing to the eye. Choose furniture that is comfortable and color coordinated, within the constraints of your library budget. Be aware of dimensions, and be sure to provide enough space around the equipment to allow for easy access and adequate flow of people. In particular, make sure that disabled patrons have access to terminals. Both patrons and staff should feel comfortable in the new setting so that a smooth transition will take place.

Other important considerations which are often overlooked relate to new work patterns that will be assumed by the reorganization of work areas. For example, integrated systems bring together the work of catalog and acquisitions librarians, since both use essentially the same tools. It may be necessary to provide working space within departments for members of the staff to share time on equipment. Library space may have to be reorganized.

Terminals for online public access catalogs will have to be placed at strategic points around the library, requiring additional power points. Be aware that most second systems include additional public access terminals. These terminals require electricity and cabling, often in the center of the library where they are most difficult to install.

As an astute project manager, think about the mechanics of your layout before putting pen to paper. For example, you wouldn't want to place online public access catalogs in congested areas, i.e., adjacent to the Circulation Desk! You must provide access to entrances and exits to conform to safety codes. Also, remember that your plans aren't cast in concrete. The proposed layout should be as flexible as possible to allow for future modification or expansion.

Once you have completed your layout chart and have gained approval, two scenarios are possible. Some libraries initiate work by forwarding work orders along with the required layouts and specifications to a higher authority, while others are required to go through the process of soliciting, receiving, and evaluating bids for site preparation. Work is generally completed by local maintenance staff, or it is contracted out. You may wish to confer with local engineers, electricians, carpenters, and heating and air conditioning specialists. The extent of preparation will depend on the complexity of the automated system selected. As project manager, it is your responsibility to see that work is coordinated and runs smoothly, according to preset timetables. Be sure to keep on top of things, know what is happening, and make yourself available to answer any questions.

> *A word to the wise:* Planning is the name of the game. Don't put yourself in the position that one project manager did . . . the new online public access catalog was about to be installed . . . an air of excitement filled the library . . . staff were awaiting training, but . . . no one had ordered the terminals.

The Project Manager or designated person in charge should monitor the installation of both hardware and software to make sure that nothing is damaged. Equipment should be placed in predetermined locations. Library files are then loaded,[12] and tests are conducted to make sure that the system is operating properly. Software is checked, using test data, to make sure that it will perform required tasks, and malfunctions are corrected before the staff training process begins. Most contracts provide that within two weeks of delivery, the library will receive written certification from the vendor that the system has been installed and is considered to be in proper working order.

Training

The automated library system will eliminate many routine duties and, at the same time, will create new ones. Staff duties, therefore, will change; and job descriptions will have to be revised. Consideration must be given to the staff who operate the system. Training can be broken down into two broad categories.

1. The entire staff is generally provided with an overview of the automated system:

---

12. The retrospective conversion process will be discussed in detail in Chapter 5.

All operators are given a basic introduction in order to gain a broad understanding of the purpose and major functions of the new system. A schematic drawing can be shown to depict how the various subsystems interact, (i.e., acquisitions, serials, catalog, circulation, and online public access modules);

A demonstration is provided for each subsystem;

Documentation, consisting of written manuals, system flow-charts, and drawings to show how the system functions, and help numbers is provided.

2. Those who are going to operate the system components must be trained to operate new hardware and software to carry out assigned tasks:

Specialist skills are taught, based on a description of job duties and responsibilities;

Detailed, hands-on system training is provided;

Staff is taught to cope with problems, such as how to proceed with work if the system is not functioning, who to call in an emergency, what steps can be taken to rectify problems;

Step-by-step procedure documentation is provided for each component.

A well-written contract will specify exactly who will be trained, where training will take place, what will be covered, the provisions for ensuring designated levels of operating proficiency, and the dates of the training. Vendors often limit operator training to a small number of staff who, in turn, train their own. Preferably, training should take place in the library environment.

Clayton and Damodaran have identified the following steps that should be considered when developing a training program:

• Identify the people to be trained;

- Identify the activities in the new system which will require special training;

- Establish the required method(s) of training;

- Prepare any training programmes which are to be run internally;

- Arrange the schedule for the programme;

- Conduct the programme;

- Review the programme (as stated in: Clayton 1987, 172-173; see Damodaran 1980)

When selecting key staff who will be responsible for supervising and training others, make sure that the trainers you choose mix well with other staff and can impart new concepts clearly and simply, without frustration. Trainers should be competent, outgoing, and supportive of the staff that they are going to teach. Each trainer is responsible for setting the stage for learning and for getting the trainees involved. The presentation given by the trainer will affect learning. Helpful hints for the trainer include:

- Create a relaxed atmosphere;

- Maintain a positive attitude;

- Go with the flow;

- Vary the teaching method, style, and pace to keep a maximum level of interest and enthusiasm;

- Vary materials used;

- Move from lecture to hands-on activity;

- Involve yourself in the learning process; listen and watch;

- Motivate trainees; exhibit support and enthusiasm;

- Relate real life workplace situations to the teaching experience;

- Be ready for the unexpected; turn problems encountered into assets by sharing group experiences to work out problems;

- Show appreciation for input; be enthusiastic about achievements;

- Make contact with each trainee on a one-to-one basis at each workstation;

- Illustrate key concepts whether on the board, at the terminal, or with visual aids;

- Make clear eye contact with members of the group;

- Review concepts; give people time to think and to formulate ideas;

- Discuss questions/answers: Use direct questioning; relay questions from one trainee to another; spark innovative thinking; energize the group; and leave room for comments.

Audiovisual aids, flip charts, overhead transparencies, etc., emphasize and clarify key points. They take complex concepts and illustrate them in an easy-to-understand form. Using audiovisual aids directs the group's attention and increases their interest. They are an excellent learning tool and an excellent source of review. They are inexpensive, flexible, versatile, can be prepared ahead of time, and quickly outline key points. Helpful hints for the trainer include:

Use simple graphics, i.e., key words or short phrases;

Condense output:	Limit each page to one topic or key idea;
	Use thick lettering;
	Use abbreviations;
	Separate lines with plenty of white space;

| Vary emphasis: | Use no more than three colors on a page; |
| | Underline for emphasis. |

Clear system documentation is essential. It serves as an instructional tool that allows staff to understand and operate each component of the automated system efficiently and in a standardized manner. It also provides immediate feedback when used as a quick-reference tool. If the library decides to develop its own training aids and support materials, be sure that training manuals/guides are uncluttered, simple to use and understand, and that they include step-by-step procedures showing how to operate each component of the system. Tutorials should be provided by the vendor for backup purposes of self-paced instruction.

Once initial training is completed, staff should be given adequate time for hands-on experiences in order to familiarize themselves with the system. Follow-up sessions should be conducted to reinforce training at work stations that are identical to the ones on which the staff members perform their assigned tasks and to correct problems encountered during the initial session. Staff should be encouraged to ask questions and build confidence. Additional workshops should be provided as software and hardware are upgraded, and the contract should state that upgrades, enhancements, adequate documentation, and further training be provided.

Library patrons are the ultimate benefactors of the new automated system. Their services might be affected temporarily as the system is installed and the workforce is trained, but inconveniences can be minimized if posters are distributed advertising the implementation of the new system. Brochures, bookmarks, and handouts describing the new system can be circulated to increase user awareness and interest. If an online public access catalog is among the modules being installed, patrons will be directly affected in the training process. An education program should be conducted by reference librarians who are stationed at designated terminals to explain the new system and orient the patron.

System Activation

Once the hardware and software have been installed and tested, supplies have been ordered, essential files have been created and loaded, and staff have been trained, it is time to activate the automated system. There are four changeover procedures that should be considered, each with its own advantages and disadvantages (Reynolds 1985: 104-105; see Clayton 1987, 154-156).

Total Approach

In the total or "all-at-once" approach, the old system is terminated, and the new system is immediately put in its place. Costs are down because it's cheaper to run one system (rather than two together), and benefits can be realized immediately. There is less disruption for the staff and patrons in the changeover.

But, be aware that this approach requires the most planning. The new system must be thoroughly tested, and staff must be trained to manage it in advance.

Pilot Approach

Your library may be one of several self-contained branches. In this multi-agency environment, the system is installed in a selected branch. Because it is done on a small scale, it can be accomplished more quickly than in a total system approach. Program errors can be immediately corrected; staff is more receptive to the new system, and overall installation progresses at a more relaxed pace. However, the implementation process can be very slow, and full benefits aren't realized until changeover is complete. A major drawback is that it is difficult to measure performance of the completed system, particularly the response.

Phased Approach

In the Phased Approach, modules or subsystems are installed one at a time. For example a cataloging module might be introduced first, followed by acquisitions, circulation, and finally an online public access catalog (OPAC). This is not always an available alternative. But, many libraries are now in the process of adding an OPAC module to their existing automated systems. You may apply the above advantages and disadvantages of the Pilot Approach to this Phased Approach. It gives staff time to adjust and learn and reduces the chances of system failure.

Parallel Approach

In the Parallel Approach, the old system and the new system are run side-by-side for a contracted period of time. The old system is left running until the new system is proved successful. Although this is the costliest of methods, it is the least confusing. Staff and patrons can compare results and see immediately the benefits of the new system. Modifications can be made with a minimum of disruption; and in the event of system failure, the old system can act as a backup.

When the system is "up and running," acceptance tests may be used to evaluate all of the system components and functions again. This is not a rehash of the benchmark process. It takes place in the library with the actual equipment installed. The requirements are fully specified either in the RFP or in the negotiated contract. Detailed logs are kept of any difficulties encountered, and final payment is not made to the vendor until each of the tests are passed. Three types of tests are generally included:

- System reliability test, i.e., "The system is expected to operate reliably for a period of (20 to) 60 consecutive days at an uptime level of 98 percent." If the system fails, the period starts again. It is a good idea to bring the system down intentionally to see if the system can be recovered and restored without loss of data.

- Functional test, i.e., performance of each function or feature is checked against requirements specified in the RFP or stated in vendor promotional literature. The process can be segmented into several sessions.

- Response time test, i.e., "The system shall exhibit average response times not exceeding:
    - six seconds for author, title inquiries;
    - eight seconds for subject inquiries;
    - two seconds for charge, renewal, discharge . . . functions."

Stop watches should be used to measure response times (elapsed time between input and output); and, if possible, vendor representatives should be present during the test.

Summary

When planning for your automated library system, follow the steps discussed in the planning process. Justify the need for automating, and be sure to support your conclusions with statistical and budgetary data. Assess the current library operations; examine costs and cost effectiveness of the new system; and show how an automated library system will streamline operations and improve service for both staff and patrons. Emphasize the climate of acceptance that has made automated library systems a favorable alternative in competitive library settings.

Ultimate success of the automated library system depends on the time, effort, and informed decision-making that goes into the planning process. The project manager must be a skillful planner and problem solver who is capable of overseeing the dynamics of the project. Committees should be broadly based to lay the groundwork for final negotiation and contractual commitment, and committee members should responsibly represent the work force in total.

Research indicates that the broader the structure, the more involved the staff, the easier the transition, and the greater the acceptance of the automated library system.

Some libraries hire consultants to assist in the design process and ultimate selection. The trend in the 1980s was for librarians themselves to become involved in the politics and dynamics of automation and to use their own expertise as much as possible in doing the leg work, writing the Request for Proposal (RFP) and in evaluating systems of competing vendors. Consultants are sometimes used to conduct feasibility studies, to assist in establishing mandatory and desirable requirements stipulated in the RFP, and/or to provide ongoing advice throughout the project. Whether your library hires a consultant or not will depend on your own special circumstances.

Writing the RFP is a time-consuming and tedious task, but an all-important one. It must be written clearly and realistically and analyzed critically. The detailed specifications give each vendor a perspective on how to satisfy the specific needs of your library in terms of functional and system requirements. It is also advantageous to include a list of questions that you would like all vendors to answer. The RFP serves as an evaluation tool for librarians and consultants who compare bids, side-by-side and negotiate for the final contract.

In the selection process, critical analysis of each system and functional component takes place. Hardware and software capabilities, guarantees, service, and updates are scrutinized. Compatibility, networking, response time, and expansion are carefully evaluated. The reliability and stability of each vendor is thoroughly investigated. Client documentation, vendor documentation, training procedures, quality of service, and projected costs are analyzed. Benchmarking is used as an additional tool to evaluate performance of required automated tasks on a selected vendor's predesigned system.

After successfully benchmarking the automated library system, the contract is drawn up by the library's legal department and signed. This is an official document that binds the library to the vendor. It should be precisely written in order to avoid future conflict or liability.

When preparing the site for installation, follow the specifications supplied by the vendor. These include layout procedures for placement of hardware, electrical lines/cabling, acceptable temperature and humidity ranges, safety and security regulations, etc. Pay particular attention to environmental considerations and design which best suit your library's needs. Your staff must be well trained to meet the needs of the patrons. The contract should include specifics on exactly who will be trained, where training will take place and when, levels of operator efficiency to be attained, and ongoing support provided by the vendor. If the library itself is involved in training, it is essential to provide (1) trainers who are "teachers," capable of motivating staff and high-lighting concepts in a step-by-step progression, and (2) clear documentation.

The staff will adjust to a total, module-by-module, branch-by-branch, or parallel system changeover as predetermined by the project team. Once the new system is up and running, it must be evaluated on site.[13] Not until all of the system components and functions are fully tested and successfully compared against the specifications in the RFP is the vendor paid.

Each step in the planning process is an integral part of the total approach. The time and effort you put into the planning process will be reflected in the success or failure of your automated library system.

References

Boss, Richard W. Sept.-Oct., 1990. The Procurement of Library Automated Systems. *Library Technology Reports* 27(2): 629-749.

Clayton, Marlene. 1987. *Managing Library Automation.* Brookfield, VT: Gower Publishing Company Limited.

Corbin, John Boyd. 1981. *Developing Computer-Based Library Systems.* Phoenix, AZ: Oryx Press.

_____. 1985. *Managing the Library Automation Project.* Phoenix, AZ: Oryx Press.

Cortez, Edwin M. 1987. *Proposals and Contracts for Library Automation: Guidelines for Preparing RFPs.* Chicago: Pacific Information Inc.

Damodaran, L. et al. 1980. *Designating Systems for People.* Manchester, U.K.: NCC Publications.

Drabenstott, Jon, ed. 1989. Truth in Automating: The Multi-Library Experience. *Library Hi Tech, Consecutive Issue 27* 7(3): 53-58.

---

13. This is not to be confused with "benchmarking" which takes place earlier in the planning process and which is usually done at the vendor's headquarters.

Epstein, Susan Baerg. Jan., 1991. Implementing a Second System: Some New Concerns. *Library Journal* 116(1): 76-77.

Heitshu, Sara C. 1989. Truth in Automating: The Multi-Library Experience, University of Arizona. *Library Hi Tech, Consecutive Issue 27*, Jon Draberstott, ed. 7(3): 62-64.

Matthews, Joseph R. 1980. *Choosing an Automated Library System: A Planning Guide*. Chicago: American Library Association.

Northland Pioneer College. Sept. 30, 1988. *Learning Resource Center Automation Study: Request for Proposal.*

Reynolds, Dennis. 1985. *Library Automation*. New York: R.R. Bowker Company.

Sources for Further Reading

Boss, Richard W. 1990. *Library Manager's Guide to Automation*. 3rd ed. Boston: G. K. Hall.

Byerly, Greg. Dec., 1990. Introducing Staff to Change. *Computers in Libraries* 10(11): 39-40.

Corbin, John Boyd. 1992. *Corbin's Library Automation Handbook*. Phoenix, AZ: Oryx Press.

Drabenstott, Jon et al. Spring, 1987. The Consultants' Corner -- The RFP in the Automation Procurement Process. *Library Hi Tech* 5(1): 99-112.

Dyer, Hillary, and Anne Morris. 1990. *Human Aspects of Library Automation*. Aldershot, Hants: Gower Publishing Company.

Fields, Keith Michael, et al. 1992. *Planning for Automation*. New York: Neal Schuman.

Gyeszly, Suzanne D., and John B. Harer. 1991. Replacement of Automated systems: Organizational and Staff Training Considerations. *Journal of Library Administration* 14(1): 87-115.

Johnson, Peggy. 1991. *Automation and Organizational Change in Libraries.* Boston: G. K. Hall.

Johnson, S. W. Sept., 1989. RFP Released for Ohio State Library System. *Information Retrieval and Library Automation* 25(4): 1-2.

Klobas, Jane E. Oct., 1990. Managing Technological Change in Libraries and Information Services. *Electronic Library* 8(5): 344-349.

Leinbach, Philip E., et al. 1990. Personnel Administration in an Automated Environment. *Journal of Library Administration* 13(1-2): 1-214.

Mikita, E. G. June, 1991. Criteria-Based Analysis of an RFP to Re-evaluate an Integrated Library System. *Information Technology and Libraries* 10(2): 140-145.

Nees, R. J. Apr., 1990. In the Eyes of the Beholder. *Inform* 4(4): 52-57.

Newhard, Robert. Winter, 1991. Leadership in an Age of Technological Change: The Significance of Technology for Public Library Leadership. *Library Administration and Management* 5(1): 20-24.

Pitkin, Gary, ed. 1991. *Library Systems Migration: Changing Automated Systems in Libraries and Information Centers.* Westport, CT: Meckler.

Predmore, L. G. Dec., 1988. The Second Time Around: Preparing the RFP for a Second-Generation System in a Consortium Environment. *Information Technology and Libraries* 7(4): 394-400.

Spyers-Duran, P. 1990. Cost of Library Technologies: The Bottomless Pit of the 1990s. *Technical Services Quarterly* 8(1): 3-16.

Thomas, M. L. March, 1991. You Only Get What You Ask For? Tips on Writing an RFP. *Inform* 5(3): 30-32.

Core Modules

Five core modules are available from most automated library systems vendors: cataloging, circulation, acquisitions, serials, and OPAC (Online Public or Patron Access Catalog). Some vendors offer other modules as well such as reserve book room, community information, media booking, bulletin board, etc. The first five, however, form the basis of the automated library system.

This chapter will examine the components of the cataloging, circulation, acquisitions, and serials modules. The OPAC module will be discussed separately in Chapter 6.

Cataloging

In many ways, the cataloging module is the most important. It is here that the integrity of the database (i.e., the library's holdings) will be maintained. The database has to be in machine-readable form, and the recommended format for achieving this is MARC II.[1] One MARC II bibliographic record represents each title in the database; it is input and maintained in the cataloging module. The MARC record is the focal point on which the system operates, the driving force behind all of the modules. The automated library system can be set up so that it is possible to view the full MARC record (or any portion of it) from the acquisitions, serials, cataloging, circulation, or OPAC module. All five modules manipulate portions of it. For example, the Circulation Desk staff accesses fields from MARC records, via item records, to link them with patron records and determine status when books are checked out; the acquisition staff links them with current vendor information.

The automated library system should be able to handle all MARC formats -- monographs, serials, maps, music, sound recordings, visual materials, archived materials, computer files, and film. In the cataloging module, the operator should have the ability to create records online by means of menus, formatted screens, and/or prompts. Records should be able to be searched by author, title, subject, call number, LC card number, OCLC number, ISSN, and

---

1. For a detailed explanation of MARC II format, see Chapter 5.

5 CORE MODULES

Figure 7.

ISBN. Mnemonic keys should be able to be defined by the library;[2] and text editing routines should eliminate the need for rekeying of entire fields or subfields. It should be easy to modify the record to add local information such as call number, accession number, extent of holdings on multi-volumes, ordering information, local notes, etc. Input of Chinese, Japanese, and Korean (CJK) characters should be possible, using an acceptable standard, preferably that used by RLIN and OCLC.[3]

The module should allow for (1) the loading of bibliographic tapes from automated cataloging services; (2) online access to cataloging sources such as OCLC, WLN, RLIN, and UTLAS; and (3) access to records stored on CD-ROM discs, such as Bibliofile by Library Corporation and Supercat by Gaylord. A check should be made against the database to see if the incoming record should be added as a new record, should be held for review, or should update an existing record. If there is a match, the existing record may be replaced by the incoming record. The library should have the option of designating certain fields in the original bibliographic record as "protected" (unchanged and not overlaid by the new record). For example, if holdings statements or local subject headings have been designated as protected, those fields should be transferred "as is" to the replacement record, along with all item and order records that are attached to the original bibliographic record. When new records are created, the system should automatically create item and order records.

The library should also have complete flexibility in deciding what bibliographic fields and subfields it wishes to index. Indexing is important as it allows the contents of a field or subfield to be searched. It should be possible to output full MARC records, thus allowing the database to be downloaded and made available in other formats, such as COM (Computer Output Microforms) and CD-ROM.

---

2. Mnemonic is an abbreviation that is easily remembered because of its relation to the actual word, i.e., "q" for quit; "e" for edit.

3. CJK records often contain information in both CJK characters and romanization. The system should be able to handle CJK records which include both characters and romanization. It should also support the electronic transfer of CJK records, including both characters and romanized fields, from RLIN and OCLC.

MITINET/marc

MITINET/marc is a recent software product which lets users create original MARC records in-house, without the user needing to learn anything about MARC. The product works through a series of prompts and instructions in English, accompanied by clear examples for every item of data. AACR2 rule numbers are also cited. When the entry is completed by the user, MITINET/marc supplies all of the additional data necessary to create a properly tagged MARC record. The software runs on IBM and Macintosh computers, and the records can be imported directly into the cataloging module. As of April 1991, 48 automated library systems cataloging modules accepted MITINET/marc records. The company is in the process of adding new vendors and expanding regional offices.[4]

Item Records

Item records are constructed in the cataloging module and used for circulation purposes. Each copy of a title is represented in the system by an item record which contains brief information about the title and can be accessed quickly and easily. The item record is linked to the full bibliographic record by a sequential control number. It is also linked to its circulating title by a unique machine-readable number on a barcode affixed to the book.[5] By running a wand across the barcode label, the staff can track the status of the library item. There should be no limit in the system to the number of item records that may be linked to a bibliographic record.

Authority Records

An authority file is a list of unique name and subject headings (authority records) authorized for a library catalog. Name headings include authors, corporate bodies, conference names, uniform titles, series; and subject headings include topics and geographical names. They are established to provide a single form of entry for a particular entity or concept and to reduce the possibility of ambiguity between titles or concepts that are similar. An authority file also

---

4. Headquarters: Information Transform, Inc. 502 Leonard Street, Madison, WI 53711; (608) 255-4800.

5. See Chapter 5 for further information on item records and barcodes.

provides (1) a system of cross-references from forms of entry that are not used to the form that is used ("See" references) and (2) references to other headings which are related in some way to the given heading ("See also" references). Therefore, it controls the types of headings that are added to the main bibliographic file.

All authority records should be stored in the MARC Authorities format; the library should be able to define which fields in the bibliographic record are to be authority controlled. The cataloging system should offer access to the authority file during data entry and include an option for automatic, global updates to old authority headings. Input and display of diacritics[6] should be supported as well. The system should incorporate standards based on the Extended Latin Alphabet Coded Character Set for Bibliographic Use: ANSI/NISO Z39.47-1985 (sometimes called ANSEL).

The library is usually given the option to retain local headings and to choose whether or not to create cross-references. The system should also offer the ability to search for and generate a list of headings which conflict in any way with the library's authority control structure, i.e., duplicate authority headings, bibliographic records attached to unauthorized headings, authorized headings which have been used as "See from" tracings in other authority records, or blind references.[7]

Circulation

Circulation is often one of the first library operations to be automated. Other technical operations are relegated to back rooms, out of public view, but the circulation process is highly visible. At the circulation desk, there are often bottlenecks, long lines of patrons, and staff that are unable to keep pace with the work. Automating circulation gives the library control over its resources.

Circulation Policies

The library's circulation policies are usually recorded in the system in a series of tables. These tables are stored in what is referred to as a "parameter file."

---

6. A diacritic is a mark added to a letter to indicate its pronunciation.

7. A "blind reference" is a reference to a heading that has been removed from the catalog.

An authorized library staff member can change or add to the tables at any time. Typical tables include the following:

1. Loan Rule table. This table specifies, for example, how long an item may be borrowed, how many times it may be renewed, when various overdue notices are produced, etc. The table can be set up to allow for the days the library is closed.

2. Patron Block table. This table lets the library set automatic patron blocks, i.e., patron card expired, too many items checked out, outstanding fines, etc. Blocks should be automatically removed when the patron has satisfied the required condition.

3. Library Calendar table. This table tells the system the days that the library is closed, or in the case of hourly loans, when the library opens and closes each day.

4. Fines table. This table lets the library enforce fines procedures. Fines allow the library to create and maintain financial records for patrons who lose items, damage them, or return overdue materials. The library can establish and maintain a rate schedule for fines. Fines should be able to be computed by a daily rate, hourly rate, flat rate, sliding rate, or a per-notice rate. The library can decide on grace periods and maximum fines. The fines due should be displayed onscreen; and options, such as the following, should be provided: charge to the patron's record; accept full or partial payment; or adjust, forgive, or refund fines.

   The patron record should reflect the total balance due as well as individual item identification with appropriate dates and the amount paid for each item. There should be an ability to post money to specific items. The system should be able to compute replacement charges as well, based on input from the library, i.e., a percentage of the existing fine, the processing charge, or the price of the copy. The fines procedure should also offer an override capability.

5. Notice and Report Contents table. This table allows the library to design the format of its notices and reports.

Check-Out/Check-In
or Charge/Discharge

The check-in and check-out functions control much of the daily transaction activity in the library. The check-out function creates a link between a patron and an item. Typically, a check-out transaction consists of (1) scanning a machine-readable label which uniquely identifies a patron and is affixed to the patron's library card and (2) scanning a machine-readable label which uniquely identifies an item in the collection. When the item is checked in, the patron-item link is automatically broken, and all appropriate statistical files are updated, i.e., fine records, recalls, etc.[8] The circulation module should have a way of dealing with circulating items which are not in the database. During the check-out process, the system should display a message to the operator that the item is not in its files. It should then be able to create an item record and attach it to a bibliographic record in the database.

Inquiry

Two types of inquiry can be run from circulation: (1) item inquiry and (2) patron inquiry.

Item Inquiry. It should be possible to search for the item by title, author, or bar code label and answer the following questions.

1. Is the item on file?

2. Does the item circulate?

3. Does it circulate to this patron type?

---

8. Typically these daily transaction activities are kept in a transactions file. While the transaction is complete and the patron has returned the borrowed item, the details of that transaction are destroyed. However, for statistical purposes, the library may keep general information, such as the number of items borrowed within a particular time period.

4. Is the item available at this branch?

5. How many copies are there of this item?

6. Is the item charged out? If so, what is the due date?

7. Is the item on hold? If so, what kind of hold? Which patron is next in line?

8. Is the item overdue? If so, has it been recalled?

9. Is the item missing, withdrawn, on order, in process, or claimed returned by a patron?

Patron Inquiry. It should be possible to search for a patron by name or bar code label, Social Security number (SSN) or driver's license number. The patron record should display onscreen, followed by a list of all items currently charged to the patron. Fines and payments made should also display as well as messages (i.e., A held item is ready for pickup at . . . Library).

Reasons for patron blocks should also be evident. It should be easy to register a new patron. The system should allow for the creation of certain defaults which are frequently common to library patrons, i.e., city, state, zip code, borrower privileges, expiration dates, etc. There is much concern with ensuring patron privacy. Libraries typically do not keep records of transactions which are completed.

Renewal

Renewal extends the due date which was set by the check-out function. The patron status should be verified, and any block messages should be displayed, such as "on hold for another patron." The item status should be verified, and renewal limits, if any, should be checked.

Holds/Reserves

Holds/Reserves allows a patron to reserve a copy of a title which is currently unavailable. The system should establish a chronological list of patrons who are waiting for each item. There are various kinds of holds:

1. Title-level hold. This hold reserves the first available copy regardless of edition, branch, etc.

2. Edition-level hold. This hold reserves the first copy of a particular edition.

3. Branch-level hold. This hold reserves the first copy owned by a particular branch.

4. Copy-level hold. This hold reserves an individual copy.

An expiration date may be specified when the hold in placed, or the hold may be indefinite. At any time, the number of holds on an item should be available.

Notices and Reports

The system should automatically generate notices. The type of notices and the format used are defined by the library in the Notice and Report Contents table. The library should also define the time lag before a notice is produced and the amount of time between notices. Examples of notices include overdues, recalls, billing, fines, hold availability, and hold cancellations. The system should also be able to produce reports on demand, i.e., by branch and system total; by categories of items, patrons, call numbers, and items added or withdrawn; by check-out date; by number of titles and copies owned by a branch; by copies currently missing or overdue; by list of titles with cumulative circulation per copy; by total number of patrons; by number of new patrons; by number of patrons registered by status, age, geographical location; and number of transactions by patron category, age, or residential location.

Acquisitions

The acquisitions module should eliminate the need for paper files of vendors, account records, selection lists, and purchase orders. It should provide for all standard acquisitions activities -- ordering, receiving, payments, claims, cancellations, fund accounting and statistics, and gift and exchange material. It should also adhere to the BISAC (Book Industry Systems Advisory Committee) standards for computerized book ordering.[9]

Orders

The system should be able to handle new orders, standing orders, subscriptions, blanket orders, approval plans, prepaid items, purchase plans, etc. Order information may be keyed in, downloaded from a bibliographic utility (such as OCLC, RLIN, or UTLAS), or transmitted to and from a vendor. If the information is keyed in from a terminal, the system should prompt for necessary information, such as author, title, number of copies, fund, vendor, etc. The library should be able to set its own prompts. It should be possible to "default" certain data so that it is not necessary to key the same information repeatedly. For example, if a group of orders is being sent to one vendor, then the vendor code should only be keyed once for the group. The system should automatically search the bibliographic file to alert the operator to unnecessary duplicate orders. If the fund amount is exceeded, the operator should also be alerted. The order record should include the order type, jobber or publisher, number of copies ordered, final destination of each copy, fund or funds to which the order is being charged, encumbered and expended prices, invoice numbers, copy-specific information, details and chronology relating to order status, and comments field.

If the information is downloaded from a bibliographic utility into the acquisitions module, the operator should be able to add the vendor, fund, and any other order information. The same duplication checks as above should be performed.

Major approval plan vendors, such as Baker and Taylor, Blackwell, Midwest, Coutts, and Yankee Approval, can download bibliographic data and invoices for books about to be shipped to the library for approval. The system should check for duplication. When the books arrive, it is easy to record the ones which are to be sent back and to pay the invoice for items which are being kept.

Funds

Funds should be given a strict security code. The system should allow for the setting up of different funds. At any time, the amount allocated, committed, and spent should be available. There should be an ability to set budget figures for

---

9. See Chapter 9 for a fuller explanation of the BISAC standards.

each fund at the beginning of a fiscal year with adjustments for carry over from the previous year. An exchange rate table should be maintained with an ability to perform automatic currency conversion. Purchase order encumbrances and invoice expenditures should be maintained automatically. When library items are ordered, the funds should be encumbered. When the item is received, the encumbrance amount should be dis-encumbered and the real cost expended. The invoice records should show the actual cost, discounts, and any shipping or handling costs. The system should be able to handle different types of payments as well, i.e., prepayment, deposit accounts, purchase orders for a single title or a list of titles.

Claiming

The system should monitor items to see that they actually arrive in the library within the required period of time. This includes claiming items that have not arrived. The library should be able to set up a claim period and have claim letters generated automatically (with the text of the letter defined by the library). The system should also monitor the performance of vendors, regarding the amount of time it takes them to deliver orders.

Suppliers/Vendors

The system should store vendor names, addresses, and claim cancellation notice cycle. It should also store information on the type of material supplied by the vendor, whether the vendor needs to be prepaid, average discounts, delivery time, etc.

Reports

Reports should be available which provide information on fund accounting, ordering, and receiving. It should be possible to produce statistical records that relate to specific vendors and show, for example, the number of titles and copies ordered along with the dollar amount. It should also be possible to produce selection lists. A selection list may be a list of titles to be accessed by branches for ordering purposes or a desiderata list of those titles that the library desires to obtain but which are not readily available. Other reports might include lists of gifts by donor, lists of titles by characteristics such as final destination, type of order, status of order, and new titles lists.

Serials

To a degree, the serials module should follow the same procedures used for the acquisitions module when ordering new titles. Although different funds are usually set up for serials, fund and supplier files should be common to both functions. The serials module should handle all types of serials: periodicals, journals, newspapers, government documents, monographic serials, etc., and deal with regular and irregular frequencies as well as cumulations, pocket parts, supplements, and serials arriving on microfilm. It should offer online access to serials vendors such as Faxon, Ebsco, and Harrasowitz, and should alert staff to subscriptions needing renewal.

Most systems present the serial record as a graphical representation of a "kardex" card. A box is drawn on the screen, showing the data of each issue, its volume and issue number, and the date it was received. Frequency information is used by the system to predict forthcoming issues; and expected issues and dates should be displayed, based on that information. The system should also allow for the check-in of unexpected issues such as an index or a supplement. Title changes and frequency changes should be dealt with by using the new frequency to automatically re-compute expected dates of arrival, new volume and issue numbers, and cover dates. Detailed information on expected, overdue, and claimed issues should be available; and claim forms for missing or overdue issues should be easily generated. The system should produce routing lists with priority levels as well as generate binding requirements, such as color, spine title, etc. Increasingly, serials modules are supporting the USMARC Format for Holdings and Locations.

Back-up Procedures

All of the library data should be copied or backed up to a cartridge tape once a week. It should be possible to perform this operation while the system is in use. Daily backup should also be performed. The system should allow the library to recover lost data and transactions up to the point when the system goes down, rather than having to use old backup tapes.

Summary

This chapter focuses on four of the five core modules of automated library systems software: cataloging, circulation, acquisitions, and serials. (The fifth --

the OPAC -- is discussed in Chapter 6.) The important features which should be present in each module are discussed below.

Cataloging

The cataloging module should:

1. handle MARC records in all formats;

2. create records online and load them into the system from automated cataloging sources, such as OCLC, WLN, RLIN, and UTLAS;

3. index on any bibliographic fields and/or subfields;

4. create and handle any number of item records linked to a bibliographic record;

5. handle an authority file, preferably in the MARC Authorities format;

6. define which fields in the MARC bibliographic record are to be authority controlled;

7. offer access to the authority file during data entry;

8. offer automatic global updates of authority records; and

9. handle diacritics, and CJK characters.

Circulation

The circulation module should:

1. customize circulation policies by means of tables stored in a parameter file;

2. check in and out books;

3. offer item inquiry and patron inquiry;

4. renew material;

5. place material on hold or reserve; and

6. generate notices and reports.

Acquisitions

The acquisitions module should:

1. adhere to the BISAC (Book Industry Systems Advisory Committee) standards;

2. offer electronic access to approval plan vendors;

3. generate orders;

4. handle funds;

5. generate claims notices;

6. keep information on suppliers and vendors; and

7. generate reports.

Serials

The serials module should:

1. offer online access to serials vendors;

2. alert staff to subscriptions needing renewal;

3. display a record of issues received;

4. predict the date of arrival of forthcoming issues;

5. handle unexpected issues;

6. handle title and frequency changes;

7. keep track of expected, overdue, and claimed issues;

8. generate claims forms;

9. produce priority routing lists; and

10. generáte lists of binding requirements, such as color, spine title, etc.

Sources for Further Reading

It is advantageous to write the automated library systems vendors who will send you information about their products, free of charge. For names and addresses, please refer to Chapter 2.

Badertscher, David A. Sept., 1988. MITINET/marc. *Information Technology and Libraries* 7(3): 326-330.

Coffey, James R. 1991. *Operational Costs in Acquisitions*. New York: Haworth Press.

Dykeman, Amy, and Bill Katz. 1989. *Automated Acquisitions: Issues for the Present and Future*. New York: Haworth Press (also published as *The Acquisitions Librarian*, No. 1, 1989).

Falsone, Anne Marie. Winter, 1986. Privacy of Circulation Files. *Journal of Library Administration* 7(4): 19-23.

Mika, Joseph J., and Bruce A. Shuman. April, 1988. Legal Issues Affecting Libraries and Librarians. *American Libraries* 19(4): 314-317.

Page, Mary. March, 1991. Authority Control in the Online Environment. *Computers in Libraries* 11(3): 8-12.

Retrospective Conversion

RECON (REtrospective CONversion) is the process of converting the library's previously created bibliographic records[1] to MARC (machine-readable cataloging) format, which simply means that a computer can read and interpret the record.

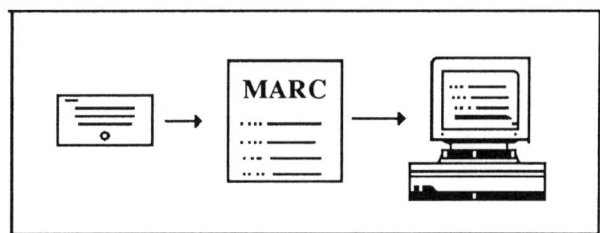

MARC II format is now the recognized national standard for bibliographic records that are exchanged and used by libraries of all types and sizes. It is the communications format recognized by automated library systems. This chapter will explain how MARC II came about; briefly trace the birth of MicroLIF (MICROcomputer Library Interchange Format); explain the relationship between automating and doing RECON; highlight the benefits and delineate problems; detail steps in the planning process; evaluate options for converting records; explain procedures followed by vendors, define points to discuss with them, and list their requirements; and consider cost implications.

Background

Before MARC II, librarians had been accustomed to ordering sets of catalog cards for new books from their jobber or from the Library of Congress. Others typed their own cards, doing original cataloging; or they obtained information

---

1. The records being converted may be in one of three formats:
(1) catalog cards, (2) paper shelf list; or (3) brief machine-readable records.

from cataloging records printed in library journals or in bibliographies. Gradually, computers became affordable to libraries; and it was no longer necessary for librarians everywhere to compose almost identical cataloging records for each item.

The basic structure of MARC was established through national and international standards. In the United States, the American National Standards Institute (ANSI) was designated as the organization for coordinating national standardization activity. It also represents the U.S. at the International Organization for Standardization (ISO) in Geneva. Its Z39 committee (now known as the National Information Standards Organization [NISO]), was given the responsibility for standardizing in the field of library work. It cooperates with other standards organizations such as the Canadian Standards Association (CSA) and the British Standards Institution (BSI).

In 1966, a pilot group of 20 libraries participated with the Library of Congress (LC) to test its newly devised MARC structure. Two years later, in 1968, MARC format was deemed a huge success. It was slightly revised, called MARC II, and offered via 9-track tapes to libraries using mainframe computers across the nation and around the world. This standardized format has opened doors to cooperative ventures. It quickly became a respected and acceptable communications format that everyone could share and understand. Libraries across the nation began to join bibliographic utilities, such as OCLC, RLIN, WLN, and UTLAS, in order to contribute and copy MARC-based catalog records. Catalogers began to talk a new language, that of MARC field tags.

What Does MARC Look Like?

A MARC record contains little tags or signposts composed of three-digit numbers that identify information that is shown on a catalog card:

000-099	Identification Numbers	
	010	LCCN
	020	ISBN
100-199	Main Entry	
	100	Personal Name or Author
200-299	Title	

245	Title Information (including Statement of Responsibility)
250	Edition
260	Publication Information

Two single-digit numbers (each being a number 0-9) follow the MARC tag. These are called indicators. One or both spaces may be used according to the rules spelled out for each field in MARC format guides. For example in the 260 0o field, the first 0 indicates that a publisher is present; the smaller second o means that the second indicator is undefined and left blank.

300-399   Physical Description

| 300 | Physical Description |

MARC fields are further subdivided into subfields (a, b, c...) which contain related pieces of data (i.e., number of pages, illustrations, and size of the item) and are preceded by delimiters.[2] For example: 300 oo _a675 p. : _bill. ;_c 24cm.

400-499   Series Statements

| 440 | Series |

500-599   Notes

| 520 | Annotation or Summary |

600-699   Subject Added Entries

| 650 | Topical Subject Heading |

---

2. Delimiters may be displayed as an underline character (_), a dollar sign ($), an "at" sign (@), or a double dagger (≠).

700-799   Other Added Entries

700   Personal Name Added Entry

800-899   Series Added Entries

900-999   Locally Defined Uses

900   Local Call Number (MicroLIF defined)

The Advent of the Microcomputer Age

When the microcomputer age arrived, smaller libraries were able to purchase microcomputer-based automated systems.[3] Software was developed especially for these microcomputers, and floppy disks were used to upload information onto hard disks. At first, storage capacity was limited, and vendors could not supply bibliographic records that contained all of the MARC fields. As a result, they each devised their own methods of selection and librarians voiced two concerns: (1) With no standards imposed, field information varied from vendor to vendor; and (2) they wanted book jobbers to offer MARC records with each new book so that they could upload new bibliographic records onto their microcomputer databases. Microcomputer storage capacity increased dramatically within a very short time; and these smaller computers quickly became capable of holding full MARC records.

What Is MicroLIF?

The MicroLIF (MICROcomputer Library Interchange Format) committee was created to establish industry-wide standards demanded by librarians. Book vendors, RECON vendors, and automation vendors met to develop standards for manufacturing MicroLIF disks as well as for programming microcomputer-based automated systems to read them. As of July 1, 1991, the full MARC record was adopted. Vendors were asked to follow the "MicroLIF Protocol," issue new

---

3. For a fuller description of microcomputer-based automated systems, see Chapter 7.

MARC on OCLC

NO HOLDINGS IN UCB - FOR HOLDINGS ENTER dh DEPRESS DISPLAY RECD SEND
OCLC: 3608963   Rec stat: c Entrd: 771222   Used: 910924
Type: a Bib lvl: m Govt pub: Lang: eng Source: Illus: a
Repr: Enc lvl: Conf pub: 0 Ctry: nyu Dat tp: s M/F/B: ^1
Indx: 0 Mod rec: Festschr: 0 Cont: b
Desc: i Int lvl: j Dates: 1978,
  1 010   77-17748/AC/r865
  2 040   DLC $c DLC $d m.c.
  3 020   0385143567 : $c $8.05
  4 041 1   engger
  5 050 0   PZ8.G882 $b Po
  6 082   398.2/1/0943
  7 090 $b
  8 049   UCBB
  9 100 1   Grimm, Jacob, $d 1785-1863
10 240 10   Selections. $1 English. $f 1978
11 245 10   Popular folk tales / $c the Brothers Grimm ; newly
translated by Brian Alderson ; illustrated by Michael Foreman.
12 250   1st ed. in the United States of America
13 260   Garden City, N.Y. : $b Doubleday, $c 1978.
14 300   192 p. : $b ill. (some col.) ; $c 26 cm.
15 504   Includes bibliographical references.
16 520   Thirty-one folk and fairy tales collected by the Grimm
brothers including "Rapunzel," "Snow White," "The Twelve Dancing
Princesses," and "Hansel and Gretel."
17 650 0   Fairy tales $z Germany.
18 650 1   Fairy tales.
19 650 1   Folklore $z Germany.
20 700 10   Grimm, Wilhelm, $d 1786-1859. $e joint author.
21 700 10   Alderson, Brian.
22 700 10   Foreman, Michael, $d 1938-

Figure 8.

software, and supply full MARC records. Any librarian presently considering RECON with MicroLIF records should check with vendors to find out (1) exactly what MARC fields are included; and (2) whether or not any other data is added to records. The following questions highlight concerns that librarians have had in the past:

1. What is the quality of the data I am receiving on MicroLIF disks?

2. Which MARC fields are present?

3. Is the data based on Library of Congress MARC tapes? If so, is the full record . . . passed on to me?

4. Is anything added to the record?
    Some vendors supply annotations with each record; others supply them only on juvenile records. Note: You can provide keyword searching of annotations on OPACs to expand access points.

5. Is one vendor's data superior to another vendor's?

6. Does [the] . . . OPAC program make full use of the MicroLIF information? Does it retain all of the data and the MARC content designators? (Furrie 1991, 11)
    In the past, some MicroLIF records did not contain subject headings or added entries. These are fields that are vital OPAC access points.

It is a good idea to ask each of the vendors you are considering to send you a sample MicroLIF disk. When you receive it, take a good look at its contents; if you have appropriate software, print out a copy of records included. Study them and compare the fullness of records in each against other vendor sources. Experiment and try to answer the following questions:

1. Are MARC tags, indicators, and subfield codes present? Are they used correctly?

2. Can you write your records back out to a disk for use with other programs, such as a union catalog project? Can they be written in MARC format?

It is important to remember that any sample diskette will represent the best records (best-case) that the vendor has to offer.

If you are automating for the first time, you may find that your library's bibliographic records do not display all of the MARC fields. Many libraries which initially automated circulation have abbreviated records that contain just a few fields, such as title, author, call number, but no ISBN or other MARC tags. Now is the time to make decisions. Retrospective conversion, or RECON, goes hand-in-hand with automation. It will bring your files up-to-date and allow you to share full MARC II format with other libraries.

Why Do You Need a Database that Works with MARC Records?

A circulation module or an OPAC cannot be run from paper records. RECON creates a single database of machine-readable bibliographic records that works within your automated library system. The database takes the place of the card catalog. Information is accessed through specially built indexes that refer back to the database files and provide the needed data onscreen upon request. Any one of the MARC tag fields and subfields can be searched and displayed. The tag tells the computer software what kind of information the field contains, i.e., author, title, imprint, subject headings, etc. Each time a unique title is added to the database, all of the fields, indicators, and subfields are filled in for the new record.

What Are the Benefits of RECON with MARC II Format?

Nothing less than full MARC is acceptable in any current system. The benefits of RECON with MARC II format cannot be emphasized enough. They include the following general and regional considerations:[4]

General Considerations

1. Improved service for users: better circulation service; improved access to the collection; improved ILL response time;

---

4. For further information, see Beaumont, Jane and Joseph P. Cox. 1989. *Retrospective Conversion: A Practical Guide for Libraries.* Westport, CT: Meckler Corporation.

2. Improved service for staff: helps staff accomplish tasks with more efficiency, i.e., elimination of card filing, more current bibliographic data; less time-consuming changes;

3. Consistent format with useful coding: MARC records can be distributed in microfiche to various points in the library or to different branches; subsets of the database, i.e., serials catalog or the library's 16mm films are no longer site-bound and can be accessed more easily;

4. Single, integrated file: RECON eliminates parallel systems. Often your present cataloging is automated, while older records remain in card format, or some records may be on microfiche or on an online catalog. When two or more files have to be maintained and searched, staff time is horrendous; patrons are unhappy;

5. Cost-effective: You maximize automation expenditures, maximize the return on your investment with full RECON. Maintaining two catalog files is not cost-effective. The computer is not being used to its full capacity if only 50 percent of the catalog records are automated;

6. Flexibility to move from an older to a newer system: Technological change is very rapid. Some libraries have automated two to three times to keep up. An integrated, machine-readable database allows libraries to update with more ease and less cost. However, care must be taken when migrating data from one system to another. Don't take the vendor's word that your database records will transfer flawlessly. Be sure to compile a representative test file which contains many different types of library records onto a floppy disk or tape; and ask the vendor to show you that they transfer cleanly to the new system.[5]

7. Portability/added protection: Machine-readable records are portable. Files can be stored at off-site locations and remain safe in the event of fire, flood, disaster. Card catalogs are not portable and are usually maintained at a single site (or must be duplicated).

---

5. For a discussion of some of the problems that can occur, read Susan Baerg Epstein's article on implementing a second system (Epstein 1991)

Regional Considerations

1. Union Lists are standardized.

2. Sharing of bibliographic data is encouraged.

3. Interlibrary loans are enhanced. Locational information makes it possible to identify an item and subsequently make a request for it.

4. Collection development is aided. Exploring holdings of nearby libraries helps you decide whether or not to purchase a specific item.

Reasons Cited by Libraries for Doing RECON

The reasons cited most frequently by libraries for doing RECON include the following:

1. Updating library holdings in MARC format.

2. Standardizing forms of headings.

3. Correcting MARC tags and subfield codes.

4. Providing de-blinded cross-references.

Why Would a Library Not Do RECON?

The RECON project manager or librarian in charge must weigh all of the considerations carefully. The following factors may suggest that the RECON project should not be attempted:

1. Cost considerations: The project is too costly: the library budget is tight; spending priorities prohibit advancing funds;

2. No justification to convert older records: Older records are not used enough; the majority of requests satisfied with recent collection or with a core collection.

The Planning Process

If you decide to go ahead with RECON, good planning is essential for the project to be successful (cost-effective and efficient). There are four areas of importance as determined by Jane Beaumont, and Joseph P. Cox (Beaumont and Cox 1989):

1. Develop a plan of action:
   determine library needs
   establish parameters
   establish standards

2. Examine and evaluate options for converting records:
   in-house RECON
   vendor-based RECON
   blend of in-house and vendor-based RECON

3. Analyze the situation:
   library resources
   library catalog
   library requirements: final decisions
   procedures followed by vendors
   points of interest to discuss with vendors
   vendor requirements
   cost implications for each option

4. Implement the plan of action.

Develop a Plan of Action

Determine Library Needs

Present needs: Examine cataloging methods already in place.

Future needs: Look at long-term plans to determine the scope, standards, quality of the RECON project.

Establish Parameters

It is helpful for the librarian to be able to estimate -- at least approximately -- how large the library's machine-readable database will be.

1. The database has to accommodate a variety of records: bibliographic, authority, item, patron, vendor, fiscal, and indexes for all fields which are to be searchable.

   a. Estimates of storage space vary from 2000 characters per title to 4000 characters per title.

   b. A library with 250 thousand titles would need to store approximately 750 million characters. A character is defined as a byte, so the amount of storage would be 750 megabytes.

2. It is also important to allow for growth, based on the average number of new titles added per year.

Examine the content of the library collection and know how it is used. This will result in a more efficient, less costly RECON project.

1. Determine the overall extent of the collection.

   a. Weed unnecessary items.

   b. Use a shelf list, if possible, to take inventory.

2. Review and become familiar with the subject form divisions within the collection.

Limit the scope of the project as needed by:

1. Collection: Look at the circulation statistics. They will tell you what parts of collection are heavily used & should be converted first.

2. Date Range: Be aware of the date range of the items borrowed by patrons. If 80 percent of circulated items fall

into the after 1975 category, you may want to convert those records after a 1975 cut off date.

Know the date range of the database you are acquiring. Older records are not always available, i.e., LC MARC database contains records after 1968. You may have to negotiate with the vendor to supply older records.

3. Classification Range:
Some libraries prefer to convert whole classification sections, rather than parts of all sections.

4. Time Frames:
Most libraries set time frames as limiting goals so that the project will not drag on.

5. Cost Factors:
With limited budgets, libraries are frequently required to detail unit costs and represent cost ceilings beyond which they cannot go.

Establish Standards

Define your classification system.

If you intend to use national library cataloging on an ongoing basis, your choices are: Dewey: (used by public libraries and public schools) and LC Classification (used by university, corporate, and special libraries).

Determine the level of fullness you want in your catalog records.

With the features of the online catalog, such as keyword and Boolean searching, a full bibliographic record is more useful. When considering level of fullness of a record, consider the needs of the library, present and future, and try to build a database that will accommodate future needs.

Implement the MARC II format.

MARC II provides a standard for communicating machine-readable versions of catalog records. If you want to share records with other systems or you want to upgrade your system in the near future, then you should be able to output MARC records.

Adopt AACR2 as a cataloging code.

AACR2 is the widely accepted cataloging code that every library should adopt. It is a standard for the content of bibliographic records. Be particularly concerned with the choice and structure of headings according to AACR2 guidelines.

> For conversion of records after Jan. 1, 1981, be aware that there is good chance that records have been created according to AACR2.

> Prior to that, there may be a conflict between pre-AACR2 and AACR2 headings.

If you don't have AACR2 records, it will limit your ability to share records and acquire records in the future.

If you are getting records from another database, be cognizant of the cataloging code, the authority control, and the impact that will have on your present catalog and its conversion.

Select a subject authority list.

Libraries provide subject access through a list of subject headings, a thesaurus, or a keyword system. Some conflicts may occur between headings of derived records and those which the library owns. LCSH (Library of Congress Subject Headings) are most commonly used by North American libraries. However, schools and some special libraries prefer the shorter form found in Sears List of Subject Headings.

Libraries use RECON as a good opportunity to acquire more up-to-date subject access at a fraction of the price it would cost to create it.

Select a name authority list.

> The best authority is the Library of Congress Name Authorities. The form of the name you are using (personal name, corporate name, conference or meeting name, uniform title, bibliographic title, topical term, or geographic name) should be checked against this authority. The vendor's database is based on LC MARC tapes. Names shown in CIP data on the verso of the title page of a book should also be based on LC authority records at the time of the publication.

Determine what authority control devices are used by your vendor.

> Check to see if the database you choose uses the same name and subject authority files as the ones you are currently using in your library. If you select a vendor that employs the same authority control devices, your per-record cost will be reduced.

> Be aware that you can arrange to have all nonconforming headings automatically changed to authoritative ones fairly reasonably. With online access, it is becoming necessary to have good authority control to facilitate access to the database.

Examine and Evaluate Options for Converting Records

There are three possible ways to convert your records:

- in-house
- through an outside vendor
- combination of in-house and outside vendor.[6]

This section will briefly define each method and present advantages and disadvantages.

---

6. See Appendix 2 for a list of RECON vendors' names, addresses, and telephone numbers.

In-house RECON

In-house RECON is the most straightforward method of converting records. However, it is very tedious, requires specific skills of the staff, and is extremely time consuming, particularly if the staff is required to code shelflist data to indicate specific MARC fields. A database is then created on appropriate microcomputer software, and staff enters information into each machine-readable record. Usually, the library obtains a copy of its shelf-list and matches its records against one of the following sources: (1) MARC records on CD-ROM, i.e., Bibliofile by Library Corporation, USMARC database by Library of Congress, LaserCat by WLN.[7]; or (2) MARC records downloaded from bibliographic utilities, i.e., OCLC and WLN.[8]

Advantages

1. The integrity of the database is maintained. There are no conflicts with authority control or library policies. Usually, a minimum of editing is required.

2. The project can be carried out during regular work schedules or overtime can be assigned as needed. Staff are familiar with policies and can deal with problems as they arise.

3. Library staff does not have to deal with an outside vendor. There will be no charges for formatting and indexing data acquired from other sources, i.e., bibliographic utility charges.

4. Files do not leave the library. Records do not have to be duplicated.

---

7. CDMARC Names and CDMARC Subjects are also available for authority control. Initial prices and update fees vary as do the number of records on the disc.

8. Special software can be obtained from the utility to do this.

Disadvantages

1. In-house RECON is very labor intensive. Quality control is not always maintained.

2. Coding is complex and requires specific skills. Staff must be letter perfect. They must be able to accurately identify and label field information (i.e., correct forms of author, title, subject, and other elements in the card) for data entry.

3. There is less opportunity to upgrade or to move to national standards when doing RECON in-house. The data is only as good as the information on the shelf-list cards. Checking each element in each record to conform to standards is wearing on staff and time consuming.

4. Online costs are high if staff must use a utility or search a host database for records that closely match the library's records. However, this can be a valid option if the library is going to continue to use the utility on an ongoing basis.

5. Error-checking is necessary and time-consuming: Supervisors must check entries to maintain quality control.

6. Extra equipment may be needed, and extra hours may be required of staff.

Vendor-based RECON

Several commercial vendors who offer full-service RECON. Suppliers have realized that there are many records out there to be converted. RECON is a big money-maker. Libraries are willing to pay "big bucks" to have their records converted. The library staff supplies the vendor with a representative sample of the shelf-list or brief circulation records. Vendors then quote a price based on that sample. When selected, they use their own staff, equipment, and facilities to match library records against their MARC databases. When there is a match or "hit," the vendor sells the record to the library. In practice, the procedure is complicated. For a more detailed explanation of the steps involved, please refer to the "Procedures Followed by Vendors" section, later in this chapter.[9]

Advantages

1. Library staff involvement is limited. Usually one person works with the vendor.

2. Costs are known in advance and are quantifiable The vendor quotes a fixed price, based on a sample of the library shelf-list (i.e., 100 records).

3. There is no additional outlay for equipment or facilities.

4. Temporary staff does not have to be hired or trained.

5. A specific time frame is established.

Disadvantages

1. There is less quality control. Records must be sampled as they are returned and loaded into the database.

2. Files must be shipped to the vendor. The shelf-list must be copied to insure against loss or damage while it is off the premises.

3. Follow-up is required. The amount of involvement by the library varies, depending upon how complicated the library's requirements are, how effective and efficient the vendor is, and how much post-load editing is required.

Blend of In-house and Vendor-Based RECON

Some libraries want to consider a blend of in-house and vendor-based RECON. Options to consider could include the following scenarios:

---

9. For a complete list of RECON vendors, which includes names, addresses, and telephone numbers, see Appendix II.

1. The library may decide to use its own staff and resources to convert some records and contract out others, limiting by a cut-off date. (For example, the library may use USMARC records on CD-ROM for the conversion of post-1967 records and have a vendor convert all pre-1968 records.)

2. The library may choose to lease a CD-ROM cataloging source for a specific period of time. Using it, the staff searches and identifies bibliographic records that match those of the library. They key holdings information for the matches onto diskettes and mail them to the vendor. The vendor generates full MARC records for the customer and returns them on disk or tape. The library may elect to have the vendor manually input records that are not on the database by sending shelflist cards as source information.

Advantages

1. The library allocates resources to the best advantage, using own staff where appropriate.

2. It is cost-effective to use an outside vendor only where useful.

Disadvantages

1. RECON planning and implementation takes much staff time and effort. Your project will be divided into two major activities.

Analyze the Situation

In order to make an intelligent choice, look at the impact on the library resources; examine the qualities/characteristics of the existing library catalog; make final decisions on library requirements; look at procedures followed by vendors; think about points of interest to discuss with vendors; explore vendor requirements; and look at cost implications.

Library Resources

Staff: Does the library have staff resources available to supervise, code, and key data?

Equipment: What equipment is required for each option? If the library must purchase a CD-ROM drive, will staff or patrons make use of it after RECON?

Location: Is there space within the library where work can be properly supervised and day-to-day problems can be dealt with efficiently?

Time: From planning to execution, management time will be involved. Unforseen problems will arise that can only be solved by experienced staff. Be sure to build in time for this. Realistic goals/milestones must be included so that RECON does not drag on.

Funds: Before evaluating the RECON options, determine what funds are available; look at constraints. Are funds available for hiring personnel but not sufficient to hire a vendor? Reject options that don't fit.

Library Catalog

Consistency: Has cataloging varied over the years?

Is now a good time to conform to national standards?
or
Has the catalog been maintained under careful authority control, and is it more appropriate to rely on existing cards rather than getting records externally?

Hit rate: Check a sample of the library's shelf-list against potential sources. A matching list or hit rate of 60-80 percent is considered adequate; 80-90 percent very good; below 60 percent not worth obtaining external records.

Quantity: Estimate the number of records in the library. This will give you an idea of how to estimate resources required to complete the RECON project.

Level of MARC: Make a final decision on the level of fullness of the MARC records.

Final Decisions on Library Requirements

Quality Control: Document requirements and procedures for sampling records regularly and consistently.

Standards: Include proposed standards in procedural manuals.

Cost Control: Determine the method of funding for the project; how and when you will receive designated funds; what services are being provided; what will not be covered; and whether vendor prices are fixed or open-ended.

Procedures Followed by Vendors

The following procedures are followed by vendors and will provide general background information that you should know to deal effectively with your vendor.

Sending, Extracting, Merging, and Verifying Records

Records are usually sent in one of four ways: (1) The shelf list may be copied and sent to the vendor that will charge for keying the information into a computer; (2) relevant field information may be extrapolated, keyed in by library staff, and sent to the vendor on floppy disk or tape; (3) the library may purchase communications software from the vendor and transmit records via a modem; or (4) the vendor will extract the library's holdings from an online database, such as OCLC. If a floppy disk, tape, or modem is used, the vendor will supply specific instructions as to the procedures to be followed and the software to be used. In any case, it is important to tell the vendor the source of your records (i.e., OCLC, Bibliofile, etc.), the number of records, the time period involved, and optionally, the sequence in which the new MARC records are to be loaded into the bibliographic database file. The vendor you select will merge your library records into a single bibliographic file. Each record will be checked as part of the initial verification and merging process.

Matching Against the Vendor's Database

The library should determine which fields are most appropriate to match. Check with your vendor to see what criteria they offer. Vendors search the LC MARC database based on criteria such as:

LCCN	ISBN/ISSN
Title only	Title/Author combination
Publisher	Imprint Date
Arabic collation	Number of volumes in a multi-volume set
Reproduction status	

Opinions vary widely. The LCCN and ISBN/ISSN are frequent choices because they are supposedly unique fields. Some libraries feel that the LCCN is a slightly better search key because there is a higher publisher error rate in printing ISBNs and because U.S. publishers began including LCCNs in books before they began including ISBNs. The exception to this is paperback reprints in which the LCCN often refers to the original publication and the ISBN refers to the reprint. For libraries with collections which include foreign materials, ISBN would be the better choice because with one exception, books published outside the U.S. do not contain an LCCN. An example of a well planned search might be: (1) Initial search, LCCN; (2) Second pass, ISBN/ISSN (to find records for nonhits and inaccurate matches); (3) Final step, Title search. The Owensboro Community College and the University of Kentucky recommend ISBN, author, and title. They argue that the LCCN gives more multiple and incorrect hits (different author or title) than does the ISBN. A library may specify some degree of latitude to accommodate minor variations which may exist between LC and local cataloging practice, for example:

> Author: Accept match on last name only;
> Publisher: Wave match if all other elements match;
> Date: Accept match within __ years;
> Pages: Accept match within __ pages.

Understanding Problems with Nonhits. There are many reasons that matching a library's records with a vendor's database may result in nonhits. Every database has its own peculiarities.

Brief Records. Libraries that are moving to a second system often upgrade bibliographic files at the same time. Some library files contain brief records have been stripped of nonessential information when they were initially loaded or downloaded from a bibliographic utility. Nonhits occur when there is no definite element, such as Library of Congress or ISBN number, in the brief record to match the MARC record in the vendor database. It is also common for such libraries to have short entries or abbreviations in the author or title field. This will also negate an exact match.

Date Conflicts. At one time, the publication date was taken from the title page of a book, and the date on the verso of the title page was of secondary importance. It is important to note that the policy has since changed. The date used in cataloging is now the first date of publication and not simply a printing date. Be aware that these conflicts may cause problems when matching records during RECON.

Edition Statements. Because editions are not easily found in books to be cataloged and the rules for handling them (as defined by LC and AACR2) can be confusing, inaccuracies in cataloging do occur. There can also be a question about whether the book is a reprint edition or simply a subsequent printing. When records are matched, edition statements do not always appear to coincide.

Removing Duplicate Records

A major portion of the database preparation process is eliminating duplicate records or "deduping." When duplicate records are identified, the record to be retained is determined by criteria which the library has supplied. The earliest or latest record can be retained, or the best record can be selected, using the hierarchy of criteria submitted to the vendor, i.e., source, library, and/or date. Holdings information, such as call number, copy number, and local information, can be kept, deleted or merged from a duplicate record. Be aware that even under the best conditions, some duplicates may slip through due to missing OCLC control numbers, upper- and lower-case differences, pseudonymous names, and data entry errors.

Defining Filing Indicators

Filing indicators specify the number of initial characters to be ignored, usually an initial article at the beginning of the title field, title subfield, or corporate heading field in a MARC record.

Adding Local Information

Local information can be added to the MARC record, i.e., local call numbers, collection prefixes (such as B for Biography or F for Fiction), branch locations, number of copies, and/or local notes.

Checking for Current USMARC Format

The USMARC format has evolved over a period of time. Many changes have been made to the format since its inception. If some of the library's records are already in MARC format, obsolete MARC tags, indicators, and subfield codes should be converted to their current formats. Missing fields should be added; and invalid fields should be deleted.

Building the Item Field

The RECON vendor puts coded information into an item field in your MARC records which identifies characteristics such as (1) barcode; (2) call number; (3) copy and volume numbers; (4) holding library; (5) branch or location information; (6) media code, i.e., book, cassette, etc.; (7) statistical category code used to generate reports; (8) fine code; and (9) period of circulation code. The item field is specially built, using formatting requirements supplied by the ALS vendor. The RECON vendor will need to know the name of the automated library system you plan to use, and your library's cataloging practices and profiles, (i.e., method of cataloging oversized books; the hierarchy of your call number selection).

The ALS vendor will construct item records from data supplied in the item field. Each copy of a title in the collection has an item record that contains some abbreviated information. Circulation systems link item records to the patrons who check out materials. If more information is needed about an item, the item record can be linked back to the full MARC record from which all of the fields can be accessed.

Deciding on Authority Control

Authority control is the process of (1) assigning a unique form to a heading and (2) using cross-references to go from an unused or related heading to the accepted heading. Selecting and using one accepted heading (i.e., "Mark Twain") brings together in one place all of the works of an author, editions of a work, titles in a series, or subjects dealing principally or exclusively with a topic.

The vendor can eliminate errors, inconsistencies, and ambiguities in the use of names, uniform titles, series headings, and subject headings. Normally, the library's holdings are compared against LC Name and Subject authority tapes. A library may also, if it wishes, supply its own local authority records which can be incorporated into custom designed authority files. Authority records can be output on tape in the

MARC Authorities Format, provided the automated library system being purchased can accept this format.

Assigning Barcodes

Barcodes look like a rectangle made up of a series of printed lines and spaces of varying widths. The lines and spaces actually represent numbers, symbols, and/or letters. The two main types of encoding schemes used in libraries are Codabar and Code 39.

Codabar is more frequently used. The rectangle of lines and spaces translates into 14 digits which are displayed below it. The first digit is used to identify whether the barcode is for a patron or an item; the next four digits identify the institution; the following eight digits represent patron or item information; and the final digit is an error-checking digit.

Figure 9. Codabar.

In the Code 39 encoding scheme, the rectangle of lines and spaces translates into 10 digits, but they are not displayed. The first digit is used to identify whether the barcode is for a patron or an item; the next two digits identify the institution; the last seven digits are a unique code which represent either a patron or an item.

Figure 10. Code 39.

    The library may purchase either "smart" or "dumb" barcodes. If "smart" barcodes are purchased, the vendor assigns them to the items in the database and sends pages of barcodes in shelflist order to the library. Staff must affix the related barcode to the item with the correct call number. If "dumb" barcodes are purchased, each item in the library must be brought to the circulation terminal(s) and individually linked to the specific item record in the database. Simultaneously, the barcode is affixed to the item.[10]

    It is rare for a library to be required to relabel when upgrading or migrating to a new system. However, be aware that some problems may develop. The new system does not always operate effectively with old barcode labels. It is possible that the vendor may have to write special software to accommodate them, and this software does not always perform the necessary check-digit calculations. Peripheral devices, such as backup and inventory, may also not work as well; and the library's custom data may be lost and have to be rewritten.

---

10. Libraries sometimes use "dumb" barcodes for on-the-fly item entry into circulation systems. For example, if a book is not cataloged, staff can create an item record and attach a barcode to the book, thus enabling a patron to check it out. It is important to remember to create a full MARC record at a designated or more convenient time.

Determining Tape Size, Density, and Format Type for the Prepared Database of MARC Records

Tape Size: MARC records are normally written to 1/2 inch, 9-track, magnetic tape.[11] Tape comes in reels of 600, 1200, or 2400 feet. (Note: 3600 ft. tape is generally regarded as too thin and easily damaged.)

Density: MARC records can be written to tape at varying densities. The most common are 1600 BPI (Bytes per inch) or CPI (Characters per inch) and 6250 BPI or CPI.

Format Type: MARC records are generally written to tape, using (1) unblocked or unspanned, variable-length records format in which a blank space of 1/2 to 3/4 inch separates each physical record (referred to as the OCLC-MARC format); or (2) blocked, spanned format in which 2048 bytes are allocated per block (referred to as the LC-MARC format). The latter increases the tape storage capacity.

The number of records stored to a tape depends on the length of the tape, the BPI or CPI density, and the format type. (For example, approximately 20,000 full MARC records could be stored on a 2400 ft. tape at 1600 BPI, using unblocked format.) Over 60,000 full MARC records could be stored on a 2400 ft. tape at 6250 BPI, using blocked format. The automated library system vendor can assist you with detailed information concerning any of the above.

Processing Gap Tapes

Gap tapes are created from new records that the library has cataloged between the time the database was processed by the RECON vendor and the time that it is loaded into the automated system. There will be an added fee when you send these to the RECON vendor.

Continuing to Convert Records

When the RECON process is completed, you may opt to have the RECON vendor continue to convert new records.

---

11. Two other alternatives are possible: MARC records can be (1) downloaded directly into the automated library system via a modem; or (2) put onto floppy disks, using a MicroLIF format.

Points of Interest to Discuss with Vendors

The following areas should be thoroughly discussed with each vendor that you consider.

Coverage: Coverage for LC MARC records prior to 1968 is very selective and incomplete. If your library has many older records, select a vendor that has access to REMARC (LC MARC records from 1898-1968); to MARC records contributed by users with similar collections; or to alternative files.

Uniqueness: Vendors obtain MARC records from many different sources, all of which may have some of the same records. Ask the vendor how many unique titles are in the database.

Quality and Consistency: Quality and consistency vary enormously among vendors. Know the source of the records. You can rely on those contributed by national libraries and academic libraries. All records should meet at least LC minimal level cataloging standards. The wider the range of your records, the more inconsistent your headings will be. Consider the vendor's approach to authority control.

Specialized Collections: The more specialized your library collection, the more carefully you will have to search for a vendor whose database matches your needs. (For example, if your library has a collection of (1) British or European material, select a vendor with access to the UK MARC (1950-) database; (2) medical material, select a vendor with access to the National Library of Medicine (NLM) database; or (3) government publications, select a vendor with access to the Government Printing Office (GPO) database.

Local Requirements: Check with the vendor to see if the library can edit records to meet local requirements.

Nonhits: Find out what the vendor does about nonhits? The library should decide whether (1) to supply more information to the vendor and hope for a match; or (2) to have the vendor create records in MARC format.

Quality of Editorial Staff:	Ask about the number and quality of the editorial staff. Most bibliographic services have qualified personnel to properly match records, but not all are competent to review the results (*Library Systems Newsletter*, June 1989).
Level of Support:	Determine whether or not the level of support suits your needs. Is there an 800 number for follow-up calls and questions?

Vendor Requirements

Vendors have unique requirements that you may have to meet. Be aware of the following conditions:

Shelf-list cards:	Vendors have requirements on how cards are to be divided into batches or edited before submission. Be sure to budget for this.
Payment Schedule:	The contract should spell out how many records will be delivered, at what cost, and when payment is to be made.
Schedule:	Since the vendor is receiving RECON projects from a variety of sources, you may need to schedule your work months in advance. Negotiate to reach a mutually agreeable timetable.
Licensing:	Licensing has been a thorny issue over the past 10 years; Who owns the bibliographic records that the vendor has created for you? Do you have the right to redistribute them after they have been loaded onto your automated system? Some vendors have attempted to copyright and limit the library's right to share. Clarify in the service contract that you want the right to use the records as you wish.

Cost Implications

Go through the planning stages step-by-step. Calculate the costs for staff, equipment, supplies, and vendor and utility charges. Be sure to include the costs of dealing with nonhits. The cost of RECON will be based on the input method, the number of records converted, and the complexity of the criteria matched. The unit price goes down as the number of catalog records increases. The more complex the library's criteria requirements, the more expensive the matching process. Vendor estimates range from $.01 to $3 per record, depending on the number of services performed. That does not include hidden costs, such as library staff time to supervise and manage the project and problem solving. The ideal situation is to obtain the highest quality product for the lowest cost and still maintain the least negative impact on the library.

Implement the Plan of Action

Whether it is to be carried out in-house, by an outside vendor, or through a combination of the two:

1. Assign someone to supervise the project who will be directly responsible for its execution.

2. Distribute written policies for the project.

3. Determine staff requirements; initiate recruitment; look at skills; and determine training requirements.

Prepare a timetable and task lists. If staff is new or unfamiliar with library policies and procedures, be sure to provide detailed user manuals for them. It is important to budget carefully and allocate resources for staff, equipment, supplies, work location, and money. When you are ready, implement the project and monitor progress. Fine-tune procedures as needed, and complete the project with as much flexibility as possible.

Summary

RECON is an acronym for retrospective conversion which means converting bibliographic records from catalog cards, shelflists, or brief machine-readable records to full MARC format. MARC format is recognized as the standard for exchange of bibliographic records between automated library systems. When RECON takes place, each category of information on a catalog card is identified and converted to a 3-digit number or MARC tag. The related information is converted to coded numerical indicators and a grouping of subfields following the MARC tag. MARC tags, indicators, and subfields provide a standardized and consistent format instantly recognized by computers and catalogers.

MARC records were initially designed to be uploaded via 9-track tapes onto minicomputers and mainframe computers. When the microcomputer age arrived, MicroLIF (MICROcomputer Library Interchange Format) records were designed to be uploaded via floppy disks onto hard drives. Book jobbers began to offer MARC records with each new book so that the library staff could upload them directly onto their microcomputer databases. To ensure that (1) all MARC fields would be represented in MicroLIF records, and (2) all automated library systems could read them, MicroLIF Protocol standards were adopted on July 1, 1991. It is still advisable to check the quality of the data you are receiving in MicroLIF records, the exact MARC fields that are present, and any data added by the vendor.

When you automate and convert your library's records to machine-readable format, the MARC tags, indicators, and subfields can be searched and displayed. This results in improved access to the collection; the elimination of the card catalog; more efficient use of staff and patron time; up-to-date or current bibliographic data; and standardized, consistent records that can easily be updated and distributed off-site. Many libraries are members of bibliographic utilities such as OCLC, RLIN, WLN, and UTLAS and both contribute MARC records and copy catalog. In this way, they are able to share resources and eliminate duplication of efforts.

Planning for RECON is a major undertaking. A responsible member of the staff should manage the operation. The project manager should determine present and future needs of the library; map out a plan of action; and work with the vendor or with staff to accomplish goals. If you are heading the project, know the collection inside out, its content and how frequently each item is used. Examine your budget and set limitations where needed, including time lines. Analyze circulation statistics; and if necessary, convert only those items most frequently used, those after a particular copyright date, or start with a designated portion of your collection. Weed unnecessary items, and take full inventory of the remaining collection. Look specifically at subject divisions used. Ask yourself: Do they reflect recent changes in AACR2? Are they consistent? Are records duplicated? Are catalog cards missing? What needs to be done before RECON? How should the staff be involved? What is their level of expertise?

Are they sufficiently trained to undertake all or part of the conversion, or should a vendor be consulted and hired? Analyze the pros and cons. Is there sufficient space? Is there proper equipment within the library to make this an in-house RECON? Will funds have to be allocated to hiring and training additional staff or purchasing equipment? Would it be cost-effective to use staff for some in-house conversion and hire a vendor for the rest?

If you choose a vendor, records may be transmitted in one of four ways: (1) paper copy of a shelf list; (2) floppy disk or tape; (3) via a modem; and (4) extracted by the vendor from an online database. The vendor will merge your records into a single bibliographic file, match them according to criteria set by you, and check for duplication/inaccuracies in your records. You determine the quality of MARC records that you want and deal with nonhits according to your contract. The vendor will work with your automated library system vendor to build an item file with information that you supply. You should also decide upon (1) the type of barcode you wish to affix to items in the library and patron cards, and (2) some form of authority control or accepted headings for authors and subjects that will be searched by your patrons.

When selecting a vendor, carefully consider the following: If you have a special collection, be sure to choose a vendor who has records that specifically meet your library's needs. If you want to edit records to meet local requirements, find out if this is a possibility. If you have records prior to 1968, check the coverage of the vendor's database: make sure it fits your needs. Vendors obtain records from many different sources and may have duplicates; determine how many unique records they have. Make a point of asking about the source of the records; they should meet minimal LC level cataloging standards. Look at the vendor's financial picture, stability in the marketplace, and support.

Above all, analyze your options and calculate your costs step-by-step. The ideal solution is to determine the lowest cost that will ensure high quality and have the least negative impact on the library. It is usually a compromise among the three.

References

Auto-Graphics, Inc. 1991. *Authority Control System.* Pomona, CA: Auto-Graphics, Inc.

_____. 1991. *Circulation Database Upgrade Project Description.* Pomona, CA: Auto-Graphics, Inc.

_____. 1991. *Conversion Services.* Pomona, CA: Auto-Graphics, Inc.

_____. 1991. *Retrospective Shelf List Conversion Service.* Pomona, CA: Auto-Graphics, Inc.

Beaumont, Jane, and Joseph P. Cox. 1989. *Retrospective Conversion: A Practical Guide for Libraries.* Westport, CT: Meckler.

Epstein, Susan Baerg. Jan., 1991. Implementing a Second System: Some New Concerns. *Library Journal* 116(1): 76-77.

_____. May 15, 1990. Retrospective Conversion Revisited. *Library Journal* 115(9): 56, 58.

Furrie, Betty. 1991. *Understanding MARC (Machine Readable Cataloging), 3rd ed.* McHenry, IL: Follet Software Company.

Hart, Amy. Oct., 1988. Operation Cleanup: The Problem Resolution Phase of a Retrospective Conversion Project. *Library Resources and Technical Services* 32(4): 378-386.

Kroll, Carol. Winter, 1990. Preparing the Collection for Retrospective Conversion *School Library Media Quarterly.* 18(2): 82-83.

Library Technologies, Inc. June, 1990. *Authority Control Services.* Abington, PA: Library Technologies, Inc.

_____. June, 1990. *Library Database Preparation Services: A Primer.* Abington, PA: Library Technologies, Inc.

Marcive, Inc. April, 1990. *Authorities Processing*. San Antonio, TX: Marcive, Inc.

Murphy, Catherine. Winter, 1990. Questions to Guide Retrospective Conversion Choices for School Library Media Centers. *School Library Media Quarterly* 18(2): 79-81.

Plezia, Sue. Winter, 1989. Retrospective Conversion. *DLA Bulletin* 9(3): 10-12.

Rockman, Ilene. April 15, 1990. Retrospective Conversion: Reference Librarians Are Missing the Action. *Library Journal* 115(7): 40-42.

Sources for Further Reading

Allan, Ann. Jan., 1990. Chasing MARC: Searching in Bibliofile, Dialog, OCLC, and RLIN. *Journal of Academic Librarianship* 15(6): 339-343.

Beaumont, Jane. 1992. *Make Mine MARC: A Manual of MARC Practice for Libraries*. Westport, CT: Meckler.

Bibi, Abd M. Nov.-Dec., 1989. CD-ROM for Retrospective Conversion: The BRAZNET Experience. *Library Software Review* 322-326.

Bossers, A., and D. Law. 1990. Guidelines for Retroconversion Projects. *IFLA Journal* 16(1): 32-36.

Byrne, Deborah J. 1990. *MARC MANUAL: Understanding and Using MARC Records*. Englewood, CO: Libraries Unlimited.

Campbell, Brian. Aug., 1987. Whither the White Knight: CDROM in Technical Services. *Database* 10(4): 22-33.

Chao, Dolly. 1989. Cost Comparisons Between Bibliographic Utilities and CD-ROM-Based Cataloging Systems. *Library Hi Tech* 7(3): 49-52.

Crawford, Walt. 1989. *MARC for Library Use: Understanding Integrated USMARC*. 2nd ed. Boston: G. K. Hall.

Epstein, Susan Baerg, et al. Sept. 1, 1989. Custom Barcoding as a Better Way: How to Barcode Your Collection Without Tears. *Library Journal* 156-159.

Urrows, Henry, and Elizabeth Urrows. Sept., 1991. Automating with Barcodes. *Computers in Libraries* 11(8): 51-52.

The Online Public Access
Catalog (OPAC)

This chapter will concentrate solely on the Online Public Access Catalog (OPAC).[1] Early OPAC studies and development will be briefly introduced; the advantages and disadvantages of online public access catalogs will be discussed; and factors to be considered when designing the OPAC for your library will be illustrated in order to give you a better understanding of what to look for. Questions to consider and those to ask user groups are detailed; problems that patrons have encountered are discussed; and concepts for training and clear documentation are emphasized. Additionally, sections are devoted to the use of the OPAC as a multidimensional tool, to its impact on colleges and universities, and to ergonomics and cost considerations. See Appendix 1 for a chart which summarizes the features and functions to rate when evaluating competing OPAC modules.

---

1. Also called the "Online Patron Access Catalog."

Background and Early Studies

In the early 1960s, some libraries began experimenting with online public access in order to catalog information and display their holdings for patrons. These early databases provided very limited access, but they were more current and more flexible than either book or microform catalogs. In the 1970s and 1980s, OPACs became more prevalent in libraries, and the whole approach to accessing information changed dramatically. Library staff began to input new information and edit records on an ongoing basis to keep information up-to-date. Patrons became familiar with the OPAC and interacted less frequently with catalog cards, printed editions, and supplements. They learned to formulate search strategies by truncating terms or using Boolean operators in order to narrow or broaden their searches. This new and interactive experience allowed patrons to access vast amounts of information more quickly. It allowed access through more points of entry and retrieved more hits or matches per entry.

How and why did this revolution take place? One of the earliest explorations was a project known as INTREX (INformation TRansfer EXperiments) conducted at Massachusetts Institute of Technology (MIT) between 1965 and 1973. Basically, journal articles were indexed, and a bibliographic record was created for each article. Author's name, title of article, and bibliographic citation were entered along with subject terms, descriptors, and abstracts. The full text of each article could be retrieved on a microfiche reader adjacent to the terminal used to access the bibliographic database. In 1970, both the bibliographic record and the full text were available online.

The INTREX database was designed for direct access by the library patron who used instruction manuals, charts, and guides provided by the library. The online system also displayed prompts to help the patron with options and commands that were available at any given point in the search. The project was supported through grant funding totalling almost $2.5 million from the Carnegie Corporation, the Council on Library Resources, the U.S. Department of Defense, the Independence Foundation, the National Science Foundation, and the Sloan Foundation. This public access catalog was far ahead of its time. It demonstrated the application of computer services in libraries, but online public access catalogs were not financially feasible on a large scale (Overhage and Reintjes 1974).

Most of the public access programs that survived in the 1960s and 1970s were outside the public and academic sectors. For example, the library at IBM Los Gatos developed an Experimental Library Management System which offered online retrieval of catalog records for books and technical reports in the early 1970s (Winik 1972); and the British Steel Corporation developed an online catalog for its Technical Information Systems Department of the Strip Mills Division. The latter was a unique bibliographic database that could be searched by patrons either within the library itself or through remote terminals (Patten 1974).

Online Public Access Catalogs came into their own during the mid- and late 1970s. One of the first academic libraries to introduce an OPAC was Ohio State University (OSU) Libraries which had a fairly sophisticated online circulation system in place during the early 1970s. The OPAC experiment in 1975 was an outgrowth of the earlier circulation system which had been designed with a broad range of access points. Through the OPAC, access was available by author, title, a combination of author and title, and call number. Subject access was added in 1978, and provisions for cross-references were in the planning stage. Refinements were made and strategies became more complex as the system was revised and updated with advanced technology. Eventually, an online authority structure was devised, and a cross-reference display was included. These developments foreshadowed the intense activity of online public access catalog development in libraries in the 1980s (Miller 1980).

During that decade, hundreds of libraries joined the march to automation when they became members of OCLC.[2] Many libraries experimented with public access to OCLC by redesigning the existing formats. Gradually, several trends began to emerge. Online public access catalogs came into being in their own right as unique and separate entities, not as an outgrowth of circulation systems. Minnesota State University System Project for Automated Library Systems (MSUS/PALS) was one such system. Libraries on the whole became interested in accommodating patron needs in terms of access, display, and program assistance. The University of California Systemwide Division of

---

2. Online Computer Library Center (OCLC) is the largest and best known bibliographic utility. In 1967, the "Ohio College Library Center" was incorporated and intended to function as a computerized regional processing center for academic libraries in the state of Ohio. In 1972, the regional membership was abandoned, and participation was extended to nonacademic libraries. The scope of the organization became national and then international. These orientations were reflected in subsequent name changes: to "OCLC, Incorporated" in 1977 and to "Online Computer Library Center" in 1981. This international computer network is primarily used by libraries to "acquire and catalog books, order custom-printed catalog cards for card catalogs and machine-readable records for local electronic catalogs, arrange interlibrary loans, and maintain location information on library materials" (OCLC Annual Report: 1988/89).

Library Automation developed MELVYL, its own public access catalog. The OPAC became a separate component in fully integrated systems which included acquisitions, serials, cataloging, and circulation. Many OPACs developed in-house in the 1970s and 1980s are now being offered for sale, either through vendors or by the originating libraries. The OPAC has proved a versatile tool, and its design is crucial to the ultimate success of the end product (Reynolds 1985, 99-100).

OPAC User Studies

The 1980s marked the decade of OPAC user studies. Frederick Kilgour was a forerunner in the field who felt that the online public access catalog should be designed solely for the user. The major impact was felt in studies sponsored by the Council on Library Resources (CLR) in 1982, when various groups of library administrators and librarians met to determine exactly what patrons wanted an online public access catalog to do. Their purpose was to study user likes and dislikes and the dynamics of their interaction with the OPAC. Through system monitoring, patron interviews, self-administered surveys of users/nonusers of online catalogs, system simulation, online controlled retrieval tests, and data collection of staff and expert observations, various aspects were carefully examined. After analyzing such components as language used, screen design, access points, format, and contents of records to be displayed, the groups funded by the CLR made the following eight recommendations that every OPAC should include:

1. author-title-subject access;

2. bibliographic details and availability for interlibrary loans;

3. a printer attached;

4. dial-up access from a personal computer outside the library which frees the patron from visiting the library;

5. access to all formats, i.e., books, periodicals, musicals, etc.;

6. contents, i.e., summaries and abstracts;

7. browsing capability;

8. Boolean searching capability. (Cochrane and Markey 1983; Markey 1982, 1983a, 1983b; Matthews 1982).

Almost all of the above components are available in OPACs today, with the exception of number 6. Not all OPACs feature summaries or abstracts, and there is still little continuity or common agreement in the major features or functions provided by vendors. Online catalogs for public use are a relatively new concept when compared with other aforementioned modules which have been in use in libraries for years. In the OPAC revolution, much design experimentation is still occurring. Some systems are simple, and others are very complex, but vendors are expanding options rapidly. It should be remembered that the more sophisticated the OPAC, the less simplistic the operation. If patrons have to master intricate techniques with which they have had little or no experience, ease of use has been defeated. Ideally, the OPAC should be simple to operate with sophisticated retrieval capabilities. The number of operations of the system should be kept to a minimum.

Comparing Competing Vendor Systems

When comparing competing vendor systems, there are certain things to look for. As a librarian, you must investigate, test, and intelligently question. If you are considering the purchase of a new OPAC, read the literature, look at comparison studies, learn the jargon, and talk with others in the field who have OPACs in place. In order to accurately compare similar systems, it is helpful to prepare lists of specific questions to ask. You will get more reliable and objective responses if you have reference librarians talk with reference librarians and catalog librarians talk with catalog librarians at installed sites. Finally, you will need to analyze the specific needs of your library patrons and match their needs with the design of the OPAC.

The vendor will gladly give you an ample supply of literature about the system, a demonstration, and a list of users. He or she is in the business of selling the OPAC and will put the system in the best light and point out its most valuable features.

Questions to Consider

How long has the company been in business? Vendors come and vendors go. The length of service and reputation of the vendor is important. You do not want to be left with a system developed by a company which has gone bankrupt. Look at annual reports and determine the financial stability of the company. A minimum of $5 million in sales is considered necessary for a company to support significant development and marketing efforts.

How long ago was the OPAC module developed? Were librarians involved in its development or in any of the upgrades? OPACs are generally the most recently developed modules in integrated systems. Newly developed modules may have many bugs to work out. Find out what other modules have been installed by the vendor, and carefully check the features and warranties offered. It is generally advantageous to purchase a tried and tested system which has had the input of librarians who work in the field. Vendors often employ librarians to hedge the gap between practical experience and business sense.

How many previous installations have been done and in what time period? What is the typical size and type of library with which the vendor has contracted? Generally, a customer base of 30 is deemed sufficient to support ongoing software maintenance, even if a vendor experiences a downturn in system sales, and 10 sales per year will generate enough income to underwrite a basic software enhancement program. Be sure to ask for a list of installations from the vendor, and consult them to determine their satisfaction. It is best to go with a vendor that has had the experience of installing OPACs in libraries of the same size and type as your own, providing that your patrons' needs match the features offered.

On what kind of hardware does the system run? If you have terminals in place in your library which you intend to use for the OPAC, you will need to determine compatibility of the software with your hardware. If you intend to purchase new hardware, be sure to discuss makes and models which will run the software and provide for future expansion.

How many terminals should the library have? The number of terminals is usually dominated by money and by the number of patrons who access information. Formulas are available to help you justify the number of terminals you purchase, i.e., 1 terminal per X number of patrons, or X number of terminals for each OCLC terminal. One terminal per 100 users is considered a quick estimate.

Where should terminals be placed? What is the optimum arrangement? OPACs should be placed at strategic points within the library to provide widespread use in several locations. They should be easily accessible. CLR studies show that OPACs should not be placed in areas where there is continuous activity. Patrons require and appreciate a certain degree of privacy when completing queries.

Does the library have any control over the design of the screens? Most vendors allow librarians great flexibility in designing OPAC screens to match patron needs. Research indicates that each screen should contain a minimum of clear, uncluttered information[3] with frequent prompts for the naive or inexperienced user. Easy-to-understand help screens should be available at any given time during the search. Commands should be simple and direct; and error messages should be short, intelligible, and to the point.

What levels of searching are available, command driven or menu-driven? OPACs must accommodate the novice, experienced, frequent and infrequent users, and cater to both simple and complex needs. Each user will have his or her own mix of expertise and level of retention. Because of the diversity of knowledge among patrons, it is best to simplify the methods of retrieval as much as possible. If your library can afford to provide only one level of searching, select a menu-driven search process that is easy to operate. If two levels are possible, include a combination of a menu-driven search process for the novice and a command-driven search process for the more experienced user.

---

3. According to Anne Lipow, an independent consultant, "No more than 30 percent of the screen should be filled with characters -- effective displays are open displays. Lines of text shouldn't exceed 65 characters. Summary displays using more than one line for each entry should have blank lines between entries. Five to nine options can be taken at a glance; more options require more thought and much slower reaction," (LITA Newsletter, Fall 1991:23).

Is the background on the screen relaxing? An aesthetically pleasing background can help promote a more positive attitude toward OPAC use. Whenever possible, the surrounding color scheme should be carefully designed to create a comfortable setting. To minimize eye fatigue, bright colors and strong contrasts should be avoided.[4]

Are touch screens available? Touch screens will be an option with some vendors. Patrons enjoy the novelty of touching the screen to make a choice. However, research indicates that they are less popular than video display monitors in libraries because they tend to become a play toy. Dirty fingers mar the image and cause the system to malfunction more frequently.

What types of keyboard layouts are available, standard or enhanced? Has the vendor rekeyed characters? Have some of the keys been disabled? An enhanced keyboard with a separate number pad is most frequently purchased by libraries today. It gives the patron more flexibility when inputting the query. Keys should be spaced comfortably so that input isn't jumbled. Vendors sometimes rekey existing keyboards or use keycaps in order to incorporate special program keys that will help the user access a variety of features with ease. Active keys are designated to be patron operative; others are disabled so that programs are not destroyed or manipulated by the patron.

Should printers be included? It is very helpful to attach printers to the OPACs so that patrons may take a copy of the results of their search with them as they attempt to locate library materials. However, noise is a disruptive factor that must be considered when placing printers in strategic locations, particularly if inexpensive dot matrix models are purchased. Some libraries have purchased printer covers to minimize noise; others have partitioned equipment; many are beginning to place desk jet or laser printers in designated locations throughout the library.

What is the projected response time? Studies indicate that the time lapse between inputting the inquiry and displaying the results on screen should fall within a range of 2 seconds.

---

4. Ergonomics will be more fully discussed later in this chapter.

What is the projected downtime? Downtime may be defined as the time when the system is not up and working due to power failure, repairs, or malfunction. If your library has abandoned the card catalog and is operating solely from the OPAC, there will be no access available to patrons during downtime. Ninety-eight percent uptime and two percent downtime is not good enough. The acceptable rate of uptime is 99.1 percent with less than 1 percent downtime.

Is there a list of appropriate subject headings available to the patron? Some OPACs have controlled vocabularies, and others vary procedures related to access. Many systems use Library of Congress subject headings (LCSH) which, because of the complexity of subheadings, often intimidate users. To compound the problem, a list of acceptable subject headings or thesaurus is frequently not available online. Optimally, terminology should represent the vocabulary used by the patron, and subject headings should be selected from all possible equivalents. Each station should be supplied with a list of acceptable subject headings, either online or in hard copy.

What fields are indexed? What are the access points? Does the design of the OPAC allow for local changes? Some vendors allow greater flexibility in designing access to OPAC records than others. An OPAC should minimally allow the patron to find library material by author, title, or subject. It should include all records by a particular author or on a given subject; and it should provide assistance in obtaining the ultimate selections through display of bibliographic records which include status information.

You may want to specify variant forms of names and titles to be included or incorporate other bibliographic elements for purposes of qualifying search queries for your patrons. You may elect to add language codes, names of publishers, and ranges of publication dates. It is becoming increasingly popular to incorporate relevant local changes. If your library has multiple branches, it may be beneficial to display codes that inform your patrons where library materials are available. These expansions will require a greater sophistication and more entries, but a depth in access capabilities results in better retrieval.

Remember that enhancements or adaptations cost money. Keep them simple. Add only what you need. If you decide to customize, be sure to outline your specific needs carefully and discuss them with the vendor. The best time to negotiate changes is before you buy the OPAC.

Does the system include a browsing mode? It is useful for the patron to be able to browse a list of selections such as authors, titles, or subjects. For example, if the patron is unsure of an author's first name and types in the last name only, the system displays an alphabetical list of adjacent last names with a marker indicating the specific name requested or the closest possible spelling. The patron can then browse previous or subsequent screens to locate further listings. The only drawback is that incorrect spellings can place the patron far from the desired name on the alphabetical list.

A title search allows the user to browse through an alphabetical listing of titles that are the same or close to the search term. The approach is appropriate if the user knows the first word of the title. The more words in the title that the user enters accurately, the closer in the listing he or she will be placed to the desired work. Some systems will also include Related Works as an option so that the patron can also see other titles by the same author.

The browse option will retrieve particular terms or subjects as well as series titles. It is helpful if the system does not require that the patron use the exact syntax of Library of Congress Subject Headings, but shows valid headings and allows the user to select one that will display citations.

Does the OPAC have keyword searching capabilities? Keyword searching enables the user to retrieve records on the basis of single terms or combinations of terms within specified fields, such as author, title, or subject heading. This means that the user does not have to know the specific name, exact title, or subject heading to retrieve the records. The search may be less precise than a full title or author's name, but it is a particularly useful feature.

Most common is title keyword searching. Libraries are attempting to improve subject access by providing access to words, strings, and phrases within titles or subject heading strings instead of just matching card catalog access points. Some OPACs have the added feature of free text or full text searching which allows the user to search for natural language words or phrases throughout the entire text.

Is proximity searching an option? Proximity searching enables the user to search for words that are next to each other or within a specific number of characters. Vendor literature is increasingly cognizant of the need to include as many options as possible in order to increase the number of accurate hits.

Can Boolean operators be used? Most OPACs allow the patron to combine two or more search terms by inserting logic operators such as "and," "or," and "not." The user may be queried or prompted for the entry of terms (e.g., subject and author and/or title) to be combined by the system in the search process. Some OPACs have limited Boolean capabilities and will process only one or two logical operations or will process them only in selected fields. The Boolean concept may be used to either broaden or narrow the search and is a particularly useful feature.

How is truncation handled? Some OPACs allow the user to abbreviate search terms by placing a symbol, such as an asterisk or an exclamation point, at the end of a search string. The more sophisticated OPAC will allow the patron to truncate in the middle of a word. For example, wom*n will retrieve both woman and women. Some OPACs permit retrieval on truncated forms of surnames, thus producing results when the author's surname and first initial are keyed in. The net effect is to broaden the set of records retrieved.

Is Dial-Up access available? Dial-up or remote access allows the patron to search the library's online catalog from another location and retrieve bibliographic citations with full status information. All the patron needs is a microcomputer, a modem, communications software, and a telephone line. This is a very useful service that enables the patron to tap into what was once library-bound information from home, college dorms, or offices. Some libraries include bulletin boards, interlibrary loans, and document delivery service, all of which can be made available in-house or through dial-up access.

Does the system have a foreign language translation capability? Access to foreign language searching is one of the more unique offerings. INLEX, for example, supports up to six different languages on a single terminal, including a simplified vocabulary for children. The patron simply selects the language of choice from a list of screen options, and the system responds by translating all of the instructions, key labels, and descriptive information into the selected language. This is a very useful feature, especially for those libraries catering to multicultural clientele. Others in the field offer similar capabilities.

Questions to Ask User Groups

When consulting with vendors, you may obtain names and addresses of user groups and gain more information by attending meetings or by writing for sample issues of their newsletters. Information gathered at user group meetings can be very revealing. You can often pinpoint problems with specific vendors and obtain information by asking pertinent questions. Your list of questions should include:

- Are professional librarians satisfied with the OPAC module, the hardware, the software, the maintenance, and the training? Is the system reliable/adequate?

- How long did it take for delivery and installation? What problems arose? Are there any tips to know that would facilitate installation?

- Why was the vendor system chosen over others? What other vendors were considered?

- How much time did it take to load and index the database?

- What features were required? Were there any that couldn't be adapted to the system? What features are most disliked? What changes would they like to see?

- Are there hidden limits to the system, such as the maximum number of hits that can be displayed on the OPAC screen? If so, can the parameters be changed?

- Who is supplying the service: the vendor, a third party vendor, the hardware manufacturer, or the software supplier?

- What is the response time for service? Are problems dealt with effectively in a professional manner or do they remain unresolved? Can diagnosis and repairs be made by dialing into the system?

- How long does it take to install new releases? Is re-indexing a background operation which allows continued use of the system, or is it a foreground operation which requires exclusive use of the system?

- Would they recommend the system to others? Would they buy the same system again?

User Group Studies

In addition to the comments of professional librarians and users at user group meetings, patron needs and user studies should be considered when planning for or designing the OPAC. Librarians must take an active role in analyzing and adapting system specifications and in providing training to meet the needs of their library's unique user group.

In the past, patrons have enjoyed the card catalog for its subject access, cross-references, and browsability. They were used to removing drawers and flipping cards. If they were unsure of the spelling, they scanned the cards. Today, OPACs present different search capabilities. They can be designed to elicit a positive reaction. Librarians should take into consideration that patrons are encountering the following problems:

1. Too many failed searches (search attempts aborted; no matches; or unmanageable large numbers of items retrieved).

2. Navigational confusion and frustration. (Where am I? What can I do now? How can I start again?)

3. Unfamiliarity with subject indexing policy and vocabulary idiosyncracies leading to failure to match search terms with the system's subject vocabulary.

4. Misunderstanding and confusion about the fundamentally different approaches to retrieval and search methods in OPACs (e.g., pre-coordinate phrase searching and browsing and postcoordinate KW [keyword]/Boolean searching).[5]

5. Partially implemented search strategies and missed opportunities to retrieve relevant materials (e.g., large sets not scanned or narrowed in size, title keyword searches not followed up with searches on call numbers or subject headings of found records). (As stated by: Hildreth 1989, 16-20; Cochrane 1989, 7-8.)

Patrons are running into problems in spite of handouts, flip charts, department and classroom instruction, computer-assisted instruction, and clear help statements on the OPAC screen. The ability of the user to understand the OPAC and to interactively pursue the search to its fullest extent is critical to the success of the OPAC and thus to the library. Users often need guidance in formulating a search. They do not use the system often enough to remember the system protocol, such as special search codes, truncation, punctuation, stopwords, abbreviations, and authority control (Aken 1988).

As information grows and the technology to access it becomes more powerful, the librarian must be willing to maintain an active role in communicating with the user so that he or she can provide valuable input in designing an OPAC that will meet patron needs. When revamping original OPAC designs or revising specifications for new OPACs, it must be remembered that searchers are not passive. User-friendly is not always user-easy. Every effort should be made to design OPACs that are clear, simple to operate, and accessible to a diverse clientele. Replicating the functions and access points of

---

5. Pre-coordinate phrase searching tells the computer to look for the exact phrase that is entered. The search is fixed to a word-for-word match. Post-coordinate keyword Boolean searching allows the user to have control over the search. Keywords are indexed in specific fields that can be searched, i.e., the title, the name of the author, the annotation, the text of the article, etc. The patron uses Boolean operators, such as AND, OR, and NOT between terms to combine or eliminate them from the resulting hits or records that are displayed.

the card catalog is not enough. Records must be well indexed for the catalog to be effectively searched online. The patron must be provided with adequate learning tools, and the setting must be conducive to research. Better system design, more front-end software, more one-to-one instruction, detailed user manuals and ready-reference guides should be available. The user must know how to exploit the strengths of the online catalog, and be able to compensate for any shortcomings.

Users Group Reactions

For the most part, users of OPACs are enthusiastically receptive to online computer access. They feel that the OPAC saves time, i.e., "Just punch your topic in and you get instant gratification." "You know whether or not a book is on the shelf. You don't have to waste your time walking." Patrons feel that the OPAC provides new services, i.e., "I like the combined author/title search; it narrows the search, and I find what I want quickly." They notice the capabilities of the OPAC as compared with the card catalog, i.e., "I don't have to look through so many catalog cards. I can get a printout instantly." They appreciate the versatility of the access points, i.e., "I can put in a subject or a call number and find books."

Users have also envisioned features to improve subject access and improve quality of retrieval, many of which have come to pass. For example, they originally stated that cross references were lacking on the early OPACs. Specifically, they wanted the OPAC to suggest related terms when they typed in unauthorized subject headings. Most vendors have addressed this need. Users also suggested that subject lists be made available online. Many systems now provide online name and subject authority lists. In particular, college and university students wanted to be able to access the library OPAC from home, work, or classroom, to place interlibrary loans from remote locations, and to order delivery of library materials through the OPAC, a modem, and a phone line. These capabilities are becoming increasingly popular among vendor systems. Staff and students at community colleges and university libraries have also made suggestions for including community information such as job ads, current events, concerts, continuing education courses, subway routes, movies, plays, restaurants, reviews, city directories, dates of festivals, etc., and campus information such as library hours, displays and exhibits, campus phone numbers, campus events, academic calendars, etc. Vendors have incorporated these requests by providing a bulletin board feature. The library can include as much or as little community and campus information as it deems necessary. In general, users want all of the library's resources to be online, from comic books to paperbacks to movies to pamphlets to records and tapes to community resources to newspaper indexes and periodical articles. Ideas for enhancing the OPAC are virtually limitless.

The OPAC is a Multidimensional Access Tool

Ken Dowlin envisioned the OPAC as "the network engine for the library of the future" (Dowlin 1987, 2). He saw it as the sole access to library information-- and emphasized that through it, the patron should have access to *all* of what the library holds. Transforming the OPAC into a multidimensional access tool is the challenge of the 90s; and vendors and librarians are beginning to meet that challenge. Gateways are used to provide transparent connections or paths to available information. Networking gives the patron access through a microprocessor to indexes, directories, online database services, and other reference tools without the user ever being aware of the location or storage format of the files.

It has become increasingly popular to connect OPACs to CD-ROM and online reference databases via front-end interfaces.

For example, NOTIS' Multiple Database Access System (MDAS)[6] allows the user to retrieve information from reference files which have been loaded onto the NOTIS OPAC module, such as Infotrac 2000, ABI/INFORM, ERIC, Medline, and PsychINFO. The search commands

---

6. NOTIS has been acquired by Ameritech Information Systems.

are identical to those used when searching any other information on the OPAC.

The CARL system allows users to search the databases of Information Access Company (IAC), for example: Magazine Index and Trade and Industry. Retrieved citations automatically indicate whether or not the library subscribes to the displayed journals. If it does not subscribe, the system gives the patron an option to order them and to deliver them in one of two ways: onscreen or via fax. The cost can be charged to a credit card or a deposit account can be established with the library. The deposit account acts like a photocopy card in that it shows a diminishing balance until the credit is used up.

GEAC users can arrange to have Data Courier's reference databases loaded onto their system and accessed via the OPAC. Included are ABI/INFORM, Business Dateline, Newspaper Abstracts, Periodicals Abstracts, and Dissertation Abstracts.

In the same vein, vendors such as CLSI, Dynix, INLEX, Innovative Interfaces, PALS, SIRSI, and VTLS offer access to journal literature through the OPAC. DRA offers access to a variety of reference databases (many in full text) through its Information Gateway module, which enables users to search reference sources using the same commands as they use to search the OPAC.

One of the most impressive product enhancements is Gaylord Information Systems' SuperSEARCH. It gives GALAXY's OPAC users access to a variety of networked CD-ROM reference databases, such as those available from Wilson and Information Access. This new development makes it potentially cheaper for a library to provide OPAC CD-ROM database access than to add reference database files, via tapes, to the hard disk of a minicomputer or mainframe computer.

The advantages for patrons of the developments mentioned above are tremendous. They include:

1. unlimited access;

2. fixed annual fees;

3. simultaneous search capability.

If vendors adhere to the NISO and ISO Common Command Language standards (Z39.58-199X and ISO/CCL), patrons can use the same search commands to search reference databases (loaded onto the local system) as they use to search the OPAC.

There are also some important implications for libraries, namely additional disk storage and additional software licensing fees. Loading journal citation files requires a significant upgrade in system storage capacity, and licensing fees can be quite expensive, depending upon (1) the databases selected; (2) the number of years of coverage; (3) the users involved;[7] (4) locations of users;[8] and (5) the maximum number of concurrent users.[9] In addition, some database producers require that the library continue paper subscriptions as well, thus elevating the overall cost.

The Impact on Colleges and Universities

The OPAC has become a sophisticated information workstation in colleges and universities. Academic institutions are incorporating campus-wide networks to allow faculty, staff, and students access to the library OPAC from anywhere on and off campus.

Virginia Polytechnical Institute is a good example of technology's resounding impact on libraries. The campus has installed more than 13,000 personal computers. Students are linked from their dormitory rooms and staff are linked from their offices through a digital PBX to the Computing Center's mainframe IBM and DEC computers. They access the library's Hewlett-Packard computer which runs Virgina Tech Library System (VTLS) software and dozens of student-run electronic bulletin boards. Campus networks provide gateways to both national and international networks. These networks allow library employees to exchange information with colleagues around the world and to interact with remote databases and library systems elsewhere.

---

7. Some database vendors offer lower rates for academic or educational use than for general or corporate use.

8. Some database vendors restrict licenses to specific locations.

9. For further information on determining concurrent users, see *Library Systems Newsletter*, vol. XI, no. 6, June 1991, pp. 47-48.

The Virginia Tech library has developed its own public information system as well, enabling patrons to obtain information ranging from the operating hours for branch libraries to the titles of books on order in various subject fields. Users can access reference service through a menu-driven electronic mail system. "Virtually all intralibrary transactions are being converted to electronic methods. Some personnel functions, such as student payroll and financial accounting, are handled largely on microcomputers. Other transactions, including supplies and equipment requests, are handled through the mainframe network. . ." (Kriz, Harry and Queijo 1989, 64). According to Harry M. Kriz and Z. Kelly Queijo,[10] "To function as a library employee within this environment is to do far more than use an automated system for a particular task. The successful employee must develop the conceptual skills necessary to navigate by keyboard through the virtual information space of the electronic environment" (ibid).

The M.D. Anderson Library at the University of Houston introduced a mediated searching service known as "Computerized Information Retrieval Services" (CIRES) in 1975. By 1986, patrons were given access to online databases such as BRS/After Dark and Knowledge Index during selected evening and weekend hours when online costs were lowest. Ready-reference computer searching was available at the Reference/Information Desk so that users could verify citations and experiment with databases that had no printed equivalents. By 1987, the library had introduced CD-ROM databases, Books In Print Plus for collection development, and ERIC and Compact Disclosure for public access. The following year, the number of workstations was expanded, and nine other products were added. Quick Search and the CD-ROM area were consolidated, and an Electronic Publications Center was developed near the Reference/Information Desk. According to Thomas C. Wilson, "This action unified database access and emphasized the relationship between this service area and the Reference/Information Desk. . . .

"In January of 1988, the M.D. Anderson Library began formally exploring the potential for expert systems applications in reference. The Intelligent Reference System project developed a working prototype of an expert system to assist users in identifying appropriate indexes in the collection. . . . Over the past couple of years the Information Services Department has explored technologies such as desktop publishing, computer projection, hypertext, electronic mail, and general office automation. While these have been pursued

---

10. Kriz and Queijo work in the Automation Services Department at University Libraries, Virginia Polytechnic Institute & State University, Blacksburg Virginia.

somewhat less formally, they represent ongoing commitments in the department, and in the library as a whole" (Wilson 1989, 67).

The online catalog is beginning to offer access to full text retrieval as well as to ready-reference sources such as Grolier's Academic American Encyclopedia, the American Heritage Dictionary, and Roget's Thesaurus. The University of Kansas has attempted to expand services with a new text-based information retrieval system called Inquire/Text. Inquire/Text allows the searcher to retrieve "textual" information such as abstracts and the full text of books and periodicals that exist in electronic format. The trend is for universities to pool electronic informational resources as well as making them available online from multiple sites as a means of sharing collections and improving service at a reasonable cost (University of Kansas, November 1991). Many libraries are beginning to display their own locally developed databases through OPACs, such as demographic data, voter information files, local services, or special collections. Libraries are simplifying access by incorporating hypermedia and expert systems in OPACs to provide optimum performance and further enlarge the scope.

A Voice from the Public Sector: Hayward Public Library

There is a feeling that in some circumstances, these sophisticated search capabilities in OPACs are not needed for everyday public library users. The staff at the Hayward Public Library (Hayward, California) feel that patrons generally want to know (1) what the library has; (2) where the item is located; and (3) whether or not it is available at the time of the search. They do not want to be presented with several display screens that force them to toggle back and forth between complicated menu systems. Consequently, the library staff[11] developed a public online catalog (Public Easy Access Catalog of Hayward or PEACH) and a separate staff online catalog in 1989. PEACH is based on the following concepts:

- Ease of use by all educational and computer-literacy levels;

- Single screen display for all information on a single title;

---

11. Bennett Jacobstein, Systems Analyst at the Hayward Public Library, was the primary developer of PEACH.

- Browsing capabilities from A to Z at each level of display; thus, patron does not ever have to go back to menu;

- Uncomplicated search process.

According to Bennet Jacobstein, the primary system developer, the PEACH online catalog has proved to be extremely popular with patrons. In 1991, they marketed an integrated library system based on the above concepts. Known as PEACH 3, the system uses POWERHOUSE fourth generation language and OMNIDEX indexing software and operates on a full range of Hewlett-Packard HP3000 minicomputers. It is said to incorporate both ease of use for patrons and more sophisticated concepts for staff.

Training and Training Materials for Staff and Patrons

Staff Instruction

As libraries continue to automate and provide external access to myriad resources, it becomes crucial to adequately train the staff. They are the conductors on the train . . . the team who will give the patrons a ride to their destinations. It is they who will support the system and in turn, train the patrons. Systems and services have widened; so, too, have the responsibilities of the trainers.

To be able to determine why the OPAC works the way it does or why it fails to retrieve needed information, the staff must be knowledgeable about "how records get into the database; how they are structured; what causes the order of display; how the searcher's choice of search strategy affects retrieval;

what types of errors are correctable and how to correct them; and which errors result from faulty inputting as opposed to system-produced flaws" (Lipow 1989, 864). Those who conduct training sessions need to be adept at translating their knowledge to patrons. They are often called upon to explain or solve problems resulting from split files, choice of wrong index, correct index wrongly used, or any other trouble spots. According to Anne Grodzins Lipow, "This requires training, with continued follow-up reinforcement until it is clear that the search-and-find benefits these features were intended to achieve are realized" (ibid).

The vendor that you choose will provide basic OPAC training for your library staff. Your contract should specify service hours, types of support, general and specific training objectives, descriptions of the areas of training support, and expectations of the library's role in the training process. The library's role should be clearly defined. Through a combination of feedback from patrons, brainstorming sessions, task force meetings, and manager's negotiations, you should develop a framework for implementation of training both during and beyond the initial implementation of the online public access catalog.

Training typically begins just prior to installation and is preferably conducted in a remote area, away from library activity. A comfortable environment promotes the learning process and emphasizes the library's commitment to continued staff development. Selected staff members are initially trained so that they can incorporate local policy decisions and train other staff. As a rule, library staff are provided with manuals which reduce the need for notetaking during the training session and serve as practice tools for subsequent in-house training.

The NOTIS Experience

Some vendors have developed detailed levels of support for the libraries they serve. For example, NOTIS Systems, Inc. (acquired in 1991 by Ameritech) has developed what it terms a "tiered" program of support. Basic training in its Library Management System (LMS) software is included in the purchase price, but it is only a segment of the more comprehensive training program and is designed as a foundation for further learning. The second tier includes special training in topical workshops for library and technical staff, presentations at annual users'group meetings, training in the use of products that are not part of the LMS, and customized training. The Technical Group offers classes in programming as it relates to NOTIS and installation seminars; and the User Services Group presents the topical workshops and specialized training courses. Libraries are encouraged to share information by publishing articles in their newsletter. A special interest group has been organized and conducts workshops around training and the instruction. Training is considered critical to the successful implementation of the system, and expertise is drawn from the users as well as the staff (Cunningham 1989).

The University of Delaware Experience

The University of Delaware Library developed a staff training program which included a needs assessment of staff experiences and expectations, a statement of goals, methods of program development and evaluation, and a generation of future projects. Specifically, it included:

- "train-the-trainers" workshops to develop skills among a core group of system trainers;

- self-paced workbooks;

- staff manuals; and

- orientation sessions which would overview general automation topics as well as provide specific sessions on local components.

The general orientation session included a review of the hardware, system software, and telecommunications that support the library system. Another incorporated security issues. The expectation was that the staff would be more comfortable with job tasks, could accept changes/enhancements confidently, and would develop a willingness or intellectual curiosity toward new applications, given the full scope of training (Gordon 1989).

The Virginia Tech Experience

The environmental approach to staff training was adopted by Virginia Tech in 1986. Rather than teach employees the procedures to follow in isolated tasks, they prepare them for the total experience. Each employee has a mainframe account and is given training in the use of electronic mail and in navigating through the library and campus information systems. Microcomputers are widely available for use: Two microcomputers for each three employees are accessible, whether or not positions involve regular use of a computer.

Trainers are encouraged to have a global view of the library's functions and of the capabilities of automation. They are heavily involved in the development, maintenance, and use of mainframe systems operated by employees, and training is considered an integral part of each employee's job. In order to avoid the uneasiness that employees might feel when being trained by an immediate supervisor, training is conducted by trainers outside the employee's department in a relaxed approach that tends to demystify computers. OPACs are designed to incorporate visual guideposts into screen displays, and informative messages and menus help the user to navigate. The employee is not expected to remember how to use everything that exists. Technical support is provided to anyone interested in understanding the diverse systems now in place, and experimentation is fully encouraged.

To support further training, the Electronic Environments Group was formed in May of 1989. Speakers come to the meetings on campus and make presentations on broad topics which have included AskSAM, a text database manager to construct an integrated database system; hypermedia; and a review of automation. An agenda is posted online, and a daily logon message reminds employees of the meeting (Kriz and Queijo 1989).

The M.D. Anderson Library Experience

Your staff may include part-time students who should also be considered in the training process. The M.D. Anderson Library at the University of Houston employs students to provide technical assistance as opposed to helping a patron build a strategy. Their training program consists of a two-hour introduction to computer searching, followed by discussion, and a hands-on session. According to Thomas C. Wilson, "Supervised practice time allows each student to investigate typical research questions online. The training is rounded out with an assignment to read the vendor manuals (BRS/After Dark and Knowledge Index) and a locally developed user manual. To ensure that quality assistance is always available, ongoing discussions take place to provide a forum for student staff to ask questions and share experiences" (Wilson 1989, 68).

Training Needs in Other Areas

As training needs diversify and OPACs open the doors to multimedia, it is particularly important to think about increasing training opportunities in other areas. Training programs which incur little cost are offered regularly by CD-ROM database vendors such as Dialog, Dow Jones, or Sociological Abstracts. Local training sessions are listed in their departmental weekly newsletters. Usually people attending these sessions are encouraged to update other members in the department. An up-to-date collection of manuals, guides, thesauri, and directories support ongoing development. For the novice, vendor-produced videotapes are available. They may be used in conjunction with practice sessions which introduce the concept of basic computer searching scenarios.

Developing Training Materials

The most time consuming part of the overall training is developing printed materials. As you prepare for the installation of the OPAC, the database is undergoing continuous change. Screens and software functions are literally being changed overnight. The key element to be provided is the user's manual which includes the database techniques and functions. Flip charts are often used to feature key concepts, and handouts are frequently presented at the terminals. Formal evaluations should be made of the completed training materials, and reevaluations should be based on input from users of the text.

The ILLINET Online Experience

The ILLINET Online experience is worth noting. It has been in operation since 1980. By the fall of 1991, 40 state and private universities and colleges, community colleges, high schools, and the state library had contributed their holdings to it. Representing five million records and over 20 million volumes, it is a union catalog, with the largest contribution from the University of Illinois (Urbana-Champaign). It also provides statewide access to 800 OCLC libraries and 2,600 other libraries through dial-up access and is used heavily for interlibrary loans (Bretthauer 1991).

Initially, an Operations Committee was established to improve library staff training, and a subcommittee was formed on user education. The User Education Committee was given the responsibility of developing training materials, sponsoring training workshops, and acting as a clearinghouse for training materials. It put together a reference manual that reflected the multi-library system, and the user services staff worked with the committee to train member libraries that joined the network.

Today, they continue their cooperative working relationship. User services staff members automatically become members of the User Education Committee and are often called upon to lead workshops and handle the administrative details, such as registration. Member libraries provide tours to new members in the network, and experienced member libraries form unofficial partnerships with these new members, based on geographic proximity or similarity of size.

In January of 1988, ILLINET Online was formally introduced to the Illinois State Library, 18 Illinois library system headquarters, and over 100 librarians representing the member libraries. A three-day lecture and hands-on workshop was presented by the User Education Committee to train the trainers of member libraries. Training materials were developed and presented by the User Education Committee, and the Illinois OCLC Users' Group provided additional workshop materials to train other ILLINET OCLC libraries. In August of 1988, the Illinois Library Computer Systems Office (ILCSO) was established as a separate office within the University of Illinois for the purpose of providing user services, i.e., staff training, for participating libraries.[12]

In 1989, services were expanded to the user community. Member libraries were provided access to PROFS, an electronic mail system, Faxon's LINX, and a test system from Baker and Taylor. The PROFS training was done by the ILCSO staff using a hands-on approach in a learning lab that had never before been used to train staff outside the University of Illinois. Since the training, the ILCSO office has documented a steady increase in incoming communications via PROFS. Training is continuing. Faxon and Baker and Taylor provided both training and documentation at library sites and will continue to do so as new members join the network.

The ILLINET Online staff continues to work toward cooperation and participation to keep pace with demands. With decreasing funds, they will call on the user community to lead staff training. A major redesign of the online system will eliminate duplication of services in the circulation component (LCS: Library Computer System) and in the online catalog component (FBR: Full Bibliographic Record). Retraining and rewriting of system documentation is an ongoing project (Hammerstrand 1989).

The MELVYL Experience

MELVYL is the online union catalog for the nine University of California campuses: UC Berkeley, UC Davis, UC Irvine, UCLA, UC Riverside, UC San Diego, UC San Francisco, UC Santa Barbara, and UC Santa Cruz. MELVYL

---

12. For a detailed history prior to 1988, see *Library Hi Tech, Consecutive Issue 28* (Volume 7; Number 4; 1989; pp. 71-72).

MEDLINE[13] was mounted into MELVYL terminals at all campuses; and dial-up access was made available for UC faculty, staff, and students. This was partially accomplished through a $521,400 National Library of Medicine Resource Grant. Two of the aims of the grant were:

1. to train users in effective searching of a file of journal citations in conjunction with a search for book holdings; and

2. to bring to the attention of all UC online catalog users the resources in the biomedical journal collection.

From the inception of the grant proposal, training was given the highest priority. Funding was requested and received to develop a workbook, brochures, flip charts, and a newsletter. A central training coordinator was named, and one person on each campus was designated as campus coordinator.

"Training for the Trainers" workshops were conducted at two centralized locations: UC Berkeley and UCLA, in October 1987. They focused on searching MEDLINE using MELVYL software via NLM, BRS, or Dialog. Campus coordinators were provided with a textbook, flip chart pages, a quick guide to system commands, and a very detailed brochure. Products could be customized as needed, and a floppy disk was available upon request. By early 1988, most campuses were holding training classes on a regular basis for staff as well as for patrons.

In June 1988, a second "Training for the Trainers" workshop was held to include an introduction to MEDLINE and Index Medicus. Overall, there was general support for the materials and training provided. Some campuses had developed transparencies and microcomputer demonstration programs. The training coordinator received monthly progress reports from all campuses as well as calls and correspondence and was able to continually improve the training materials. Scheduling of classes at each campus was flexible and determined by specific needs. There was one distinct advantage: All training materials used

---

13. MEDLINE is one of the international databases included in NLM's Medical Literature Analysis and Retrieval System (MEDLARS). It includes citations which appear in Index Medicus, the Index to Dental Literature, and International Nursing Index. Approximately 4,000 journals are indexed in MEDLINE, some cover-to-cover and others selectively, and about 75 percent are published in English.

were developed by the single training coordinator. According to Beverly L. Renford,[14] this training model was considered very successful (Renford 1989).

Patron Instruction

Once the staff has been trained, workshops should be provided for patrons. The ultimate goal of any OPAC is to provide the path through which users can locate materials to meet their needs. Whether you teach library patrons in a classroom setting, as part of a public demonstration, or on an individual basis, the same guidelines may be followed:

> **Identify yourself and your position.**
>
> **Get a feel for the level of competence among your patrons.**
>
> **Define the scope of the database:**
> > the types of materials available (books, periodicals,
> > > videos, cassettes, microforms. . .);
> > the dates of coverage;
> > special codes and special collections;
> > affiliated libraries within the system.
>
> **Briefly overview the function and purpose of the OPAC:**
> > Demonstrate how the equipment is operated.
> > Discuss the keyboard and point out the function keys.
> > Explain help screens and prompts.
> > Describe the relationship between the card catalog and
> > > the computer catalog; review types of materials that can be accessed through the OPAC; note special collections, such as maps, recordings, and software that cannot be found in the OPAC.
> > Emphasize patron interaction.
> > Stress the librarian's role of assistance.

---

14. Beverly L. Renford is the head of public services and project training coordinator for MELVYL MEDLINE, University of California at the San Diego Biomedical Library.

Demonstrate a search:
> Go over the access points -- author, title, subject,
> > keyword, call number. . . .
> Construct a simplified mock search
> > by author;
> > by title;
> > by subject.
> Take the patron(s) through each type of search.
> Point out the elements of a bibliographic record.
> Explain locational codes.
> Highlight the system prompts.
> Demonstrate online assistance.

The object of the lesson is to make the patron a self-confident, self-reliant searcher. The selection of good examples is crucial to illustrate system points. Be sure to prepare them in advance and vary them according to level of difficulty. After the lesson is completed, the same examples can be used by patrons as supplements during practice time. Repetition cements new-found knowledge. It is helpful to provide brief handouts or quick-searching guides to highlight concepts just learned.

The content of your demonstration will depend upon the capabilities of the OPAC you purchase and the level of expertise of the clientele you teach. In any case, it is beneficial to point out features that seem to cause the most difficulty for users. For those who are more sophisticated, managing the size of the retrieval through the use of Boolean operators and truncation should be emphasized. After adapting an outline to fit your needs, the outline will serve as a means to ensure continuity of instruction.

Users bring a variety of experiences and learning styles to the online catalog. Linda Wilson, Project Manager for User Education at Virginia Tech, states, "Written instructions should be as brief as possible; active rather than passive verbs should be employed; examples should be shown and small print and jargon should be avoided. Graphics, underlining, and use of thematic titles help to simplify and organize information." She suggests the use of flip charts to display pertinent information compactly, but with ample spacing and an uncluttered look, and lauds online tutorials. Her article, "Preconditions to Teaching the Online Catalog User," emphasizes ergonomics in teaching.[15]

---

15. Ergonomics encompasses appropriate kinds, quantities, and placements of chairs, tables, and video display terminals, as well as the design and placement of instructional aids. It is the "study of human capabilities and psychology in relationship to a working environment and equipment" (Wilson 1989).

The OPAC and Ergonomics

Librarians responsible for the installation of the OPAC must make decisions about the kinds of terminals and furniture to be purchased. When planning your layout, there are a number of complex decisions regarding the shape and design of the OPAC workstation that should be considered. The library must be flexible. The OPAC is here to stay and will serve the needs of the library for several years to come. Research has shown that users base 80 percent of their impressions on what they see in the first few seconds.

As card catalogs are replaced with OPACs, ergonomic considerations need to be addressed, i.e., how much space is available for the terminals? What kinds of furniture will support the OPAC terminals, printers, and peripherals? How will electrical needs be met (cable, acoustical requirements, lighting considerations, handicapped needs, etc.)? The OPAC workstation should be planned with features that support the health and comfort of the patron.

Cost, flexibility, and simplicity are key words to remember. According to Ed Pennybacker of OCLC, "When designing a facility, it is important that current requirements be met, and that potential future needs be identified so that they can be accommodated with the fewest future modifications. This can be accomplished to a degree by designing a facility that can support multiple uses. Removable partitions, open office concepts, and underfloor or ceiling access for utilities can contribute to flexibility in building design" (Pennybacker 1987, 47). Furniture now comes equipped with features to secure and route cables and electrical wiring. Improper wiring and cable extensions are dangerous and should be avoided.

Work surface is required for additional equipment, such as a printer, a CD-ROM player, and a paper holder. Unfortunately existing furniture, offered in most furniture company catalogs, does not keep pace with current trends. Research indicates that the ideal worksurface should be 27 to 27 1/2 inches in height with adjustable guides that allow the work surface to be raised at least three inches. This allows for ease of reading materials with bifocals at a downward angle. The top of the terminal should be positioned at eye level so that the user looks downward and reduces stress on the neck and back. Regulations require that libraries provide some workstations for handicapped users. In that case, work surface should be adjustable to provide adequate clearance for wheelchairs which are approximately 30 inches in height (Martin 1989, 21).

Sufficient workstation width and depth are also imperative. Studies show that space must be allowed for left-handers and right-handers and sufficient accommodations must be made for bookpacks and coats, etc. A minimum width of 66 inches is recommended. A minimum table depth of 30 inches is recommended to accommodate room for the keyboard, terminal, electrical cords, cables, and plugs. Take into consideration that most furniture companies offer tables depths between 24 and 28 inches (ibid., 21-22).

Privacy is another consideration. Some workstations are designed for a high level of privacy with a height of five feet, while others are designed with lower heights of three feet for semi-privacy. In general, enough height should be provided to prevent one user from viewing the adjacent user's screen. A height of 44 to 46 inches is recommended. The height of the back of the workstation should match the height of the sides (ibid., 22).

For the user who sits at the workstation for just a few minutes to do an author, title, or brief keyword search, seating at the workstation is not an overriding concern. However, for the patron doing extensive searching of 30 minutes or more, an adjustable swivel chair is recommended. The costs for ergonomic chairs have decreased and are comparable in price to conventional chairs (ibid., 25).

A great deal has been written about the glare of light on the computer screen. Overhead fluorescent lighting is most frequently used, and terminal screens may be turned downward to decrease glare (ibid., 23). Antiglare screens can be purchased from vendors. Those that are constructed of a very fine mesh tend to attract dust, while others are etched or coated to prevent dust from gathering.

Designing the OPAC workstation is a complex and time-consuming process, but the time spent doing so is worth the effort (ibid., 26). The OPAC environment should be inviting to library patrons and should be balanced with light colors and appropriate art work or other interior decorations. Decisions will be mandated by your particular library environment and by funds allocated for the project.

Cost Considerations

Most libraries appoint a system manager and automation committee to oversee the OPAC specification and procurement process. The system manager should have a good background knowledge of the library environment, budgeting, and excellent interpersonal skills. He or she will deal directly with the vendor to conform with standards and coordinate contract negotiations, installation, and training. It is essential that the system manager possess the expertise to determine the true costs and available options. As a rule of thumb, when evaluating vendors, costs are projected over a five-year period, the period during which no major additional hardware or software should be incurred through obsolescence. Libraries often prepare checklists that take into consideration the full price of the OPAC (to include one-time costs, such as site preparation and record conversion; and ongoing expenses, such as supplies). Comparisons should be made on selected systems of the same size because system capabilities, projected hardware life, and frequency of upgrades vary. Any unprojected addition to the system or change in activity level will alter the cost.

Because hardware quickly becomes obsolete and must be replaced, the library can expect a major upgrade every five to seven years. To ensure a fully operable system, a reserve fund should be established into which 6-8 percent of the purchase price is paid each year.

Summary

Online public access catalogs have come into their own right as a means of helping patrons access the information available today. The card catalog is quickly becoming a tool of the past. With the OPAC in place, librarians no longer have to file catalog cards in a linear fashion, drawer after drawer. Patrons simply type in the author, title, or subject of their query. Boolean search techniques and truncation aid in broadening or narrowing searches, and more hits are retrieved per entry in less time than was ever possible before.

Forerunners in the field included INTREX (INformation TRansfer EXperiments), conducted at MIT between 1965 and 1973, in which journal articles were indexed and a bibliographic record was created for each article; IBM Los Gatos which offered online retrieval of catalog records for books and technical reports in the early 70s; and the British Steel Corporation which developed on online catalog with remote access. Academic libraries, such as Ohio State University, joined the march; and during the 1950s, hundreds of libraries followed suit by joining OCLC and redesigning existing formats in OPACs which were made available to patrons. The OPAC proved to be a versatile tool, and its design became crucial to its ultimate success.

Fred Kilgour was a contributor to the field who felt that the OPAC should be designed solely for the user. The Council on Library Resources (CLR) funded studies which (1) researched user likes and dislikes and (2) made eight recommendations that every OPAC should include. Vendors expanded systems rapidly but not uniformly, and patrons had difficulty in mastering protocol and formulating searches. To perform effective searches, it is helpful for users to understand how to exploit the strengths of the online catalog. They must be armed with information that will make them self-reliant searchers.

Librarians must take charge. They must not only be prudent buyers who do their homework before comparing vendors and purchasing a new system. They must learn the jargon, read the literature, look at comparison and user studies, attend user meetings, talk with others in the field who are using the system, and prepare lists of relevant questions to ask vendors. They must become active participants, aware of the problems patrons are experiencing, and be willing to help.

Ken Dowlin describes the OPAC as the "network engine of the future through which the patron can access *all* of what the library holds." This includes accessing gateways to retrieve information from other sources such as indexes and directories on CD-ROM as well as online database services. Colleges and universities are providing access to journal articles through OPACs. Campus systems are linked to mainframe computers or minicomputers, thus allowing patrons to access information both nationally and internationally. Hypermedia and expert systems add an element of user friendliness and increase interaction.

In order to function in the complex world of the OPAC, we must understand the whole picture, design the OPAC to meet patron needs, encourage initiative, and provide adequate training. Contract negotiations should include concise training policies. Research shows that patrons want to learn how to operate the OPAC efficiently. They are not passive learners. Clear and simple training materials should be developed, and training sessions should be presented on an ongoing basis.

The library environment should be conducive to learning, yet private enough to foster individual initiative. Comfort and aesthetically pleasing colors are suggested. Proper lighting should be provided to prevent glare, furniture should be roomy and adjustable, and specifications should conform to regulations.

The system manager is the key to the success of the project. He or she will oversee and coordinate the entire project. The person selected should be an integral part of the library, one who is aware of all of its functions, who can deal effectively with vendors and ameliorate complex problems, who can work within the confines of a predesigned budget, and who can competently project future needs.

References

Aken, Robert A. Fall, 1988. Meeting the Patron at the OPAC Crossroads: The Reference Librarian as an Online Consultant. *RQ* 28(1): 42-46.

Bretthauer, David. Fall, 1991. System Design for the Consortium Environment. *LITA Newsletter* 21.

Cochrane, Pauline A. Oct., 1989. Subject Access Problems of Different Types of OPAC Users OR, The Double Challenge. *Technicalities* 9(10): 7-9.

Cochrane, Pauline A., and Karen Markey. Winter, 1983. Catalog Use Studies-Since the Introduction of Online Interactive Catalogs: Impact on Design for Subject Access. *Library & Information Science Research* 5(4): 337-363.

Cunningham, Katherine V. 1989. Vendor Training of Library Staff. *Library Hi Tech, Consecutive Issue 28* 7(4): 77-79.

Dowlin, Kenneth E. 1987. Influencing the Systems Designer: The Second Time Round. *Online Public Access to Library Files: 3rd National Conference.* England: University of Bath.

Gordon, Richard. 1989. Staff Training for Support Agencies: The ACS Ex perience Supporting DELCAT. *Library Hi Tech, Consecutive Issue 28* 7(4): 79-83.

Hammerstrand, Kristine. 1989. Library Training for ILLINET Online. *Library Hi Tech, Consecutive Issue 28* 7(4): 70-73.

Hildreth, Charles. 1989. *The Online Catalogue: Development and Directions.* London: Library Association.

Kriz, Harry M., and Zl Kelly Queijo. 1989. An Environmental Approach to Library Staff Training. *Library Hi Tech, Consecutive Issue 28* 7(4): 62-66.

Lipow, Anne Grodzins. Oct., 1989. The Online Catalog: Exceeding Our Grasp. *American Libraries* 20(9): 863-865.

Markey, Karen. 1982. *Final Report to the Council on Library Resources: Pilot Test of the Online Public Access Catalog Project's User and Nonuser Questionnaire.* Dublin, OH: OCLC.

_____. 1983a. *Online Catalog Use: Results of Surveys and Focus Group Interviews in Several Libraries.* Volume 2 of the Final Report to the Council on Library Resources. Dublin, OH: OCLC.

_____. 1983b. *Online Catalogs: Users' Problems and Needs.* Final Report to the Council on Library Resources. Dublin, OH: OCLC.

Martin, Ron G. 1989. Design considerations for an OPAC Workstation: An Introduction to Specifications and a Model Configuration. *Library Hi Tech, Consecutive Issue 28* 7(4): 19-27.

Matthews, Joseph K. 1982. *A Study of Six Online Public Access Catalogs: A Final Report Submitted to the Council on Library Resources.* Grass Valley, CA: J. Matthews & Associates, Inc.

Miller, Susan L. 1980. The Ohio State University Libraries Online Catalog. In *Closing the Catalog.* edited by D. Kaye Gapen and Bonnie Juergens, 79-84. Phoenix, AZ: Oryx Press.

Overhage, Carl F. J., and J. Frances Reintjes. 1974. Project INTREX: A General Review. *Information Storage and Retrieval* 10(5-6): 157-188.

Pennybacker, Ed. Winter, 1987. Designing Facilities for a High Tech Future: The OCLC Online Computer Library Center, Inc. Headquarters -- A Case Study. *Library Hi Tech* 5(4): 47.

Renford, Beverly L. 1989. Staff Training Systemwide on MELVYL MEDLINE. *Library Hi Tech, Consecutive Issue 28* 7(4): 73-76.

Reynolds, Dennis. 1985. *Library Automation: Issues and Applications.* New York: Bowker.

University of Kansas Purchases Infodata's Inquire/Text. November, 1991. *Information Today* 8(10): 45.

Wilson, Thomas C. 1989. Training Reference Staff for Automation In a Transitional Environment. *Library Hi Tech, Consecutive Issue 28* 7(4): 67-70.

Winik, Ruth. May-June, 1972. Reference Function With an Online Catalog. *Special Libraries* 63: 217-221.

Sources for Further Reading

Akeroyd, John. March, 1990. Information Seeking in Online Catalogues. *Journal of Documentation* 46(1): 33-52.

Allen, Bryce. April, 1991. Topic Knowledge and Online Catalog Search Formulation. *Library Quarterly* 61(2): 188-213.

Azubuike, Abraham, A. 1988. The Computer as Mask. *Journal of Information Science* 14(5): 275-283.

Belkin, N. J. 1990. Taking Account of User Tasks, Goals and Behavior for the Design of Online Public Access Catalogs. In *Information in the Year 2000: From Research to Cooperation*, 69-79. Medford, NJ: Learned Information.

Boss, Richard W., and Susan B. Harrison. Sept.-Oct., 1989. The Online Patron Access Catalog: The Keystone in Library Automation. *Library Technology Reports* 25(5): 633-722.

Cargill, Jennifer, ed. 1990. *Integrated Online Library Catalogs*. Westport, CT: Meckler.

Cherry, J. M. 1989. A Profile of User Background and User Satisfaction with the University of Toronto OPAC and the Implications for User Training and User Interfaces. In *Managing Information and Technology*, 121-128. Medford, NJ: Learned Information.

Cherry J. M., and M. Clinton. 1990. Online Public Access Catalogues (OPACs): Design of Instructional Software for User Training. In *Information in the Year 2000: From Research to Cooperation*, 143-150. Medford, NJ: Learned Information.

Crawford, Walt, ed. 1992. *The Online Public Catalog*. Boston: G. K. Hall.

Culkin, Patricia B. June, 1989. Rethinking OPACS: The Design of Assertive Information Systems. *Information Technology and Libraries* 8(2): 172-177.

DeHart, F. E. 1990. Subject Enhancements and OPACs: Planning Ahead. *Technical Services Quarterly* 7(4): 35-52.

Drabenstott, K. M. 1990. Improving Subject Searching in Online Catalogs. In *Annual Review of OCLC Research July 1989-June 1990*, 42-45. Dublin, OH.

Efthimiadis, Efthimios N. July, 1990. The Growth of the OPAC Literature. *Journal of the American Society for Information Science* 41(5): 342-347.

_____. 1990. Online Public Access Catalogues: Characteristics of the Literature. *Journal of Information Science* 16(2): 107-112.

Elsbernd, Mary Ellen Rutledge, et al. Winter 1990. The Best of OPAC Instruction: A Selected Guide for the Beginner. *Research Strategies* 8(1): 28-36.

Epstein, Susan Baerg. April 1, 1990. Training for Automated Systems. *Library Journal* 115(6): 89, 92.

Fetch, D. Jan-Feb., 1991. Staff Training for an Online Public Catalog: A Practical Approach. *Library Software Review* 10(1): 3-8.

Fokker, Dirk W. Feb., 1989. Requirements for a User-Friendly OPAC. *Electronic Library* 7(1): 4-10.

Freeman, Gretchen, and Russell Clement. April, 1989. Critical Issues in Library Automation Staff Training. *Electronic Library* 7(2): 76-82.

Freivalds, Dace, and Sylvia Carson. March, 1990. Extending the OPAC With Microcomputers. *Information Today* 48.

Frost, C. O. Oct., 1989. The Literature of Online Public Access Catalogs, 1980-1985. *Library Resources and Technical Services* 33(4): 344-357.

Hardin, Steve. March, 1991. Multiple Database Access: More Users, More Considerations. *CD-ROM Professional* 4(2): 32-34.

Hickey, T., and C. Prabha. 1990. Online Public Catalogs and Large Retrievals: Methods for Organizing, Reducing, and Displaying. In *Information in the Year 2000: From Research to Cooperation*, 110-116. Medford, NJ: Learned Information.

Holloway, Mary. Sept., 1990. The Media Center Online Catalog: A Modern Day Instructional Tool. *Wilson Library Bulletin*: 26-30.

Lancaster, F. W. 1990. Identifying Barriers to Effective Subject Access in Library Catalogs. In *Annual Review of OCLC Research July 1989-June 1990*, 46-49. Dublin, OH.

MacDonald, Linda, et al. 1990. *Teaching Technologies in Libraries: A Practical Guide*. Boston: G. K. Hall.

Meyer, R. W. 1990. Management, Cost, and Behavioral Issues with Locally Mounted Databases. *Information Technology and Libraries* 9(3): 226-272.

Michael, James J. 1989. Beyond the Online Catalog: James J. Michael, Data Research Associates. *Library Hi Tech, Consecutive Issue 27*, Chris Sugnet, ed. 7(3): 90-91.

O'Brien, Ann. 1990. Relevance as an Aid to Evaluation in OPACs. *Journal of Information Science* 16(4): 265-272.

Powell, J. H. Spring, 1990. Printed Documentation for the OPAC User: A Study of the Design and Production Process at Cornell University. *Journal of Educational Media and Library Science* 27(3): 294-310.

Schuyler, Michael. 1991. *Dial In 1992: An Annual Guide to Library Online Public Access Catalogs in North America*. Westport, CT: Meckler.

Sutton, B. March, 1990. Extending the Online Public Access Catalog into the Microcomputer Environment. *Information Technology and Libraries* 9(1): 43-52.

Tiefel, Virginia. Oct., 1991. The Gateway to Information: A System Redefines How Libraries are Used. *American Libraries* 22(9): 858-860.

Wilson, Flo. June, 1989. Article-Level Access in the Online Catalog at Vanderbilt University. *Information Technology and Libraries* 8(2): 121-131.

Woodward, B. S. 1989. Strategies for Providing Public Service with an Online Catalog. In *Questions and Answers: Strategies for Using the Reference Collection*, 132-143. Urbana, Il: Graduate School of Library and Information Science, University of Illinois.

Yee, Martha M. March, 1991. System Design and Cataloging Meet the User: User Interfaces to Online Public Access Catalogs. *Journal of the American Society for Information Science* 42(2): 78-98.

Yee, Martha M., and Raymond Soto. March, 1991. User Problems with Access to Fictional Characters and Personal Names in Online Public Access Catalogs. *Information Technology and Libraries* 10(1): 3-13.

Zink, S. D. 1991. Monitoring User Search Success Through Transaction Log analysis: The WolfPac Example. *Reference Services Review* 19(1): 49-56.

Microcomputer-Based
Automated Library Systems:
A Growing Field

This chapter will discuss the technological advances which made the microcomputer a vehicle for integrating automated library systems in small libraries; outline tips and traps when purchasing a micro-based system; briefly reiterate planning guidelines; and highlight features. A list of microcomputer-based automated library system vendors is provided in Appendix 3.

The Advent of the Microcomputer in Automated Library Systems

Until the late 1980s, it was not possible to run an integrated automated library system on a microcomputer. The hardware was simply not powerful enough in terms of memory (or RAM) and disk storage. If a small library (defined as a collection of no more than 100,000 titles) wished to automate, it had to be content with stand-alone software. Stand-alone software is software which performs only one function, for example circulation or cataloging. In the last few years, however, microcomputers have changed dramatically in the following ways:

1. Greatly increased storage capacity;

2. Greatly increased memory (or RAM);

3. Greatly increased speed, which has affected (a) the number of tasks which can be performed, and (b) the number of tasks which can be performed simultaneously;

4. An ability to link several terminals to a single microcomputer;

5. An ability to link multiple microcomputers together to form a LAN or Local Area Network.

At the same time, the cost of microcomputer hardware has fallen.

"If the same technological progress that has characterized the computer industry had taken place in the automobile industry, today's Mercedes Benz would cost about $100 and would travel nearly 5000 miles on a gallon of gas. Of course, the same car would also be about the size of a penny," (Matthews et al 1990, 133).

As a result of these changes, integrated automated library system software, running on a microcomputer, is now available. Several companies have come into existence which are exclusively targeting the small library market (see Appendix 3). Some of the established automated library systems vendors are also looking seriously at the small library market, notably Data Trek (Manager Series and ULS), Dynix (Scholar and Marquis), ILS, IME (Information Navigator), Inlex (the Assistant), and VTLS (Micro-VTLS).[1]

"The rate of adoption of micro-based automated library systems in small libraries of all types during the last four years has been most impressive. At the beginning of 1991, there [were] more than 30,000 known copies of automated library system software installed in libraries. By contrast, in 1986, there were approximately 1,000 copies of library software installed" (Matthews 1991, 8).

Tips, Traps, and Planning Guidelines

A word of caution should be inserted here. Currently, the most volatile sections of the automated library system marketplace are the microcomputer-based systems.

"Microcomputer software is the modern day equivalent of a better mousetrap. It seems that practically any bright young programmer can develop a new idea and find a market for it . . . the transition from product development to ongoing maintenance and enhancement can be a difficult one for many entrepreneurs" (ibid., 138). It is especially important, if you are buying a microcomputer-based system, to check the business foundation of the vendors.

---

1. For addresses and telephone numbers, see Chapter 2.

As with any automated library system purchase, whether on a microcomputer for a small library or on a minicomputer for a larger library, careful planning should be conducted. The points discussed in Chapter 3 (The Planning Process) all apply to the selection of the small system and should be examined. The small library may not need to have more than one or two committees; it may not need to use a formal RFP, as it may be allocated a certain amount of money with which to automate. But the underlying considerations remain the same and will be briefly reiterated here:

1. *Form a project team.* Assign a project coordinator. Involve the library staff, especially those with expertise in each functional area of the library.

2. *Establish the goals of the automation project.* What are the reasons for automating? To provide new services to patrons? To improve patron service? To gain greater control over the collection?

3. *Conduct a requirements analysis.* What does your library automation system need to do? Analyze the current operations. What functions should be automated? Identify repetitive tasks which now occupy a large amount of staff time. What unique features of your collection must be accommodated? How may your needs change over time? Will several library sites share the system?

4. *Analyze hardware requirements.* Will a stand-alone PC system suffice? How many users need to access the system? Is dial-in access required? What kind of microcomputer do you want -- IBM -- (or compatible) or Macintosh?

5. *Investigate processing and storage requirements.* How many titles, volumes, patrons, orders placed, number of vendors, notices sent do you have? How much do you expect the collection to grow? What additional types of information will be managed on the new system (i.e., journal citations, reports, non-print items, equipment, kits, software, etc.)? What volume of activity do you expect: for Circulation? for Acquisitions? for Serials? Are your

records in machine-readable form? If not, what will it cost to put them in that form?

6. *Develop system specifications and a requirements checklist.* Specifications should outline what you expect the system to do, rather than how it should be done. Prioritize your requirements. Which are mandatory, and which are optional? The requirements checklist should deal with the following:

General Features
Vendor support and assistance;
Ease of use;
Data input screens and techniques;
File updating;
Management reports;
Flexibility for customization;
Multi-site networking;
Security.

Cataloging
Bibliographic record types;
Bibliographic content and fields;
Authority control;
MARC records;
Editing records;
Interfaces with other systems.

Circulation
Patron records;
Loan period definitions;
Check-out functions;
Renewals;
Holds;
Overdue notification;
Returns.

Acquisitions
Types of orders;
Order processing;

Fund Accounting;
Vendor files;
Claims capability;
Deposit accounts;
Interfacing with other systems.

Serials
Serials control records;
Check-in procedures;
Arrival prediction;
Claims capabilities;
Bindery control;
Routing;
Subscription monitoring;
Interfacing with other systems.

Public Access Catalog
User-assistance features;
Retrieval capabilities;
Construction of search statement;
Authority control and cross-references;
Truncation;
Keyword searching and controlled vocabulary;
Subject access;
Screen displays;
Response time.

7. *Identify available systems.* Scan the professional literature; talk to other librarians; attend library conferences and exhibits.

8. *Request information from vendors.* Request product literature, and ask to see the system demonstrated. Microcomputer automated library systems vendors offer demonstration disks (usually, for a small fee which is deducted from the price if you buy the system). Ask vendors to review your specifications, and respond to your checklist. Ask about specific hardware requirements. Get price quotes for the systems and related services. Make sure that all optional items are quoted. Ask about ongoing developments.

9. *Eliminate systems that are not appropriate.* Systems can be eliminated because they do not operate on hardware platforms available to you or do not offer functional modules that you need.

10. *Talk to current system users.* Ask for references from current users. Ask how the system is used in their library. What do they like? What don't they like? What was the biggest surprise? What would they do differently? How long have they used the system? What type of vendor support do they receive?

11. *Match the systems against the requirements checklist.* Use the checklist and specifications to evaluate all products on the same basis. If there are trade-off decisions to be made, go back to the overall goals of the automation project.

12. *Contract Negotiations.* The vendor will present a purchase agreement which details all costs (including options and services), warranties, and maintenance.

13. *Site Preparation.* Purchase any necessary hardware.

14. *Data Conversion.* If you have existing machine-readable data, the vendor can convert it to your new system. If you do not have machine-readable records, you will have to convert your records to machine-readable form.

15. *Installation.* The vendor will install the software and set up system management procedures, such as system back-up routines.

16. *Staff Training.* Schedule staff training. Let the staff know what type of impact the new system will have on job responsibilities and library services.

17. *Keep library patrons informed.* Let them know how the new system will save them time and improve their access to information. Provide instructions for successful use of the system.

Features to be Considered

When purchasing a microcomputer-based automated library system, several important features should be examined.

1. Hardware Platform

> The library will be responsible for obtaining the hardware platform. It will be necessary for the project director and staff to familiarize themselves with CPUs, RAM, and disk storage, etc. The two hardware platforms for microcomputer-based automated library systems are IBM (or IBM compatible) and Macintosh.
>
> The approach from the user's point of view is different. On the IBM (or IBM compatible),[2] the user makes extensive use of the keyboard. On the Macintosh, the user moves a mouse to direct a pointer on the screen to a particular picture of an object called an icon. Choices are indicated by pressing a button or "clicking."

2. Full MARC records

> With any automated library system, your records have to be in machine-readable form. The accepted standard for records in machine-readable form is MARC II (see Chapter 5). Libraries that have records in full MARC are able to share resources, participate in networks, and move easily from system to system. It is important to ensure that your microcomputer automated library system software can handle full MARC records for all formats and that you have enough storage on the hard disk to store records with all of the MARC tags. It is also important that the system can output and/or export MARC records.

---

2. IBM compatible is the term applied to a computer which uses the PC-DOS or MS-DOS operating systems but which is not manufactured by IBM.

In an effort to come up with an easy way for MARC data to be loaded into microcomputer-based automated library systems, book vendors, retrospective conversion vendors, and vendors of automated library systems got together and devised MicroLIF (Microcomputer Library Interchange Format). The purpose of the MicroLIF Committee was (a) to devise a way of placing a MARC record on a floppy disk; (b) to adapt the information to the capabilities of microcomputer keyboards; and (c) to retain full compatibility with the USMARC Format for Bibliographic Data (LC).

The MicroLIF Committee has adopted the entire MARC record as a standard. Vendors and data suppliers have agreed to conform to the standard by issuing new software and supplying records under the MicroLIF Protocol.[3]

3. *Item File*

The item file is used in the Circulation Module and contains a barcode number for each copy of a title (along with shelf location number, call number, etc.). Multiple copies of the same title have multiple records in the item file but are linked to only one bibliographic record. If the system does not support an item file, it is necessary to duplicate the bibliographic record for each copy of a title.

4. *Authority Control*

Although microcomputer-based systems are constantly improving, they vary in the amount of authority control offered.

5. *Indexes*

In small systems, it is important to find out whether or not there is a limit to the number of indexes that can be built. Each field

---

3. For a fuller discussion of MicroLIF, please refer to Chapter 5.

that you want to search on (or offer the patrons an ability to search) must be indexed.

6. *Speed of Transactions*

The system should react quickly to input and output. Record input should take no more than 10 seconds. Circulation-related transactions should take no more than 2-5 seconds to complete.

7. *Ease of Use*

A good system should be both simple and easy for staff and patrons to use. When examining a microcomputer-based system for your library:

    a. menus should be clear and easy to understand;
    b. you should be able to move freely among options and modules;
    c. help should be readily available;
    d. the number of keystrokes needed to perform tasks, such as check-in or check-out, should be kept to a minimum.

8. *Training*

Most vendors claim that the microcomputer-based systems are so easy to use that no training is required. It is usually available, however, at a price.

9. *Documentation*

Many of the microcomputer-based automated library systems are so new that documentation is still in the process of being written.

10. *Customer Support*

It is important to determine the level of vendor support. Ask the following questions:

    a. Is toll-free telephone support available?
    b. Is there a local users' group?
    c. Is a newsletter published?

11. *Upgrade Policy*

Ascertain the vendor's policy on upgrades. Much of the microcomputer-based automated library systems software is recently developed and is constantly being upgraded.

12. *Multi-user Capability*

If the software offers multi-user capability, the price will go up. If you want multi-user capability, you will probably have to consider a LAN or Local Area Network. A LAN or Local Area Network is a combination of hardware and software which enables several microcomputers in one physical location to "talk" to each other. More precisely, it allows several computers to share resources, such as printers, software programs, and hard disk drives.

In a LAN, there is usually (though not always) a central or main computer, called the "server." The server has a hard drive large enough to store all of the data required by the system. It is frequently located at the Circulation Desk, and its hard drive holds all of the catalog and circulation data for the library. At other locations within the library, there are additional computers, called "workstations." These computers usually have no data files of their own, but provide access for other users to the data stored on the hard drive of the server. Each computer in a LAN must be equipped with a Local Area Network card and must be physically connected by network cables. Each computer must also have network software.

There are four major types of LAN cards: Ethernet, Token Ring, Arcnet, and Appletalk. The major LAN software vendors are Novell (Netware), 3 Com (3 Plus), IBM (Token Ring), Artisoft (LANtastic), and Apple (Appleshare). There are many different types of cabling, including coaxial (essentially the same as that used for cable TV), twisted pair (typically used for telephones), and fiber optic. Coaxial is probably the best, as it can handle high speed, is not affected by electrical "noise," and is relatively inexpensive.

LAN TOPOLOGIES

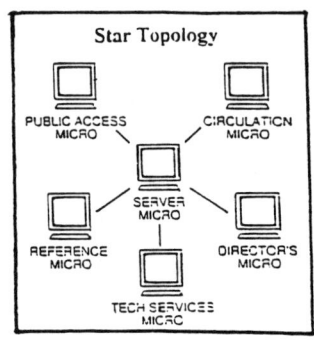
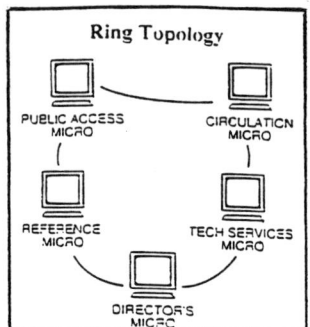

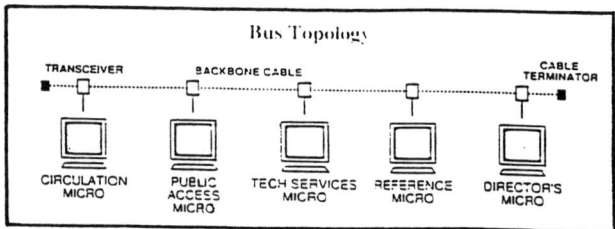

CABLE

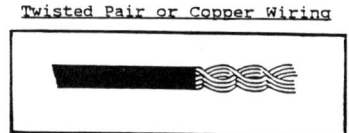
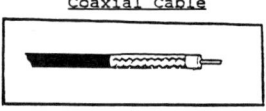

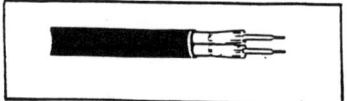

Figure 11.

Summary

This chapter focuses on automated library systems running solely on microcomputers. Until recently, small libraries (defined as having a collection of no more than 65,000 titles) were unable to have a fully integrated automated library system due to microcomputer limitations in memory (RAM) and disk storage. This has changed within the last few years. Microcomputers now have greatly increased storage capacity, memory (RAM), and speed. They have an ability to link several terminals to a single microcomputer and an ability to link multiple microcomputers together in a local area network (LAN). In addition, hardware costs have fallen.

Planning issues should be addressed with care. The steps involved in planning are briefly reiterated. Special concerns about microcomputer-based automated library systems are isolated and discussed. These concerns are:

1. the hardware platform used;
2. the system's ability to handle full MARC records;
3. the ability to create an item file;
4. the ability to have authority control;
5. the ability to build multiple indexes;
6. speed of transactions;
7. ease of use;
8. training;
9. documentation;
10. customer support;
11. upgrade policies;
12. multi-user capability.

References

Matthews, Joseph R. Nov. 1991. An Explosion in Micro-Based Systems, *Small Computers in Libraries*. 11(10): 8-12.

Matthews, Joseph R., et al. March-April and May-June, 1990. Microcomputer-Based Library Systems: An Assessment. *Library Technology Reports* 26(2, 3): 131-443.

_____. May-June, 1991. Microcomputer-Based Library Systems: An Assessment. Part 3. *Library Technology Reports* 27(3): 217-398.

Sources for Further Reading

Breeding, Marshall. 1992. *Integrated Library Systems*. Westport, CT: Meckler.

Burlingame, Dwight F. 1989. The Small Library and Fund-Raising for Automation. *Library Hi Tech* 7(2): 49-52.

Clement, Russell, and Dane Robertson. Aug., 1990. Small But Pristine -- Lessons for Small Library Automation. *Electronic Library* 8(4): 244-248.

Library Systems Newsletter. April, 1991-. Annual Survey of Automated Library Systems Vendors -- PC-Based Systems. *Library Systems Newsletter*.

Mandelbaum, Jane. 1991. *Small Project Automation for Libraries and Information Centers*. Westport, CT: Meckler.

Saffady, William. 1991. *Automating the Small Library*. Chicago: ALA.

CD-ROM-Based Automated Library Systems: A Field in Limbo

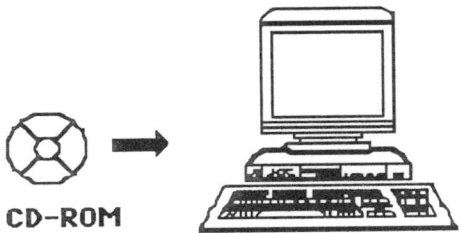

CD-ROM

CD-ROM, or Compact Disc-Read Only Memory, is a high storage capacity optical disc. This means that "The data is recorded by using a laser and burning pits into the surface of the compact disc. The pits and flat areas on the disc represent binary digits which are then read by a computer. This information cannot be altered or written over" (Langlois 1990, 13). Like the audio compact disc, a CD-ROM disc is approximately 4 3/4 inches in diameter and weighs only one-sixtieth of an ounce. Made of durable plastic, with a reflective metal coating and lacquered surface, it can hold approximately 600-700 megabytes of data (i.e., approximately 300 thousand typewritten pages.) In combination with search software, it has become a very popular publishing and storage medium.

Libraries and information centers account for the largest installed base of CD-ROM technology today. (Beiser and Nelson 1989, 285) The four main uses in libraries are (1) reference databases of bibliographic information, such as ERIC on disc, PAIS on disc, encyclopedias; (2) resource data files for retrospective conversion, copy cataloging, and ongoing cataloging needs, such as LC MARC records; (3) union catalogs which display member library holdings and identify owning libraries for interlibrary loan purposes; and (4) CD-ROM PACs. CD-ROM PACs contain a library's bibliographic records stored on compact disc (ibid., 286).

This chapter will concentrate specifically on CD-ROM PACs (Compact Disc-Read Only Memory Public Access Catalogs). A library's holdings on CD-ROM discs can be easily searched by patrons using microcomputers with attached CD-ROM players. ROM (Read Only Memory) means that the discs may be read but not written upon by staff or patrons.

Some vendors offer CD-ROM Public Access Catalogs as alternatives to integrated online public access catalogs. They appeal to small libraries which cannot afford the expense of online automation, to those with unique collections, to larger libraries in transition, and to those which can afford to offer them as a backup tool. The chapter will include a brief historical overview of the emergence of CD-ROM PACs; highlight vendors; discuss the role of standards; and outline system requirements and characteristics. Additionally, it will discuss librarians' perspectives; identify advantages and disadvantages of CD-ROM PACs as a storage medium; review system selection and preparation guidelines/possibilities; and present synopses of what others have done in the field.

Historical Development

At the American Library Association's midwinter meeting in January 1985, Library Corporation introduced Bibliofile, the first commercially developed CD-ROM discs containing Library of Congress MARC cataloging records. Shortly thereafter, in June 1985, Brodart marketed the first CD-ROM PAC, called LePac. Since then, several vendors have offered their wares, and librarians have enthusiastically accepted them.

By and large, CD-ROM products have been developed by companies that have a history of association with libraries. Many vendors, that now offer CD-ROM Public Access Catalogs or "ROMCats" for library use initially developed CD-ROM products to complement their existing lines. (Many originally put library records on computer-output microform or put them on magnetic computer tapes; now, they are offering the same records on CD-ROM.) They specifically targeted libraries as a principal market, aggressively promoted sales, and continued to add new CD-ROM products to their lines. Basically, they are solid contenders with established records in the marketplace (ibid., 288-289). As of this writing, vendors listed in the next section are actively selling CD-ROM Public Access Catalogs to libraries across the nation.

Vendors/Systems

1. Auto-Graphics: IMPACT

2. Brodart: LePac and Precision One

3. CLSI: CD/CAT

4. General Research Corporation: LaserGuide

5. Library Corporation: Bibliofile
     a. Intelligent Catalog (sound, pictures, maps, and graphics; monthly update fee);
     b. Generic Catalog;
     c. ColorCat;
     d. BibCat.

6. Library Systems and Services: CD-CAT

7. Marcive: Marcive/PAC

8. Western Library Network: Lasercat (The library must first be part of the WLN online system; regional focus)

9. Utlas: CD-PAC

The Role of Standards

CD-ROM technology is based upon the same CD technology that was introduced in 1982 as a medium for digital music recording (CD-Audio). Philips and Sony, co-holders of the compact disc license, extended the CD format to include text and pictures. In 1985, they introduced CD-ROM. It was intended as a mass storage medium for computer-readable text.

The essential differences between CD-Audio and CD-ROM lie in the unique encoding, decoding, and formatting schemes needed for the kind of digital data specific to each type of CD technology. Incompatibilities existed in the ways in which information files were organized and worked with the drive and operating system.[1] Different drives interpreted the formatted disc information in different ways; and software programs tied up varying amounts of memory while conducting routine chores. Librarians, who adhered to system requirements, were locked in to a specific vendor package. Upgrading systems and changing vendors meant that a variety of hardware and software had to be purchased, and funds had to be reallocated for new equipment.

The High Sierra Group, composed of ad-hoc members of Philips, Sony, Digital Equipment Corporation, Apple, Hitachi, Microsoft, 3M, VideoTools, LaserData, TMS, Xebec, Yelick and vendors, recognized the need for standardizing products (Elshami 1990, 33). At the High Sierra Hotel and Casino in Lake Tahoe, Nevada, they hammered out a mutually compatible proposal which addressed location, size, structure, and mapping of files on CD-ROM. It is now incorporated as ISO (International Standards Organization) 9660. Although some incompatibility still exists in the marketplace, as vendors and manufacturers conform to the imposed standards, there will be fewer problems of compatibility.

System Requirements

A typical CD-ROM delivery system consists of:

Hardware

1. IBM PC (Personal Computer)[2]
   AT or compatible recommended;
   at least 640K memory;
   one floppy disk drive, 1.2 MB or higher;
   monochrome, CGA, EGA, or VGA monitor;
   standard or enhanced keyboard;

---

1. For more in-depth coverage, "The Yellow Book for CD-ROM" describes the physical characteristics and format of CD-ROM discs, specifying the size of the disc, the physical layout and characteristics of the data storage areas, and two modes of recording.

2. It is also possible to use a Macintosh computer (SE or higher) with a CD-ROM player.

2. CD-ROM drive ("reader" or "player") which meets High Sierra standards (ISO 9660 data and file format standards) and incorporates a laser to read the disc.
   The reader can be either:
   > a standalone unit attached to the PC via a cable; or
   > a built-in unit inserted in place of a second floppy disk drive;

3. Controller board or "card" that fits into a slot inside the computer and signals the PC that it has a CD-ROM attached;

4. Printer (optional).

Software

1. Operating System: MS-DOS or IBM-DOS 3.1 or higher;

2. Microsoft Extensions 2.0 or higher: software that allows the disk operating system to treat the CD player as a network device in order to access the storage capacity of the compact disc;

3. Search software: a program that provides microcomputer screen displays and keyboard commands that enable users to access the data stored on CD-ROM disc(s);

4. CD-ROM disc(s): a library's bibliographic records.
   > Some vendors offer juke box players which allow the user to search within a group of stacked CDs that amass different collections.

Characteristics of CD-ROM PACs

CD-ROM workstations are most frequently purchased by libraries as independent single-units. The advantage to this is that when one CD-ROM workstation goes down, other standalone units remain unaffected. Their characteristics are as follows:

1. High-density, compact storage mediums.
   > A single compact disc stores:

600-700 megabytes or 600-700 million characters;

750,000 MARC records and their accompanying indexes;

300,000 pages of print;

550 1.2MB floppy disks.

2. Read-only mediums.

> Once recorded, data cannot be changed, deleted, or added without remastering the disc which is an expensive process. However, new breakthroughs in technology may alter this. Rewritable optical storage discs offer gigabytes of storage.[3] Several vendors are poised to ship a new generation of erasable optical drives that will be faster and more affordable than the current generation.

3. Easy-to-use delivery mediums.

4. Accessible by personal computer.

5. Inexpensively produced, depending on features, number of records, etc.

6. Able to be produced in quantity (with the purchase of a multi-user or site license)

   multi-user license: more than one site

   site license: one site, several locations within the building;

---

3. A gigabyte is one thousand megabytes.

Librarians' Perspectives

Librarians Are Active Supporters

Librarians actively support CD-ROM PACs as transitional catalogs, as practical alternatives to OPACs, and as inexpensive backups to online systems (Beiser and Nelson 1989 285, 286). They are considered the "wave of the present not the future" (Hegarty 1988, 109). Computer-based public access systems appeal to patrons. Users can search library holdings by title, by author, by subject and by other fields or locations as designated by the library. Discs can be remastered with updated holdings on an annual, semi-annual, or quarterly, basis; and most vendors offer monthly updates on floppy discs or cartridges that interact transparently with the CD-ROM to show patrons new and modified acquisitions. Some systems support an interlibrary loan function; others provide maps of the library to indicate to the patron exactly where the item is located; and some are interfacing with library circulation systems to show status of items. Vendors are constantly improving their products to meet anticipated needs.

Why Choose a CD-ROM PAC?

1. Patrons find CD-ROM PACs easier to learn and simpler to use than their online competitors.

2. The software can be easily enhanced or modified in response to user needs, and changes can be made at lower cost.

3. They are less risky than online systems. Librarians can use a CD-ROM PAC on a trial basis without committing so much money. Hardware is generic and can be redirected to other uses if the project is unsuccessful. There is no long-term commitment. In addition, there is no communications cost and no downtime due to communications failure.

4. Costs are fixed, known, and controllable.

5. They can be expanded, unit by unit, or networked if the venture proves successful.

6. They store vast amounts of information that can be shared. After the first disc is mastered, copies can be ordered at greatly reduced prices.

7. A small number of people can coordinate the effort to distribute them.

8. Several vendors are contenders in the marketplace which keeps it competitive.

9. Small libraries that don't use a bibliographic utility have found it advantageous to copy-catalog from a union database that contains titles from a variety of sources. For them, this is a giant step forward.

10. Libraries, which automated circulation as a first step, have found online systems incompatible and have opted for CD-ROM union catalogs (Beiser and Nelson 1989, 290-292).

Librarians Are Concerned Buyers

Librarians' concerns rest with system cost, CD-ROM standardization, and vendor stability. With limited library budgets, funding for any new system is a serious consideration. Hardware and software, offered by vendors as a unique package, is taxing on library budgets, particularly if it is an interim solution. The money available for new and replacement equipment is typically a line item in the budget and represents a small portion of the total annual funds.

Vendors have been slow to standardize. Up until recently, CD-ROMs have been written to work with one specific operating system; there has been no transportability among operating systems. The compact discs and the software that goes with them have not been exchangeable across vendor systems. (For example, a library could not purchase Auto-Graphics and share with libraries using Brodart.)

Librarians consider themselves forerunners in development of standardization related to information sharing in various areas: MARC Format; AACR2; ISBN; ISSN; Standard Address No.; Use of Conventions: LCCN; OCLC Control Number; Active in National Information Standards Organization.

They want to have a voice and be heard. Within the past few years, they have found it necessary to purchase and maintain a new brand of CD-ROM drive for each CD-ROM system. They have had to install compatible interface systems on their existing microcomputers to compensate for inconsistencies. They have had to train staff and patrons over and over again to compensate for vendor specific search protocols. Fortunately, some of their concerns are now being addressed by the High Sierra Standard ISO 9660.

As concerned buyers, librarians will continue to be uneasy about the stability-shakeout of the marketplace. Although the market is relatively stable and competitive, they ask, "What happens if their vendor is forced out of the marketplace?" "Where does that leave me?" Consequently, the financial stability of each qualified vendor is investigated in depth.

Potential Problems in a CD-ROM PAC

1. Currency can be a problem if the only way to update is to master a new disc. Calculate a lag time of 60 days.

   Cost benefit questions should be investigated: Ask "How important is it that the library catalog be 100 percent up-to-date? How much would be lost by only updating quarterly?" Supplemental files, offered by most vendors, allow you to update as frequently as daily, but be sure to weigh all of the factors. Look at logistics of interim updating, i.e., the required hardware and its storage capacity, software, staff time, etc. before you make your decision.

2. Networking can be difficult. It is easier to put an OPAC into a LAN (local area network) than it is to connect CD-ROMs. Currently, a single CD-ROM drive can accommodate five users in a network with acceptable response time.

   Look at the installed base of network hookups available in your library before making that choice.

3. The dial-up function is still under development in CD-ROM systems. In contrast, it is generally supported by integrated online systems.

4. The process of interfacing with circulation systems has been a problem in the past. As a result, more and more CD-ROM vendors are offering the capability of integrating with online circulation systems. It is a valued commercially available feature in integrated online systems. Online systems that are integrated with circulation modules display status information, i.e., tell you whether an item is on the shelf. It is harder to justify a CD-ROM catalog that does not offer this feature.

5. Response time or speed of retrieval is becoming less and less of a problem in CD-ROM PACs. Due to clever indexing approaches, CD-ROM retrieval is getting closer to the response time expected on OPACs. In addition, advances are being made in software drivers to allow a personal computer to control a CD-ROM drive more efficiently.

6. Individual maintenance is needed at each station (Beiser and Nelson 1989, 292-293).

Successful Vendor Strategies

Vendors have reacted to librarians' concerns in a variety of ways to make their CD-ROM PAC products more attractive. They have done the following:

1. Set up affordable pricing structures to attract customers:[4] Library Corporation has a "no frills" product which includes both an uncomplicated software package and an inexpensive IBM compatible workstation.

2. Bundled hardware with CD-ROM systems or sold it at cost.

3. Individualized features.
   General Research Corporation has designed a locally configured library map and incorporated it into its CD-ROM Pac, Laserquest.

4. Built-in the capability to update CD-ROM PACs through a microcomputer hard disk system.
   The database is no longer out-of-date between the times that new CD-ROMs are mastered and sent. A floppy disk with updated records is sent into the vendor by the library staff. When returned, the contents are placed on the microcomputer hard disk. Without realizing it, patrons transparently search the CD-ROM system and subsequently the hard disk for their requests.

---

4. Prices vary with database size, number of locations, nature of bibliographic data processing task, frequency of update, level of business activity of the vendor, amount of original software development called for, contractual obligations required, duration of the contract, etc.

5. Worked with individual libraries to integrate with circulation modules so that status information can be displayed on CD-ROM PACs. A few vendors, such as Library Corporation and Brodart, are now offering integration with circulation. Watch for progress in this area.

6. Helped organize user groups.
   Brodart and Marcive:
   > a. publish newsletters about systems, services, and users;
   > b. provide financial support for articles in library literature.

7. Provided users with support.
   > All have 800 telephone numbers. Beyond that, support varies. Some offer training at extra cost, and some provide manuals, but most systems are designed to require little or no training (ibid., 1989, 289).

"Most of the CD-PACs are offered at reasonably moderate prices. Workstations range in cost from around $1500 to $3000, depending on features chosen, and can be purchased independently or bought or leased from vendors. Database preparation is commonly offered on a per record basis (3-5 cents per record). Mastering a compact disc will cost another 3-5 cents per record. Flat rates for mastering run between $800 and $1000. Copies of the master disc are inexpensive by comparison ($40 to $50). Maintenance fees amount to $300 to $500 annually for maintenance of database and production of updates. Other fees may be charged for a software license, software upgrades, and maintenance of leased equipment. With a typical configuration, first-year costs range between $3000 and $4000 per workstation. Second -- year costs might typically run between $300 and $1000 per workstation" (Nolan 1990, 65). Price structures vary from vendor to vendor. Be aware that prices quoted here are subject to continual change. They are included in this section to give you an idea of prices in the early 1990s.

Planning for the System

When planning for the system, library needs should be assessed clearly and accurately.[5] That includes knowing exactly what you want to accomplish by selecting a CD-ROM PAC. Goals and objectives should be mapped out, and a

---

5. See Chapter 3, "The Planning Process."

preliminary analysis of current operations and future needs should be completed. A project manager should be appointed early in the implementation process and must assume overall responsibility, oversee and coordinate the implementation, serve as a contact person for the vendor, and establish paths of responsibility for others involved in the project. The attributes of a good project leader are outlined at the beginning of Chapter 3 under the heading, "Justification for Automating/Migrating."

Libraries tend to delegate responsibility in different ways. Some appoint the head of the reference department; others select an automation expert; still others divide the responsibility among legitimate candidates. Those selected make provisions for developing a timeline for implementation of the system; establishing profiles for database indexing and tape processing; planning a schedule for retrospective conversion and phasing out the card catalog; determining the number of CD-ROM PACs and printers needed and where to place them; maintaining equipment and supplies; training staff and patrons; obtaining and creating adequate documentation; assisting users with search questions; monitoring bibliographic control as well as copyright and licensing restrictions; evaluating the effectiveness of the new system; and recommending future modifications.

If you use good judgment and think carefully about placing the right person in the right job, your goals will fulfill your needs. For example, training patrons and illustrating search strategies should be done by someone who is adept in bibliographic instruction and able to get concepts and ideas across clearly and concisely. A clear writing style and an eye for graphics design are assets for this type of work. Hardware maintenance is best delegated to someone with mechanical ability and a love for computers. Student assistants are often used to carry out basic duties and give latitude, based on their abilities and expertise. Any combination of staffing works well if strengths are appropriately utilized and staff is adequately trained.

Selecting and Preparing for the System

When selecting the system, you may use the same guidelines as those suggested for selecting an online public access catalog (OPAC) in Chapter 6. Look at alternate system features and display formats. Prioritize system design components, i.e., searching features, that meet your needs. Investigate, test, and ask questions. Read the literature, look at comparison studies, learn the jargon, examine user studies,[6] and talk with others in the field who have CD-ROM PACs in place. You may base your RFP on models from other institutions, but remember that your planning efforts must be institution specific.

Comparing Competing CD-ROM Vendor Systems: Features to Evaluate and Questions to Ask

As you compare systems and get input from various groups, be aware of the following features and functions. System requirements should be written into your RFP and evaluated. The specific needs of your library should match the elements of the CD-ROM PAC as closely as possible. In addition to those listed in Chapter 6, examine the following areas:

1. *Compatibility*
   Most retrieval software on the market today runs on IBM-compatible hardware. However, don't take anything for granted. . . . Some software will *not* run on IBM PS2 models that use Micro Channel Architecture (the new bus design introduced in some IBM computers in 1987). Some vendors sell a proprietary bundle of hardware as a part of the package. Hard drives are usually required to accommodate high-level indexes. Ask about compatibility with your present system.

2. *Hardware*
   If you are buying a turnkey CD-ROM PAC, you will not be mixing and matching hardware. All computers will be of the same make and model, with the same CD-ROM drives and video capabilities. The vendor's default settings should meet your needs.

---

6. Review "Questions to Ask User Groups" in Chapter 6: The Online Public Access Catalog (OPAC). When consulting with CD-ROM PAC vendors, you may also obtain names and addresses of user groups and gain more information by attending meetings or by writing for sample issues of their newsletters. Information gathered at these user group meetings can be just as revealing. You can often pinpoint problems with specific vendors and obtain information by asking pertinent questions of the users in attendance.

If you are mixing and matching computers (i.e., using the CD-ROM as an ILL, technical services, or reference tool), you should be able to run an installation routine or reconfiguration routine to specify:

a.   the make and model of the CD-ROM drive;

b.   the device or "port" address at which the CD-ROM interface card will operate;

c.   which hardware interrupts and Direct Memory Access (DMA) channels should be used;

d.   the type of display adapter (monochrome, Color Graphics Adaptor [CGA], Enhanced Graphics Adaptor [EGA], Video Graphics Array [VGA]) and monitor in use.

Conflicts do occur.   Some computers, such as Leading Edge Model D, some Epson Equitys, and some Acer models, contain features that conflict with CD-ROM interface cards.   Some controller cards (Western Digital hard disk controller card) and interface cards (Network interface cards) compete with CD-ROM interface cards for the same system resources.   Fortunately, these conflicts can be resolved.

3. *Bibliographic Records*

If you are paying for retrospective conversion, be sure to check the vendor's track record with other institutions. Has the vendor accurately and effectively represented bibliographic records in other databases, merged duplicates, and cleaned up existing records? Have obligations been met in a timely manner?

If you are sending in your library's MARC records, the MARC format should be retained. Vendors should be willing to preserve original MARC tapes so that if the library changes vendors or transfers records, the records will be usable in another system. The database records should belong to you. Check licensing agreements.

4. *Supplemental File*

A supplemental file allows the library to record new titles and make modifications to existing titles on a floppy disk or tape periodically and send them to the vendor. The vendor then ships a recumulated supplemental file on a floppy disk, tape, or hard disk cartridge. If a floppy disk or tape is sent, the new file is transferred to the hard drive of each workstation; if a hard disk cartridge is sent, the new file is inserted in place of the previous one. When a user searches the CD, the hard drive should be scanned concurrently and transparently to provide updated information. Does the vendor allow you to contract for updates, additions, changes, and deletions at agreed upon intervals to compensate for the static, read-only character of the CD-ROM disc? Are supplemental files delivered in a timely fashion? Are they integrated into the system in a way that is transparent to the user?

5. *Configuration or System Administration Module*

It is helpful to be able to modify the system to meet local needs. Some vendors prefer to handle customization as a service, requiring the library to go back to the vendor to make changes at an additional cost. Others provide a configuration or system administration module that allows library staff to make changes to at least a few of the system defaults. This can be a problem if branch libraries get "out of sync," but if done cooperatively, the system can be more closely molded to local conditions.

6. *Locational Information*

Several CD-ROM products provide for the display of locational maps of the library, with or without textual labels to depict locations of titles on library shelves. Is there a facility for creating or modifying a map of the library or the location of a particular title on the shelf? Does the vendor create this, or must it be produced locally? As the library layout changes, can library staff make modifications? If an administrative mode is available, how is access controlled? Is a password required? Can the password be changed?

7. *News/Notes*

Some CD-ROM PAC vendors offer a facility for creating an onscreen bulletin board. Can your library include such items as a calendar of events; library hours; borrowing rules; a list of library names, addresses, and phone numbers; interlibrary loan or walk-in policies; additional help information? If so, is the amount of information to be displayed limited? Can ASCII text files be imported into the system and modified for display? Are calendar events automatically deleted (or at least suppressed from display) once they have occurred?

8. *Help Screens*

Help screens should be self-explanatory. Are directions onscreen clear and concise? Is additional help available at any given point during the search process? If so, are menus and commands relevant to each given situation? Do they remain consistent throughout? Can help messages be changed by staff, or are they vendor-dependent?

9. *Keyboard Functions*

Vendors use three methods to define keys on the computer that will work with the software: onscreen labels; keyboard keycaps; a combination of the two. Are online explanations and diagrams clear? Are keycaps plainly marked? Are the meanings of a given key fixed, or do they change from screen to screen? No single approach is deemed best. If you are aware of the variations, you will be in a position to compare and choose the system that meets your library's mission and best suits the needs of the patrons.

10. *Modes of Retrieval*

What search modes are available? Are retrieval options separated into Novice and Expert modes? Do they allow users to determine whether to use the more powerful and complex searching capability?

11. *Searching*

Most CD-ROM catalogs allow users to look up information by HEADING or KEYWORD. Typical HEADINGS include TITLE, AUTHOR, and SUBJECT (or some combination of the three),

CALL NUMBER, ISBN, LCCN, etc. Text is matched, character by character. The vendor will build indexes to provide access to other less commonly requested fields, such as PUBLISHER or SERIES, but it will cost more. If an additional menu must be included to access these choices, more funds must be allocated.

Cross-reference structures are of the utmost importance. They allow the user to explore alternative terms or variant forms of a name. Be sure that they support "back-stepping" and allow the user to branch off to explore and then to return to the previous step easily.

If the database includes KEYWORD searching, i.e., searching for any word in any position within specified fields, exactly what fields are indexed? Keyword access to TITLE is most frequently used and widely accepted; access to AUTHOR'S NAMES is also helpful. For example, if the user can recall only two words in the title or part of an author's name, this feature can be used to pull up the record. Keyword access to SUBJECT HEADINGS is also extremely useful.

You will want to know: Which MARC fields are indexed for keyword retrieval? Does the library have input? Can you opt for phrase searching? . . . full text searching? How is authority control handled, i.e., variant forms of names and related subject headings? Can the user highlight the alternate suggestion and automatically search? Are Boolean search techniques (AND, OR, NOT) incorporated? Can you browse name and subject files? Can you truncate? Can you substitute a wildcard character at the end of a search term or imbed it in the middle of a search term to replace characters, i.e., "wom?n" for woman or women.

Remember, cost and space are required for additional indexes. Each additional feature will bludgeon your budget!

12. *Scoping*

Most systems allow users to limit the search by location, date, format, language, etc. If so, a default is set for each type of scoping. The library should have control of these defaults. Be sure that setting the scoping defaults is a part of the system configuration.

13. *Record Display*

It is reasonable to expect a brief and fuller record display to be available to the public, and a MARC display for the library staff. How many record display formats are available? Is there a short form that displays TITLE, AUTHOR, and CALL NUMBER as well as a longer form that displays other MARC tags? Can the user switch freely among available display options? Can the complete MARC record be displayed upon command?

The library should be able to change options or set the default: Can the display labels be renamed by library staff? Can the order of the display be changed? Can individual fields or subfields be suppressed? In the case of union catalogs, is it possible to change displayed names of libraries and/or the order in which the holdings are listed?

14. *Extended Select*

Is there a facility that allows the user to choose a number of items for closer inspection from a list of brief entries? This often reduces the amount of backstepping required; however, be aware that it tends to confuse novice users.

15. *Shelf-Browsing*

The browsing capability is considered an asset. Can the user scroll among titles with adjoining call numbers, lists of authors, etc.? Can he or she page forward and backward?

16. *Highlighting*

Does the system automatically highlight matched search terms in the retrieved item? This is a nice feature that calls attention to the search terms that are present in the results.

17. *Downloading*

Downloading is the gateway to other functions. If you can download a record in MARC, it can be transparently transferred to an online integrated library system, dumped into a MARC-based catalog card production program, or moved into a database program for creation of bibliographies or other lists. A powerful added feature is the ability to download groups or ranges of records, rather than just one at a time.

18. *Printing*

Printing options differ from vendor to vendor. Be aware of the options. Can selected retrieved items be printed one at a time? Can multiple records be stored and printed at the end of the search? Are format choices similar to those for onscreen displays? Exactly what fields are included?

Vendors are in a features race. Examine the changes being made in the vendor's software and the rate at which each change is taking place.

Preparing an Iron-Clad Contract

Many of the above requirements should be recorded in your RFP as well as in your contract. The contract is an important document that should be prepared by your legal department. It should protect your rights and cover all loopholes. Be sure to provide for licensing agreements; maintenance, delivery and implementation schedules; cut off dates for inclusion of new records; delivery dates for compact disc catalogs; production dates for interim supplements on hard disk (optional); provisions for training and documentation; site visits; duration of the contract; and warranties.

Placing the Hardware

Place your microcomputers and CD-ROM players appropriately in strategic points throughout the library to provide widespread use in several locations. They should be easily accessible and are frequently clustered in public libraries. As indicated in the CLR OPAC studies discussed in Chapter 6, it is best not to place them in areas where there is continuous activity, such as adjacent to the circulation desk. Most research indicates that it is helpful to place them fairly close to the Reference Librarian who provides assistance.

But, before you prepare a layout for your library, read the latest literature. Some libraries have found that placing optical disc stations in close proximity to the reference desk have increased workload. Evans Library at

Texas A & M University reported that after the reference staff was asked to monitor CD-ROM stations and man the reference desk, their time was so divided that they could not serve either population adequately. Hahnemann University library reported that placing CD-ROM stations close to the reference desk increased the total number of reference questions by 20 percent and indicated that 31 percent of all reference questions dealt with CD-ROM searching (Eaton et al. 1989). Location may be dictated by hardware and wiring restrictions. Recommendations on technical specifications are available from the vendor.

Networking CD-ROMs

Developments in technology have permitted chaining or networking CD-ROM players together to allow access by multiple users. Workstations onsite can be connected via a LAN (Local Area Network). The advantage is that updates can be written to a much larger file on the hard disk of the LAN server which can be accessed transparently and simultaneously (with the CD-ROM disc) by the workstations connected to it. As a result, remastering the CD-ROM disc is needed less frequently.

Some problems have arisen. Local area networks generally cable workstations together in a star, ring, or bus (straight line) configuration, and instructions are issued back and forth along the cable which connects them and through an interface card in each computer. Microsoft Extensions works with device driver software to emulate a data stream which DOS can interpret. In the process, DOS perceives the compact disc as a network, and the network capabilities are usurped. In order to chain CD-ROM workstations, new network capabilities have to be added. Although networks are configured to handle simultaneous traffic as efficiently as possible, response time frequently suffers when several users access the same disc at the same time. Networking companies, such as Meridian (CD-Net), CBIS (CD Connection), Online Products (Optinet), Artisoft (LANtastic), and Novell (Netware) have designed CD-ROM networking systems to operate in this environment. The technology is still relatively new, and database producer licensing agreements vary.[7] It is considered a field in limbo, one to watch with anticipation (Elshami 1990).

New on the networking horizon, OCLC and Auto-Graphics have teamed together to promote a resource sharing system. "SharePAC" links Auto-Graphics CD-ROM PAC to the OCLC Interlibrary Loan network. Once you locate a

---

7. The basis for network pricing is often determined by the number of potential, simultaneous (or concurrent) users.

record on compact disc, you can generate an interlibrary loan workform offline without leaving your workstation and without incurring telecommunications costs. The form can be stored, retrieved, and modified as many times as you wish before sending it. You may save workforms and batch process them together. For items not on your CD, you may also link to the OCLC Online System to identify the records and create interlibrary loan requests for them. Requests sent to your library can be downloaded and updated offline. Union list libraries are also included.

Three levels of searching capabilities are offered: BROWSING, EXPERT, and RESEARCH. All include menus and an on-screen function key map and may be made accessible to staff as well as to patrons via the CD-ROM PAC.

What Others Have Done in the Field

Federal Reserve Bank of San Francisco Research Library

The Federal Reserve Bank of San Francisco is one of 12 regional reserve banks. Along with the Board of Governors in Washington, D.C., it makes up the nation's central bank. Approximately one-quarter to one-third of the library's collection is concentrated in the areas of economics and banking; it has been cataloged on RLIN since 1982. Since 1988, the Research Library has been using Library Corporation's "Intelligent Catalog" on a CD-ROM PAC on a single workstation. The bank considers it a transition vehicle from card to mini- or mainframe computer and eventually envision an integrated library system. In the meantime, it feels it has a very effective MARC record-based public access catalog that is extremely popular and does the job.

The bank specifically cited the following attributes:

1. Installation was a nonevent; we simply decided where we wanted the workstation, and then we plugged it in.

2. No special staff training was necessary, as the system is remarkably self-explanatory.

3. The low price made it easy to purchase. No special budget justifications were required.

4. Users are unanimously enthusiastic. The most common problem they have arises when they assume there is far more in the computer (such as journal articles, working papers, corporate reports) than they had ever expected to find in the card catalog (as stated by: Ciochon 1990: 72).

Alameda County Library

The Alameda County Library wanted to implement an online catalog, but when it came time to make the transition, the library found that it was not financially feasible. It would have required purchasing additional terminals and upgrading storage requirements of others as well as increasing communications costs. It examined CD-ROM PAC proposals from Brodart, Auto-Graphics, CLSI, and Library Corporation and awarded the contract to Auto-Graphics' IMPACT system in 1987 because all of the staff who had tested the different systems found it easiest to use. Initially, it had 125 CD-ROM PACs installed within its branches to which it added 15.

A committee was selected to design screen displays, introductory screens, and record displays and to write the help screens. It worked with the scoping feature and felt that the IMPACT system offered a great deal of design flexibility and local control. Each workstation could be equipped with its own scoping combinations, record displays, and introductory screens. There was also a Library News Feature that could be created and maintained locally. Advantages and disadvantages of the system, as noted by the staff, are listed below:

Advantages

1. Patrons needed little instruction. A brief set of instructions was devised on a book mark; nothing else was needed.

2. Staff got fewer questions about how to find a book. When conducting library orientations, catalog demonstrations are left until the end to entice youngsters and keep their interest.

3. Keyword searching is a boon! It has proved effective for patrons who cannot remember the full title of a book.

4. Patrons like to browse an alphabetical list of authors, subjects, titles, or a combination of the three. They can also browse call numbers in shelf-list order and easily spot headings.

5. Catalog maintenance is much easier; the call number search provides staff with a shelf list; mistakes are more visible and easier to correct; blanket subject heading changes can be implemented.

6. Cost is much less than online charges. No expansion of the present system was necessary; no new terminals were needed.

7. Storage was not a problem. Full MARC records could be stored.

8. The CD-ROM workstations are IBM compatible and may be used for other purposes as well.

9. Every workstation is independent. If one goes down, the rest are functional.

10. The workstations are portable and can be moved as easily as an electrical appliance.

11. Library of Congress Subject Headings (LCSH) and local cross-references are maintained in a file of LC MARC records, which is added automatically to the catalog.

Disadvantages

1. Without a supplement option and with only quarterly remastering, up to 5000 records are not represented in the catalog for four months.

2. A search can take from 1-10 seconds. Unlike OPACs, response time is not tied to the use of the system by others.

3. Freezing of the system occurs periodically. When a workstation freezes, the only way to correct the problem is to turn it off. For the most part, Auto-Graphics has corrected the problem.

4. There is no integration or connection to circulation status.

5. The scoping feature allows the display of branch holdings. However, it is difficult to maintain such information at a current

level; the information can be displayed on the CLSI circulation module.

A survey was conducted of the users of the new catalog; the result was that 93 percent were happy with the CD-ROM PACs. Patrons found them easy to use and found what they were looking for without assistance from the library staff (Pisano 1990).

Sacramento Public Library

The Sacramento Public Library (SPL) in Sacramento, California, consists of a city and county library that have been merged together. Over the years, it has automated in four stages: (1) Computer Output Microfilm (Auto-Graphics); (2) automated acquisitions and circulation (CLSI); (3) CD-ROM CAT (Auto-Graphics Impact System); and (4) OPAC in process (CLSI).

In the late 1970s, SPL secured a grant which helped to pay for microfilm readers for its new COM catalog provided by Auto-Graphics. Staff typed an identification number for each of 220,000 titles (including county and city where necessary). If no LC card number was available, an algorithm was made up from a portion of the author, title, publication date, call number, branch, and copy number. The final shelf list was sent to the vendor, which had the information scanned before it was put onto microfilm and input into the new database. In comparison with CD-ROM and integrated databases today, the searching process was very primitive, but it provided a new and better service. Despite the "PAWS" in service, COMCAT was well received; it was a less expensive new toy!

The collection kept growing, and the library staff continued to maintain it. However, the computer output microfilm was finite in size. Auto-Graphics compressed fields, divided the information on microfilm into two tapes (one author-title and one added entry), and then finally deleted the branch codes on tape when SPL contracted with CLSI for an automated circulation system. Funds for the CLSI system were secured through a municipal bond issue, and a shelflist was provided through RLIN. Staff was trained to clean up and maintain the database and to keep up with new releases.

In the meantime it had been 10 years since the purchase of COMCAT. The life expectancy of the microfilm readers was only five years, and they were breaking down. Some had been cannibalized to keep others going. No one manufactured the readers anymore, and only one vendor manufactured the microfilm for them. Not one more piece of information could be compressed on the tapes. It was time to rethink! A method for searching had to be devised.

Auto-Graphics suggested that SPL consider a CD-ROM public access catalog. The most logical step was to purchase furniture, personal computers, CD-ROM players, make a master CD-ROM disc, and duplicate it for use in all branches. CD-ROMs were a far better product than microfilm. They were simple to use, easily searched, and the same vendor that provided COMCAT offered a product called IMPACT CD-ROM CAT. In addition, the SPL database could be transferred to IMPACT.

The new system was a little trickier to maintain than the microfilm readers, but IMPACT CD-ROM CAT was a huge success. No public relations work was necessary to interest patrons. It was found that children trained their parents. Very few individuals needed help. The screens were so simple and self-explanatory that people were able to locate items in the library on their own. Primarily they searched by subject, author, or title. However, the more adventurous expanded the scope to include the Mountain Valley Library System or searched by keyword in the author, title, or subject field. Others who we're looking for a special medium searched the call number field for specific areas, e.g., CAS searches for cassettes.

New patrons we're always coming in, looking for the card catalog. Some we're wary of the CD-ROM CAT at first, but within a few minutes, even the elderly could be found in front of the screen. They soon felt part of the computer age and could talk computerese with their children and grandchildren. In April 1991, 125 CD-ROM readers were operating successfully in 25 SPL branches. Occasionally, lines formed behind them, but for the most part, patrons we're served efficiently and complimented the system.

SPL has since built a new $20 million central library. It needed more terminals and decided to automate again. All of the branches are equipped with CLSI OPACs and an e-mail system. Patrons are able to display status information (the particular branches that have an item on the shelf), a feature that could not be utilized in the IMPACT system simply because the branch codes had been deleted from the COM tapes to condense information. The automation process is never-ending. In this case, the CD-ROM CAT was a good interim solution, one with which SPL has been fully satisfied.

Summary

Although CD-ROM is used widely in retrieving reference materials, identifying union holdings for interlibrary loans, and copy cataloging, this chapter deals solely with CD-ROM PACs (Compact Disc-Read Only Memory Public Access Catalogs), offered by automated library system vendors. CDs are small (4.75-

inch in diameter), round, polycarbonate discs that fit inside a slot on a CD-ROM player or reader. Their main claim to fame is high density and vast storage capacity. Three-quarters of a million MARC records fit tightly onto a single CD-ROM disc and can be accessed from a menu screen on an attached stand-alone microcomputer. Libraries use read-only discs which cannot be altered or revised by either patron or staff because the cost of "erasable" discs is prohibitive.

Vendors offer CD-ROM PACs as less expensive alternatives to OPACs. They appeal to small libraries, those with unique collections, larger libraries that acquire them as backup systems, and those that use them as interim solutions until they can purchase an online system. They are often marketed as a package which includes hardware (PC, CD-ROM player, controller card, and optional printer) and software (operating system, menu or option array, and CD-ROM disc).[8]

The first company to introduce the concept of putting a library's holdings onto CD-ROM discs was Brodart (LePac) in 1985. Since then, vendors such as Auto-Graphics, CLSI, General Research Corporation, Library Corporation, Library Systems and Services, Marcive, Western Library Network, and Utlas have entered the scene. These are companies with established records in the sales of library products that offered CD-ROM PACs or ROMCats to complement existing lines. When first marketed, each system required a different CD-ROM player which interpreted disc information in proprietary ways and produced a line of incompatible systems. As a result, a group of businessmen, including representatives from Philips and Sony, met with vendors to draft a set of standards that would address location, size, structure and the mapping out of files on CD-ROM, now recognized as International Standards Organization (ISO) 9660.

With the adoption of these standards, some of the concerns of librarians have been met. Vendors have also improved retrieval time by incorporating clever indexing approaches; they have addressed the problem of currency by providing supplemental floppy disks with updated records which can be searched concurrently and transparently on the hard disk of the microcomputer by the patron; and they are devising methods to link the CD-ROM module with the online circulation system to display current status information of the location of library items. The CD-ROM PAC or ROMcat offers additional options such as graphic orientation maps of the library, a news and notes feature, an administration module, and patron-accessed interlibrary loan capabilities. User

---

8. It is usually up to the library to purchase MS-DOS extensions which allows the computer to access the full storage capacity of the CD-ROM disc.

groups have been formed to increase awareness; you may subscribe to newsletters in the field; and 800 Help numbers are provided by CD-ROM PAC vendors.

In general, librarians have supported CD-ROM PACs. They are relatively inexpensive, as compared with OPACs. Vendors have set up affordable pricing structures, bundled compatible hardware and software, and individualized features. Patrons find them easy to learn and simple to operate. They provide a wide variety of access points; they are relatively current; and results are instantaneous.

As with the implementation of any new system, planning for the CD-ROM PAC is important and should be done with forethought. Features to evaluate include the adequacy of help screens; keyboard functions; searching and scoping capabilities; display of record formats and locational information; browsing, highlighting, extended selection, downloading and printing options; and the possibilities of having news/notes screens and updating with supplemental files between remastering discs. Be sure to look carefully at the compatibility of the new system with existing or contemplated hardware and at licensing agreements. Go over your RFP with a fine toothcomb; clone parts of it into an ironclad contract that includes all of the system and functional specifications of your library, protects your rights, and covers all loopholes. The CD-ROM PAC that you select should meet the needs of your staff and patrons. Take an active part in its design and implementation, be flexible, and stay on target. Many libraries have found it to be a successful retrieval tool, one devoid of online charges.

References

Beiser, Karl, and Nancy Melin Nelson. May-June, 1989. CD-ROM Public Access Catalogs: An Assessment. *Library Technology Reports* 25(3): 285-451.

Ciochon, Miriam. 1990. Using CD-ROM for Technical Services: A Panel Discussion, The Federal Reserve Bank of San Francisco Research Library: Experiences with "The Intelligent Catalog." In *CD-ROM in the Library Today and Tomorrow,* edited by Mary Kay Duggan, 71-72. Boston: G.K. Hall.

Eaton, Nancy L., et al. 1989. *CD-ROM and Other Optical Information Systems: Implementation Issues for Libraries.* Phoenix, AZ: Oryx Press.

Elshami, Ahmed M. 1990. *CD-ROM Technology for Information Managers.* Chicago: ALA.

Hegarty, Kevin. Spring, 1988. The Compact Disk-Circulation System Interface at Tacoma Public Library: Beyond Stand Alone CD ROM. *Library Hi Tech* 6(3): 103-110.

Langlois, Jennifer M. Fall, 1990. CD-ROMs: What to Consider Before Leasing or Purchasing. *Show-Me Libraries* 42(1): 13-19.

Nolan, Charlotte. 1990. Technical Services and PACS. In *CD-ROM in the Library Today and Tomorrow,* edited by Mary Kay Duggan, 63-70. Boston: G.K. Hall.

Pisano, Vivian. 1990. Using CD-ROM for Technical Services: A Panel Discussion, CD-ROM at Alameda County Library: Advantages Outweigh Disadvantates. In *CD-ROM in the Library Today and Tomorrow,* edited by Mary Kay Duggan, 78-84. Boston: G.K. Hall.

Sources for Further Reading

Bills, Linda G., and Linda W. Helgerson. 1988. CD-ROM Public Access Catalogs: Database Creation and Maintenance. *Library Hi Tech* 6(1): 67-86.

_____. 1988. User Interfaces for CD-ROM PACs. *Library Hi Tech* 6(2): 73-115.

Butcher, Karlye S. Aug., 1990. The Rewards and Trials of Networking. *Database* 13(4): 103-105.

Desmarais, Norman. Nov.-Dec., 1989. CD-ROM Public Access Catalogs: A Bibliography. *CD-ROM Librarian* 4(10): 26-33.

_____. ed. 1991. *CD-ROM Local Area Networks: A User's Guide.* Westport, CT: Meckler.

Eckwright, Gail Z., and Mary K. Bolin. Summer, 1990. No Card Cat--No Problem: WLN's Lasercat Provides Another Opportunity for Cooperation. *RQ* 29(4): 525-533.

Harrison, Nancy and Brower Murphy. Fall, 1987. Multisensory Public Access Catalogs on CD-ROM. *Library Hi Tech* 5(3): 77-80.

Hegarty, Kevin. July, 1988. Build Your Own CD Public Access Catalog. *Library Journal* 113(12): 40-43.

Hoffman, Irene, and James S. Koga. Oct., 1989. CD-ROM: A Selected Bibliography. *OCLC Micro* 5(5): 6-8.

Kriz, Harry M., et al. July, 1991. An Environmental Approach to CD-ROM Networking Using Off The Shelf Components. *CD-ROM Professional* 4(4): 24-31.

Landrum, Hollis. Nov.-Dec., 1988. The Intelligent Catalog in Special Libraries. *CD-ROM Librarian* 3(10): 21-28.

McQueen, Howard. March, 1990. Networking CD-ROMs: Implementation Considerations. *Laserdisk Professional*: 13-16.

_____. July, 1990. Remote Dial-In Access to CD-ROM LANs. *CD-ROM Professional* 3(4): 20-23.

Masters, Deborah C. Jan., 1988. Implementation of a Public Access Catalog on Compact Disc: One Library's Experience. *CD-ROM Librarian* 3(1): 10-16.

Nelson, Nancy Melin, and Norman Desmarais. Oct., 1989. CD-ROM: An Overview of U.S. Developments. *Program* 23(4): 377-383.

Nicholls, Paul Travis. March, 1990. CD-ROM in the Library: Implications, Issues and Sources. *Laserdisk Professional* 3(2): 100-103.

Nissley, Meta, and Nancy Melin Nelson, eds. 1990. *CD-ROM Licensing and Copyright Issues for Libraries*. Westport, CT: Meckler.

Reese, Jean. Jan.-Feb., 1989. CD-ROM Technology at Vanderbilt University: Impact on Library Staff and the Educational Community. *Optical Information Systems* 9(1): 38-43.

Rosen, Linda. July, 1990. CD-Networks and CD-ROM: Distributing Data on Disk. *Online* 14(4): 102-105.

Smorch, Tom. April, 1990. CD-ROM Public Access Catalogs: One Way to Get There. *CD-ROM Librarian* 5(4): 30-39.

Stewart, Linda, ed. 1990. *Public Access CD-ROMs in Libraries: Case Studies.* Westport, CT: Meckler.

Trends Which Will Continue into the Future

Overview

As we have stated in the previous chapters, the trends of the electronic age of which we are so much a part continue. Without technological advance, the automated library system could not have been born. With it, our needs are becoming fully integrated. Trends which have made this phenomenon possible are:

>   an increase in computer storage capacity;

>   an increase in memory;

>   a decrease in size;

>   a decrease in cost.

We, as librarians, must have an unlimited ability to adapt with change and advancement. There is no end to the ability to link information, wherever it may be, and to present it to the patron. In this concluding chapter, we will summarize the directions in which we feel automated library systems are heading and the impact they will have on libraries and librarians. Our conclusions are based on voluminous readings in the field, addresses given by guest speakers who have attended class sessions;[1] and personal knowledge gained by working in the field. The chapter will bring together the concepts outlined in previous chapters, categorize areas of importance that will shape the future, and include new trends on the horizon.

---

1. Beverly K. Duval and Dr. Linda Main co-teach Automated Library Systems in the Master of Library and Information Science Department, San Jose State University, California.

A Look into the Future

Gathered research indicates that the computer of the future will most likely be the microcomputer, which will take the place of the mainframe and come equipped with an erasable optical disk. As personal computers become more prevalent and affordable in the private sector, more and more people will directly access the local library system. According to a U.S. Census survey, one in three Americans have a computer at home, work, or school (Datamation 1991).

Adoption of standards will lead to cheaper compatible hardware and easier-to-use interfaces which include transparent connections. Gateways will provide pathways to information around the world, and networks will shift the focus from the local integrated automated library system to the end user outside the library.

The compact disc will continue to provide greater storage capacity and an alternative to online charges. Electronic publishing, using this medium, will boom, creating a wealth of digitized information in full text. Concerns will continue to grow relating to ownership, copyright, and censorship. However, the printed page will not disappear. It will continue to be a competing medium of exchange.

New technologies will create an ever-changing role for librarians. Traditional planning skills will require some alteration; the need for databases will increase; technical skills will be needed; management skills will be at a premium; and public relation skills will be mandated. Libraries will continue to do more and more copy cataloging and require less specialities as original cataloging diminishes. Hypertext and hypermedia will play an increasing role in ALS modules. At the same time, expert systems, artificial intelligence, and natural language technologies will enable the user to interact with the computer more personally and will eliminate the need for command language.

As the library moves from being a storehouse of information to a gateway of information, the concept of resource sharing will become increasingly important. The OPAC will become the information station through which the patron will search indexes, directories, online databases, and services on both compact disc, hard disk, or erasable disc transparently, across town and across the country.

More and more, academic institutions will employ widespread networks available to students, faculty, and staff, both on and off campus. Online searching and online interlibrary loans will take on new dimensions. Hardcopy material will frequently be scanned and electronically sent, and services for the disadvantaged will increase.

Trends

Every librarian should be aware of the following trends as well as the implications that they have for libraries in the future. They are grouped as follows:

Standards
MARC   BISAC
ISO/OSI   Patron Record (Z39.69)
Z39.50   Networking
SISAC   Transaction Files

Networking

Terminal Load Units

The OPAC
The Face of the OPAC
Visual Information or Imaging
Hypertext and Hypermedia
Expert Systems
Robotics
Viruses

CD-ROM PAC
Networking and Dial-in Access
Integrating the CD-ROM PAC with the Circulation Module

Special Modules for the Disadvantaged

Circulation
Scanner/Security Device in One
Self-Service Circulation

Fiscal Term Rental

Changing Role of the Consultant

Standards

"A library should not implement an automated system in isolation. It should be prepared to interface or electronically link its system with those of other libraries to facilitate resource sharing" (Boss and Espo 1987, 54). Accepting the truth of this statement, librarians are looking at standards in a very serious way.

MARC. The machine-readable database is the only part of an automated library system which has the potential for an unending life span. MARC has become the accepted standard for creating and maintaining machine readable bibliographic records. A database constructed according to MARC standards can be moved to a new automated system. MARC also offers the possibility for sharing and cooperation among libraries.

ISO/OSI. In order for one library's automated system to communicate fully with another library's automated system (from a different vendor), it is necessary to get hardware, software, operating systems, and different data formats to "talk to each other." The International Standards Organization Open Systems Interconnection (ISO/OSI) establishes a model which can be followed to achieve this. The standards lay down specific communication protocols which define formats and rules for the exchange of messages between communicating systems.[2] They are made up of seven parts, called layers.

> The lower layers are concerned with and define the electrical and mechanical aspects of connecting to a communications medium, error free transmission, and communication to the right location. The upper layers process and interpret the data so a user can understand it. More specifically layer 1 connects to the network; layer 2 controls error free communication and recovery; layer 3 sets up the path for transmission; layer 4 provides communication control between users; layer 5 controls system dependent dialog; layer 6 converts data formats between different vendor systems; layer 7 provides services to support user applications. These 7 layers provide easy to use

---

2. A protocol is a predetermined and mutually agreed upon step-by-step procedure whereby the parties participating in communications understand how the communication process will begin, proceed, and end.

standards to facilitate communication in a multi-vendor, multi-hardware environment to permit users of varied systems to communicate any data, anywhere, at any time (Michael 1988, 1).

Z39.50. Z39.50 (an American National standard approved by NISO in 1988), is a standard which tries to implement a portion of the OSI model.[3] Its purpose is "to allow one computer operating in a client mode to perform information retrieval queries against another computer acting as an information server" (Lynch n.d., 1). For example, one library's OPAC from one vendor can access another library's OPAC from a different vendor.

"Compliance with Z39.50 . . . offers a means whereby a single system can provide a uniform user interface and means of access to a large number of remote information resources" (DataLine 1991, 1). An experiment is underway to connect MELVYL, the University of California's online catalog, to the circulation module of the DRA automated library system installed at the University of California, Davis. The MELVYL catalog will be able to display the circulation status of materials in the UC Davis library. The connection from one system to the other will be transparent to the user. NOTIS in conjunction with Indiana University is developing PACLink. PACLink will use the Z39.50 standard to link the Indiana State University Library Automation Network (SULAN) and the State University of New York campuses (SUNY). A NOTIS OPAC at one site will have a transparent connection to a NOTIS OPAC at another.

Gaylord Information Systems is using OSI and Z39.50 protocols with SuperLINK for electronic mail, file transfers, and online public access communication.

SISAC. Since 1982, the Serials Industry Systems Advisory Committee (SISAC) has been working to develop a standard method for uniquely identifying specific issues of serial publications. It recommended representing the issue-level identifier in the barcode on the cover of professional, scientific, and technical journals. The committee's recommendations were incorporated as ANSI/NISO standard Z39.56-1991: Serial Item and Contribution Identifier (SICI). The major journal publishers have agreed to print the SISAC barcode symbol on their journals. Many of the automated library systems vendors are

---

3. Z39.50 will be known as international standard, ISO 10162/63.

programming their systems to recognize it. This permits automatic check-in of serials and better tracking of serials circulated to patrons.

BISAC. The Book Industry Systems Advisory Committee (BISAC) has developed standards for computerized book ordering. "The standards are intended for anyone who buys or sells books and has access to a computer. The common communication paths will be between any two of the following: wholesalers or jobbers; publishers; libraries or bookstores" (American National Standards Institute 1985, 7: Section 1). The standards cover the order record, the order acknowledgment, and the invoice record. In the order record, data elements are divided into a series of tagged fields which look similar to MARC tags; for example, a 10 record is the purchase order header, 40 records are the purchase order line items. The order acknowledgment and invoice records contain the data elements required to update the library's own system with bibliographic and accounting information. "Adapting to these standards means that the systems that support them are required only to understand and process these industry-defined formats. . . . As the MARC standard has affected automation and resource sharing of cataloging data, the BISAC formats will ultimately revolutionize both the way orders are placed and the way they are filled" (Larew 1990, 29).

Patron Record (Z39.69). One of the continuing problems with migrating to a new automated library system is the difficulty of moving the patron file. Many vendors have a proprietary method of storing patron records. Librarians have found that transferring them from one automated library system to another is not always possible and often results in lost or incomplete data. In response to this, a national standard for a patron record, Z39.69, has been devised. The standard "defines a format for the representation and com-munication of the library patron information in machine-readable form. It provides for all the data elements that might be contained in any patron file and includes elements to protect patron privacy" (Library Systems Newsletter 1991, 5). "Libraries will be able to exchange patron records with other libraries and will be able to migrate patron records from one system to another more efficiently and economically" (ibid.; Library Hi Tech News 1991, 19).

Transaction Files. One of the remaining areas which needs to be standardized is that of transaction files. Transaction files are volatile in that they are constantly changing. It is extremely important to a library which is migrating to a second system, that their transaction files can be moved intact.

Networking

More and more libraries are linking their library catalogs together in a online network. Typical advantages of being a member of a network are:

1. Increased patron satisfaction. When a patron searches networked catalogs, he or she can determine the circulation status of requested items. The network also provides users with a wider range of sources for loans.

2. Expanded public service benefits. Reference staff of member libraries have access to the catalogs of other member libraries and benefit by using them as research and verification tools.

3. Decreased turnaround time for interlibrary loans. Networking allows staff to determine availability and circulation status of requested items. Requests go out immediately online and usually result in decreased turnaround time.

4. The ability to download good quality cataloging. Because member libraries have access to catalog records of other member libraries, they can download and manipulate applicable records inexpensively. Thus, retrospective conversion can be facilitated.

5. Access to remote information services. In particular, more and more libraries are accessing the Internet.[4] The Internet is essentially a network of interconnected networks which offer connections to over 1000 regional, government, and campus networks. It grew out of the Advanced Research Projects Agency of the Department of Defense (ARPANET), a network that linked academic, military, and commercial organizations in North America and was founded in 1969. Gradually, ARPANET was transformed into a new network (called the Internet) which segregated users into groups according to their organizational

---

4. The Internet uses TCP/IP (Transmission Control Protocol/Internet Protocol). This refers to the step-by-step procedures governing the communication process. TCP/IP is not compliant with the emerging ISO/OSI protocol standards. It is likely that the ISO/OSI protocols will emerge as the dominant standard, but mechanisms to accommodate TCP/IP will probably be included.

activities. For example, the education and research groups form a major inter-university network.

Internet is growing rapidly. By accessing the Internet, one may search library catalogs and access other information services around the nation and around the world, such as the Information Access Company databases and OCLC.

For libraries that are thinking of networking their systems internally in a local area network, it might be useful to know that the IEEE (Institute of Electronic and Electrical Engineers) has approved a standard for running 10-Mbit Ethernet LANs over unshielded twisted pair (UTP) wiring instead of coaxial cable. The new standard has been designated 802.3i or 10 Base-T and works with star topology. The star configuration is said to be easier to maintain than bus topology because all communications go through the hub of the LAN. It is easier to efficiently monitor, control, and troubleshoot the network. In addition, 10 Base-T is less expensive, is easier to install, and has greater data transfer capability. It is expected to be used by every major manufacturer (Library Systems Newsletter 1991).

Terminal Load Units

When a vendor and a library sign an agreement for the installation of an automated library system there is a statement in the agreement as to the maximum number of terminals supported by the system. Increasingly, vendors are moving toward using terminal load units or terminal units as the basis for quoting system capacity. Each terminal is given a weighted value, according to its potential impact on computer resources. For example, a circulation terminal might have a value of 1.0, an acquisitions terminal 1.5, a patron access terminal a value of 2.0. Librarians should understand how the system capacity is calculated, especially if they intend to add more terminals in the future.

The OPAC

The role of the OPAC is changing daily as technology makes it possible for the patron to access information using graphics, imaging, hypertext and hypermedia, expert systems, and robotics. There are distinct advantages to its enlarging role, but beware of the hidden agents of infection that lurk in its path.

The Face of the OPAC. Work continues in a big way on the appearance of the OPAC. INLEX has introduced a new OPAC (using Hewlett-Packard equipment) which has colored, labeled function keys. All instructions are clearly presented on the keyboard. The monitor is high resolution and flicker free.

More and more vendors are introducing GUIs (Graphical User Interfaces) which incorporate icons and windows as well as cut and paste options. For example, VTLS offers the Intelligent Workstation which provides windows, pop-up menus, and natural language commands. Also offered is the VTLS InfoStation, a multimedia information access system which operates only on the NeXT computer. It provides high resolution, graphics, and playback of images and music. Data Trek uses Microsoft Windows with its OPAC and calls the end result GoPac (Graphical Online Public Access Catalog).

Visual Information or Imaging. INFORMA (an advisory group of information professionals formed in 1989 by IBM Academic Information Systems) has addressed technology's role in information access and delivery in the electronic library. It has been especially concerned with the digital storage of images in all forms: slides, photographs, maps, videotapes, etc. The group wants to see the online catalog evolve to include the full text of an article with accompanying images.[5] Vendors that provide access to visual files include:

GEAC offers an image collection system which can be accessed through the OPAC module;

Carlyle offers a multimedia, image management system which integrates with its online catalog;

CARL provides the ability to link photo images to the online catalog;

DRA offers an Information Gateway module which allows users to view illustrations and pictures from the OPAC workstation;

---

5. Imaging requires high resolution monitors, a great deal of memory or RAM, and specialized software. Images can require up to 25 times as much space as a page of text and color expands this requirement still further. Processing of images necessitates scanners, optical storage systems, and telecommunications planning. Hardware, however, is improving rapidly, its capabilities are increasing, and prices are dropping.

Information Dimensions has added image management capabilities to BASISplus. The company provides hypertext links between text stored in BASISplus and images residing on Xerox, Filenet, Laserdata, Digital, and Unisys image management systems.

IBM and Winnebago are exploring the possibilities of multimedia on a microcomputer-based automated library system.

Hypertext and Hypermedia. Both are concepts which allow the reader to move rapidly on the OPAC from one part of a document to another, or from one document to another, by means of associative links. These associative links consist of words/phrases, pictures, voice, or video. The reader can look into another document that further explains the concept highlighted in the first document. Alternatively, material related to the concept highlighted in the first document is presented in the second document. The reader may return to the initial text and continue reading or go from document to document in this fashion. The sequential pattern of reading is replaced by this interactive format.

One of the first commercial applications of hypertext in the automated library systems field is called *The Information Navigator.* It is a joint product of IME Systems, Inc. and IBM; works with DOS and UNIX operating systems; and is designed for special libraries such as corporate, legal, technical, and government libraries. The application is rather unique in that one can move from an author search to a subject search, from a book to an article, or from a title to a keyword, all without leaving the initial search. VTLS has also been experimenting with hypertext.

Expert Systems. Expert systems are interactive computer programs that contain the knowledge of one or more human experts in a particular subject area. By asking the user the same questions as the expert would, the system determines and gives the appropriate advice onscreen. The intelligence displayed is based on the quality of information provided by humans and the structure and design of the information flow. Such systems start with a knowledge base of information which includes a dictionary of words that the computer translates into symbols as well as various facts about objects, actions, and processes and how they are related. When the patron types natural language into the computer, the words and concepts are translated into symbols and then examined. If the expert system can match enough input to a set of stored symbols and patterns, it links relationships and comes up with natural language suggestions and solutions. Otherwise, the program prompts the user to clarify and broaden or narrow the query so that it can search again. Expert systems, therefore, are really computer-bound resident experts in designated fields which are able to interact intelligently with users.

Researchers are just beginning to realize the importance of incorporating the techniques used in expert systems to assist OPAC users with online queries. They can be programmed to think, brainstorm, and meditate in order to suggest alternative search terms, propose quick solutions, give detailed information on highly technical subjects, and assist with difficult decisions.

Robotics. CLSI has developed a special interface to its OPAC (CL-CAT) which is in use at the Bordeaux Public Library in France. The interface enables the OPAC to work with an automated robot which performs storage and retrieval functions. After a search result appears on the OPAC screen, a request is sent to the robot via one of six personal computers. The PC assigns a number to each user's request, and the item barcode number activates the robot to retrieve the item. The system informs the user that the item has been delivered by automatically listing the assigned number on an overhead sign. To shelve the materials, a PC scans the item's barcode, and the robot returns the materials to the correct location in the library.

Viruses. As the OPAC widens its role and allows downloading via floppy disks,[6] the librarian will have to protect the library's hardware and software from viruses. The development of computer viruses has caused havoc with the information retrieval world. The more patrons share disks and download information, the higher the risk of infecting the library OPAC with a virus.

A virus is actually a little software program that someone has deliberately written to attack hardware and other software. It can replicate itself and fill up the computer's memory, freeze the computer, reformat or damage the hard disk, or cause you to lose all of the information you have copied or written. It may be programmed to activate at a special time or date in the future. A virus can be picked up and transferred via floppy disk without the owner even knowing of its existence.

---

6. Several automated library system vendors have developed interfaces which allow the use of specialized microcomputer software, such as Pro-Cite, to download records from the database and generate bibliographies, new book lists, etc.

Librarians should be aware of the consequences of viruses and equip automated library systems with anti-viral programs that have been specially devised to target and eliminate viruses before they do any damage. Consultants, such as the "Bug Busters" in the California Bay Area, are frequently hired by large companies to come in on an established basis to wipe out viruses and update anti-viral programs. This may be a consideration for the future for large libraries. For small libraries or those that wish to do it themselves, Norton offers a very good anti-viral program for IBM and IBM compatible computers that includes free updates and an 800 telephone number.

CD-ROM PACs

Networking and Dial-in Access. There is increasing interest in networking CD-ROM PACs in order to provide greater access to CD-ROM reference databases and to the library's CD-ROM PAC. Maryland's public libraries have been very active in this field. Dial-in access is also becoming very popular. However, network licensing continues to be a very thorny issue. Currently, vendors consider any workstation physically in the building to be a part of that network site. The question is being asked. "Is remote dial-in access a violation of the network license?" No clear answers have as yet evolved.

Integrating the CD-ROM PAC with the Circulation Module. Work is also underway to fully integrate the CD-ROM PAC with the integrated automated library system. One of the forerunners in the field was Henrico Public Library (Richmond, VA) which connected its LePac ROMCat (from Brodart) to its circulation file, stored on a mainframe computer in the Data Processing Center. At the present time, the searcher has to toggle between LePac and the circulation file (by using the Alt and the Esc keys). Several vendors are working on a transparent link so that the circulation information appears automatically on the CD-ROM PAC screen. When linked, patrons can immediately see whether or not an item is on the library shelf. This new breakthrough will eliminate one of the big drawbacks of CD-ROM PACs -- lack of up-to-date circulation status.

Special Modules for the Disadvantaged

Homebound modules are becoming available for shut-in, blind, or physically handicapped patrons. DRA has always been active in this field, especially in servicing blind patrons. Dynix offers a module that handles special loan situations, tracks visits, deliveries, material preferences, and reading histories. The module is fully integrated with all other modules in a Dynix automated library system.

Circulation

Scanner/Security Device in One. In most libraries, two steps are involved when books are checked in or out. At the circulation desk, staff routinely scan the barcode label and then put the book through the security sensor. They have been waiting for someone to come up with a one-step procedure which would make their work less labor-intensive. 3M has devised a combination laser-scanner and library security sensor whereby a circulation clerk can scan a barcode label on the outside of a book and sensitize or de-sensitize a target inside the book -- all in one step. The sensor will connect to any automated library system circulation module which uses a serial port for connection. The combination unit costs about the same as the separate components.[7]

Self-Service Circulation. No, this is not available yet! However, it is on the way if the San Francisco City Librarian, Ken Dowlin, has his way. Mr. Dowlin wanted self-service circulation in the new San Francisco Public Library building which is scheduled to open in 1995. This is unlikely to happen due to financial considerations. Mr. Dowlin, however, feels that patrons are so used to ATM cards that they would adapt easily to the concept of slipping their library cards into a slot and having a machine take care of the check in and check out process. Make sure your fines are paid if you want your card back.

Fiscal Term Rental

Fiscal term rental is a short-term rental agreement which helps libraries with limited capital budgets to acquire an automated library system. A short-term purchase order covering only the time from delivery to the end of current fiscal year is issued. The purchase order is renewable for a number of years. In times of recession this approach may become very popular.

---

7. 3M Library Security Systems, Building 225-4N-14, 3M Center, St. Paul, MN 55144-1000. Tel: (800) 328-1684 Ext.111. (612) 792-1072 Ext. 111.

Changing Role of the Consultant

The automated library systems field has always had three chief groups of players: librarians, vendors, and consultants. As librarians have become more confident in their dealings with vendors and more comfortable with technology, the role of the consultant has changed. Consultants are used much less to supervise the entire automated library system selection process and much more to confirm that what has been done -- or written -- by the librarians is accurate. The role of the consultant may change even further if a service offered by GEAC becomes popular and starts a trend. A special department, called Professional Services, has been set up. A GEAC analyst will visit a library site, review the environment, procedures, and resources. The analyst is hired to help maximize system potential, provide consulting services, and suggest any customization that needs to be done.

References

American National Standards Institute. 1985. American National Standard for Information Sciences Z39.49-1985. *Computerized Book Ordering.*

Boss, Richard W., and Hal Espo. Oct. 1, 1987. Standards, Database Design and Retrospective Conversion. *Library Journal* 112(16).

DataLine. Winter, 1991. University of California, Digital, and Data Research Connect for Z39.50 Implementation. *DataLink.*

Datamation. May 1, 1991. Expensive Toys. *Datamation* 37(9): 22.

Larew, Christian K. 1990. Electronic Interfacing for Material Acquisitions. In *Convergence, Proceedings of the Second National Conference of the Library and Information Technology Association,* edited by Michael Gorman, 28-30. Chicago: ALA.

Library Hi Tech News. Jan.-Feb., 1991. Format for Patron Records. *Library Hi Tech News* 78:19.

Library Systems Newsletter. Jan., 1991. Format for Patron Records Out For Review. *Library Systems Newsletter* XI(1): 5.

Lynch, Clifford. n.d. *Z39.50 in Plain English.* St. Louis, MO: Data Research Associates.

Michael, James J. Oct., 1988. The ISO/OSI standards and Computer Networking. *Data Research Papers* 2.

Sources for Further Reading

Bailey, Charles W. June, 1989. Public Access Computer Systems: The Next Generation of Library Automation Systems. *Information Technology and Libraries* 8(2): 178-185.

Besser, Howard. Spring, 1990. Visual Access to Visual Images. *Library Trends* 38(4): 787-798.

Birchfield, N. Nov., 1990. *Searching Library Catalogs Via the Internet.* ED 329 295.

Boss, R. W. April, 1990. Linked Systems and the Online Catalog: The Role of the OSI. *Library Resources and Technical Services* 34(2): 217-227.

Crawford, Walt. 1991. *Technical Standards: An Introduction for Librarians.* 2nd ed. Boston: G. K. Hall.

Henry, Marcia Klinger et al. 1991. *Search Sheets for OPACs on the Internet: A Selective Guide to U.S. OPACs Utilizing VT100 Emulation.* Westport, CT: Meckler.

Kalin, Sally W., and R. Tennant. Aug., 1991. Beyond OPACs: The Wealth of Information Resources on the Internet. *Database.* 14(4): 28-33.

Raeder, Aggi W., and Karen L. Andrews. Sept., 1990. Searching Library Catalogs on the Internet: A Survey. *Database Searcher.* 6(7): 16-31.

Sloan, Bernard G. 1990. *Linked Systems for Resource Sharing.* Boston: G. K. Hall.

Stahl, J. Natalia. Fall, 1990. Using the Internet to Access CARL and Other Electronic Information Systems. *Science and Technology Libraries* 11(1): 19-30.

University of Houston Libraries. 1990-. *The Public Access Computer Systems Review.*

Appendix 1:
What to Look for When
Evaluating an OPAC

The following chart summarizes the key design components, features, and functions to evaluate when comparing competing OPAC modules:

SCREEN	SEARCH	RESULTS
Is the background color on the screen relaxing? Are colors sharp? bright? Are contrasting colors comfortable to the eye?	What kind of keyboard layout is available? Standard? Enhanced? Are some keys disabled?	What kind of information do you get? Brief record? Abstract? Full text?
Are touch screens available?	Is two-level searching available (menu and command driven)? Menu driven: lots of prompts for the inexperienced; Command driven: faster method for the sophisticated user.	Are you prompted to broaden or narrow your search?
Is a help screen available?	Are appropriate subject headings available?	Are confusing symbols used in retrieved information?
Is the screen cluttered, i.e., too much information on each screen?	What are the access points? Is keyword or Boolean searching available?	Are your hits accurate?
Do you get error messages, i.e. "Syntax		

error 24, Invalid
function, Catastrophic
error?"

Are the commands
clear?

Are both uppercase
and lowercase
available?

SCREEN

SEARCH

RESULTS

Is there a problem
with ergonomics, i.e.,
lighting; screen
position; properly
positioned chairs?

Are pseudonyms used,
i.e. Mark Twain vs.
Samuel Clemens?

Can you browse
through lists of
authors, titles, and
subjects?

Do all searches follow
similar formats?

Do screens display
consistent symbols
throughout?

Is dial-up access
available?

Appendix 2:
RECON Vendors

Below is a list of RECON vendors' names, addresses, and telephone numbers.[1]

Amigos Bibliographic Council,
Inc.
11300 North Central Expressway,
Suite 321
Dallas, TX 75243
(800) 843-8482
(214) 750-6130

Auto-Graphics, Inc.
3201 Temple Ave.
Pomona, CA 91768
(800) 776-6939
(714) 595-7204

Blackwell North America
6024 S.W. Jean Rd.
Building G
Lake Oswego, OR 97035
(800) 547-6426 (USA only)
(800) 626-1807 (Canada)
(503) 684-1140

Brodart Automation
500 Arch Street
Williamsport, PA 17705-9977
(800) 233-8467
(717) 326-2461

EKI, Inc.
140 Weldon Pkwy.
Hazelwood, MO 63042-3180
(800) 325-4984
(314) 567-1780

Gaylord Information Systems
P.O. Box 4901
Syracuse, NY 13221-4901
(800) 962-9580
(315) 457-5020

General Research Corporation
5383 Hollister Ave.
P.O. Box 6770
Santa Barbara, CA 93160-6770
(800) 235-6788
(805) 964-7724

Information Transform Inc.
502 Leonard St.
Madison, WI 53711
(608) 255-4800

Library of Congress
Processing Services, Cataloging
Distribution Service,
Washington D.C. 20541
(202) 707-6100

The Library Corporation
Research Park
Inwood, WV 25428
(800) 624-0559
(304) 229-0100

Library Technologies, Inc.
1142 E. Bradfield Road
Abington, PA 19001
(215) 576-6983

---

1. CLSI offers a full RECON service to its customers.

Marcive, Inc.
P.O. Box 47508
5616 Randolph Blvd.
San Antonio, TX 78265-7508
(800) 531-7678
(512) 646-6161

National Library of Canada,
Canadiana
Editorial Division
395 Wellington St.
Ottowa, Ontario K1A ON4
Canada
(819) 994-6913

OCLC
6565 Frantz Rd.
Dublin, OH 43017-0702
(800) 848-5878 (USA)
(800) 848-8286 (Ohio)
(614) 764-6000

Ontario Library Services Center
141 Dearborn Place
Waterloo, Ontario, Canada
N2J 4N5
(519) 746-4420

Retro Link Associates, Ltd.
175 North Freedom Blvd,
Suite 108
Provo, UT 84601
(801) 375-6508
(800) 765-6508

RLIN (Research Libraries Group)
1200 Villa
Mountain View, CA 94041
(415) 962-9951

SAZTEC International
975 Oak St., Suite 615
Eugene, OR 97401
(503) 343-8640

SOLINET
Southern Library Network, Inc.
Plaza Level, 400 Colony Square
1201 Peachtree St. N.E.
Atlanta, GA 30309
(404) 892-0943

Utlas International Canada
80 Bloor St. West,
2nd Floor
Toronto, Ontario, M5S 2V1
Canada
M5S 2V1
(416) 923-0890

Utlas International U.S. Inc.
8300 College Blvd.
Overland Park, KS 66210
(800) 338-8527
(913) 451-3111

WLN
P.O. Box 3888
Lacey, WA 98503-0888
(800) DIALWLN
(206) 459-6518

Appendix 3:
Microcomputer-Based
Automated Library Systems
Vendors

Below is a list of microcomputer-based automated library system vendors' names, addresses, and telephone numbers. Only companies which specialize in microcomputer-based systems are listed here. Those which offer microcomputer and mini-based systems are listed in Chapter 2 (such as Ameritech, Dynix, Data Trek, IME, INLEX, VTLS).

IBM and IBM Compatible Computers

Automated Library System
Foundation for Library
Research
2764 US 35 South
Southside, WV 25187
(304) 675-4350
(304) 675-1825

BIB-BASE
Library Technologies, Inc.
1142 E. Bradfield Rd.
Abington, PA 19001
(215) 576-6983

Bibliotrac
Novara Software
95 College Street
Antigonish, Nova Scotia

B2G 1X6
Canada
(902) 863-3361

Brodart Library Automation
Brodart

500 Arch Street
Williamsport, PA 17705
(800) 233-8467
(717) 326-2461

Columbia Library System
CTB MacMillian/McGraw-Hill
2500 Garden Road
Monterey, CA 93940
(800) 663-0544
(408) 649-8400

Davex Plus
Faxon Canada
P.O. Box 2382
London
Ontario N6A 5A7
Canada
(519) 472-1078

Eloquent Librarian
Eloquent Systems
1501 Longsdale Ave.
Suite 25
North Vancouver, BC

V7M 2J2
Canada
(800) 663-8172
(604) 980-8358

Follett Software
809 N. Front Street
McHenry, IL 60050-5589
(800) 323-3398

Impact/SLiMS
Auto-Graphics
19029 East Plaza Drive
Suite 200
Parker, CO 80134
(800) 347-6939

Innovation Plus
Scribe Software
4435 N. Saddlebag Trl 1
Scottsdale, AZ 85251
(800) 443-7890
(602) 990-3384

LION
Calico
P.O. Box 15916
St. Louis, MO 63114
(800) 367-0415
(314) 863-8028

Mandarin
Media Flex
P.O. Box 1107
Champlain, NY 1219-11107
(518) 298-2970

MicroCat
TKM Software Ltd.
P.O. Box 1525
839-18th Street
Brandon, Manitoba
Canada R7A 6N3
(800) 565-6272
(204) 727-387

Molli
Nichols Advanced Technology
3452 Losey Boulevard South
La Crosse, WI 54601
(800) 658-9453
(608) 787-8333

Professional Software
21 Forest Ave.
Glen Ridge, NJ 07028
(201) 748-7658

Ringgold Management System[1]
Ringgold
P.O. Box 368
Beaverton, OR 97075
(503) 645-3502

Surpass/2
Educational Solutions, Inc.
129 S. Phelps Drive
Suite 911
Rockford, IL 61108
(800) 443-3229
(815) 227-0527

Macintosh Computers

Alexandria
COMPanion
3755 Evelyn, Suite 201
Salt Lake City, UT 84124
(801) 278-6439
(800) 347-6439

Library Works (formerly
Mac Library System (MLS);
Library Browser (formerly
Mac Library Access Program
[MacLAP])
CASPR
20111 Stevens Creek Blvd.
Suite 270
Cupertino, CA 95014
(408) 446-3075
(800) 85C-ASPR

MacBook
Library Interface Systems
7900 International Drive
Suite 632
Bloomington, MN 55425
(800) 234-5183

MacSchool
Chancery Software
4170 Still Creek Drive
Suite 450
Burnaby, BC V5C 6C6
Canada
(800) 999-9931
(604) 294-1233

Mac The Librarian
Richmond Software Corporation
500 Aston Hall Way
Alpharetta, GA 30202
(800) 222-6063

TLC: Total Library
Computerization
On Point, Inc.
2606 36th Street N.W.
Washington, D.C. 20007
(202) 338-8914

Winnebago[2]
Winnebago Software
310 West Main Street
Caledonia, MN 55921
(800) 533-5430

---

1. Uses the UNIX system on a microcomputer.
2. Also runs on Macintosh computers.

Glossary

AACR2. See Anglo-American Cataloging Rules.

Abstract. A condensed, representative description of a document, which includes pertinent data and occasionally critical comments.

Acceptance Test. Evaluation of the system components and functions after the automated library system is "up and running" in the library. The tests typically cover reliability, response time, and the performance of the functions or features. Final payment is not made to the vendor until the tests have been passed.

Access Point. A search term that may be used to retrieve information from the automated library system, such as title, author, keyword, call number, ISSN, etc. Several access points can be searched at once. See also Boolean.

Acquisitions. The term given to the ordering, receiving, payments, claims, cancellations, and fund accounting work of the library. Acquisitions also deals with gift and exchange material.

Acquisitions/Serials Control Committee. The committee set up to make recommendations on what is required for the automated library system in the area of automated acquisitions and serials control. Committee members prepare statistical reports on number of purchase orders, renewals, standing orders, monographs and serials received, claims, cancellations, item records, binding records, fund accounting records, and vendor/jobber records. They project future needs and prepare a list of functional requirements for the RFP.

Advisory Committee. See Automation Committee.

AIX. Operating system. IBM version of Unix.

Alphanumeric. A mixture of letters (upper and lower case), numbers, and punctuation marks.

ALS. See Automated Library System.

American Standard Code for Information Interchange. A standard digital code for information exchange among computers.

Analog. A signal which is represented by continuously oscillating waves. The telephone system is analog.

Anglo-American Cataloging Rules. A cataloging code which lays down rules covering main entry, added entries, bibliographic description of an item, and the form they should take.

ANSI. American National Standards Institute.

Application software. A software program, or a combination of programs, that direct the computer in the execution of a specific task, such as word processing, information retrieval, etc.

Artificial intelligence. The branch of computer science that is concerned with making computers smarter. More specifically, the field of study that explores the ways in which computers can be used for tasks requiring the human characteristics of intelligence, imagination, and intuition.

ASCII. See American Standard Code for Information Interchange.

Authority control. The process of (1) assigning a unique form to a heading and (2) using cross-references to go from an unused or related heading to the accepted heading.

Automated Library System. The application of a computer and software to the various functions of a library such as circulation, acquisitions, serials control, cataloging, and the patron access catalog.

Automation. See Library automation.

Automation Committee. The primary or first-level committee with responsibility for establishing the goals and objectives of the automation process, analyzing existing operations, and setting up sub-committees. Its members report directly to the project manager.

Barcode label. A rectangular sticker, made up of a series of printed lines and spaces of varying widths and affixed to a library book or patron identification card. The lines and spaces represent numbers, symbols, and/or letters. See also CODABAR and Code 39.

Batch processing. Accumulating tasks over a period of time and then processing them; grouping together similar computer tasks and sequentially processing them in order to simplify operations.

Baud. The speed with which information is transmitted across the phone lines.

Bibliographic record. See Record.

Bibliographic utilities. Automated library networks that provide services to member libraries, such as cataloging. Examples of bibliographic utilities are OCLC, RLIN, UTLAS, and WLN.

Bidder. An automated library system vendor that submits a price quote, based on specifications, in an attempt to match those requirements and secure a contract to automate the library.

Bidders' conference. A conference or meeting held by a library at which interested vendors may ask questions before submitting their automated library systems bids.

Bidding process. Procedures which are clarified in the RFP and include a schedule of the following events: distribution of RFP; Bidder's conference;

deadline for receipt of vendor proposals; opening of bids; and guidelines for proposal evaluation and contract negotiations.

Binary. A number system using base 2 mathematics which assigns only two values -- 0 or 1 -- to every character that is typed into a computer. These two values can be expressed in an on/off form and can be combined to represent any number.

Binary digit. See Bit.

BISAC. Book Industry Systems Advisory Committee. This committee has developed standards for computerized book ordering. The standards cover the order record, the order acknowledgment, and the invoice record.

Bit. The basic unit for recording information in machine-readable form (the form that allows the computer to assimilate information). A bit has a value of 0 or 1 as determined by the computer's recognition of an electronic condition of on or off.

Blocked, spanned record format. The way in which MARC records are stored on magnetic tape. In this arrangement, 2048 bytes are allocated per block until the tape is full. Usually called LC-MARC format.

Boolean. The use of AND, OR, and NOT functions to combine search terms for selecting information during an online search.

BPI. Bytes per inch; the density with which MARC records are written to tape. The most common densities are 1600 BPI and 6250 BPI. BPI is sometimes referred to as CPI (characters per inch).

Browsing. Examining automated library systems records onscreen by scrolling through them, one after another. In an OPAC browsing usually takes the user to an alphabetical list of titles, authors, or subjects, as opposed to keyword searching which takes the user to a particular word contained in a document or a record.

Bulletin board. Messages and information posted on a computer screen that are accessed via special software. Patrons can access data via a modem. Bulletin board data may include library hours and activities.

Bundled hardware. A unique package or all-in-one unit, marketed by vendors and offered to libraries. For example, CD-ROM vendors include hardware (PC, CD-ROM player, controller card, and optional printer) and software (operating system, menu or option array, and CD-ROM disc).

Bus configuration. One of the ways in which equipment can be physically connected in a local area network; an arrangement of computer terminals and peripherals each linked through a cable, with two open ends; straight-line configuration.

Buzz words. Words or terms which are in fashion at a particular time and unique to the trade.

Byte. A sequence of binary digits or bits (typically 8 or 16) in a specified combination of 1's and 0's used to represent a letter of the alphabet or a number. Such sets of bits are called bytes. One byte is equivalent to one character.

C. A computer programming language.

Catalog. A list of the library's holdings. In automated library systems, the records are in machine-readable form in a database.

Catchword indexing. A 19th century term for keyword in context indexing or KWIC. See also KWIC.

CD-ROMCat. The name given to a library's catalog when it is stored on CD-ROM discs and made available to the public; also called CD-ROM PAC.

CD-ROM disc. An aluminized disc, 4.75 inches in diameter, which stores large quantities of digital or computer data. The data is read by a laser beam. The contents of the disc cannot be changed by a user.

CD-ROM drive. See CD-ROM player.

CD-ROM PAC. Another name for CD-ROMCat.

CD-ROM player. A machine designed to read digital data from a compact disc to computer memory or RAM. The information is displayed onscreen on a personal computer.

CD-ROM reader. See CD-ROM player.

Central Processing Unit. A chip containing many integrated circuits that is thought of as being the heart of the computer. It interprets and executes program instructions and communicates with the input (keyboard, mouse, tape), output (screen, printer, tape), and storage devices.

CGA. Color Graphics Adapter which enables a monitor to display up to four different colors on the screen from 16 available hues. The resolution or sharpness of the image is low.

Changeover. See System changeover.

Chip. A tiny piece of semiconductor material (usually silicon) containing microscopic electronic circuitry. Examples include CPU chip, ROM chip, and RAM chips.

Circulation. The process whereby a library makes its holdings available to patrons. In an automated library system, this includes computerized check-in and check-out of items, patron and item information and procedures, etc.

Circulation Committee. A committee set up to study the automated circulation needs of the library, i.e., number of books and other library materials circulated inhouse, interlibrary loans, loan periods, fines, renewals, holds, recalls, overdues, reserves, bibliographic records of circulated titles as well as titles to be circulated, and borrower records.

Circulation desk. The work area where circulation activities, such as check-in and check-out, take place.

CLR. See Council on Library Resources.

CODABAR. The most popular way to encode barcode labels in libraries. The rectangular label, consisting of lines and spaces, is translated into 14 digits which are displayed below it. The first digit is used to identify whether the barcode is for a patron or an item; the next four digits identify the institution; the following eight digits represent patron or item information; and the final digit is an error-checking digit.

Code 39. A way to encode barcode labels in libraries. Although the rectangle of lines and spaces translate into 10 digits, they are not displayed. The first digit is used to identify whether the barcode is for a patron or an item; the next two digits identify the institution; the last seven digits are a unique code which represent either a patron or an item.

Committee process. Groups of people who work together within an or ganization to facilitate decision-making and lay the groundwork for negotiations and contractual commitments in a particular project. (such as securing an automated library system.)

Common Command language. A proposed ANSI/NISO standard (Z39.58) which would allow uniform search commands to be used in information retrieval systems. For example, the exact same wording or set of commands could be used to search both reference databases (loaded onto the local system) and OPACs. The same commands could also be used to search OPACs from different vendors.

Compact Disc - Read Only Memory. See CD-ROM disc.

Compatibility. The ability of a computer system to handle data and run programs devised for another type of computer system.

Computer. An electronic device for performing high-speed, arithmetic, and logical operations.

Computer program. A set of instructions which enables a computer to perform a specific task.

Computer programming language. The language in which applications software is written, such as BASIC, C, PASCAL.

Connectivity. The process which allows the components of different automated library systems to interact with or talk to each other. Sufficient ports and expansion capabilities are mandatory.

Consultant. An independent expert who is often hired to assist with the formalities of the library automation project. Typically the consultant helps with the preparation of bid documents, evaluation of responses, and negotiation of contracts.

Controller board. See Controller card.

Controller card. A computer circuit board that controls the flow of data between a computer and tape or disk drives.

Contract. A legal document which is usually drafted by the library's legal representative in conjunction with the project management staff. It protects the interests of the library and ensures that the automated system performs as described in the vendor's proposal.

Convert. To change the library's records from card form to machine readable form.

Council on Library Resources. A foundation established in 1956 which is concerned with: the utilization of technology in all aspects of library operations, library management, international aspects of library operations, professional and continuing education for librarians, and the preservation of library materials. CLR supports programs and services by granting funds to academic institutions, organizations, and individuals.

CPI. Characters per inch; the density with which MARC records are written to tape. The most common are 1600 CPI and 6250 CPI. CPI is sometimes referred to as BPI (bytes per inch).

CPU. See Central Processing Unit.

Cross-reference. The use of (1) see references to guide searchers from where they are in an index to where they should be, and (2) see also references to guide searchers to where they should also be to locate relevant entries and headings.

Database. An organized collection of information. This information is usually stored in a computer in the form of files. In a library, the database typically contains bibliographic information, patron information, fund information, and vendor information.

Database Management System. Software which administers the information stored in a database on the computer.

DBMS. See Database Management System.

De-blinded cross references. "Blind references" are references that have been referred to by headings that have been removed from the catalog. To de-blind is to either restore the headings or remove the references.

Debug. To fix software that is not running correctly.

Descriptor. A preferred subject heading.

Desirable specifications. Requested, but not mandatory, requirements for the new automated library system as detailed in the RFP.

Desktop publishing. The use of microcomputer software and a laser printer to input, edit, format, illustrate, and publish documents from single page announcements to lengthy newsletters, magazines, and books.

Dial-up access. The process of connecting computers via modems and telephone lines so that information can be transferred back and forth.

Digital. A signal made up of separate and discrete binary elements or pulses. A computer works with digital signals.

Directory. See Record directory.

Disk Operating System. See Operating system and DOS.

Documentation. Printed instructions which explain how to operate the functions and features of computer software, i.e., how the components of an automated library system work.

DOS. Disk operating system. PC-DOS and MS-DOS are common operating systems for personal computers.

Down. Not working. Automated library systems are said to be "down" when they freeze or cannot be accessed; the opposite of "up" or working.

Download. Computer programs and files are transmitted from a mainframe computer to a remote terminal and stored on that terminal for local use.

Downtime. The amount of time the automated library system, or a part of it, is not working.

Dumb barcoding. The process by which each item in the library is brought to the circulation terminal(s) and individually linked to the specific item record in the database. Simultaneously, a barcode is affixed to the item by the library staff.

Duplicate record. Information about the same library item which has been placed in the database twice.

EGA. Enhanced Graphics Adapter which can display up to 16 colors on the screen simultaneously and offer 64 tones and hues.

Electronic bulletin board. See Bulletin board.

Electronic mail. A system for transmitting, receiving, storing, and forwarding textual information and messages in electronic form. Mail is directed to particular individuals or groups of individuals.

Electronic publishing. Writing or displaying full textual information on a computer screen for the purposes of online production and access as opposed to paper output.

Enhanced keyboard. A computer keyboard which includes a full set of standard keys, additional function keys, and a numeric keypad.

Ergonomics. The science of incorporating human factors into equipment design and the working environment in order to make it a more comfortable setting. It encompasses appropriate kinds, quantities, and placements of chairs, tables, and video display terminals, as well as the design and placement of instructional aids.

Error checking. A process of detecting mistakes in the transmission of data.

Expansion capability. Allowing for growth of a system to include new or improved features or performance.

Expert system. A software package which asks the patron questions and attempts to analyze input, based on stored knowledge. It displays appropriate advice onscreen. In this way, a computer can be used to answer simple queries.

Fault tolerant. Ability to localize a problem or malfunction. If one part of the automated library system malfunctions, the whole system will not fail.

Feasibility study. A formal investigation conducted before an automated library system is acquired to determine if the proposed automation project is practical, economical, or possible.

Field. An element in a record. The fields in a patron record might consist of name, address, telephone number, driver's license number, etc.

File. A collection of related and usually similarly constructed records that are treated as a unit, i.e., a library catalog or a list of patrons with relevant details.

File conversion. The process of changing the library's records to machine-readable form.

Filing indicator. The number of initial characters to be ignored for filing purposes at the beginning of the title field, title subfield, or corporate heading field in a MARC record (usually an initial article).

First-level committee. An advisory committee, consisting of members with particular expertise in circulation, cataloging, search methods, acquisitions/serials control, and automation. In a small library, this may be the only committee. In a larger library setting, members of the advisory committee may be selected to head a number of smaller secondary or second-level committees.

Forms analysis. Examining forms used by the library in order to determine what tasks are performed.

Front-end interface. A piece of software that makes it easier to access programs through a menu.

Functional specifications. The part of the RFP which details the components which are desired in the various automated library system modules. Major functional components include acquisitions, serials control, database/catalog management, circulation/reserves, online public access catalog, and reports/statistics. Other functional components include interlibrary loans, binding, inventory control, item tracking, booking, journal citation access, information and retrieval files, other bibliographic databases, data files, and electronic mail.

Functional test. Checking the performance of each function or feature against requirements that are specified in the RFP or stated in vendor promotional literature.

Gateway. A piece of software which allows exchange of information between dissimilar systems. A gateway allows the user to move from one system to another without knowing any of the communications specifics to do so.

Gantt Chart. A graphical display of the critical path of a project. Daily, weekly, or monthly timeframes are generally used as column headings. Activities or tasks are listed down the left side of the chart and lines are drawn to denote starting and ending points of each task.

Graphics. Visual images appearing on a display screen.

Hardware. The physical computer equipment and its peripherals, such as printers, CD-ROM players, etc.

Hardware maintenance. The process of keeping the hardware serviced and in good working order.

High Sierra Group. Ad-hoc members of Philips, Sony, Digital Equipment Corporation, Apple, Hitachi, Microsoft, 3M, VideoTools, LaserData, TMS, Xebec, Yelick, and various vendors of CD-ROM products that met at the High Sierra Hotel and Casino in Lake Tahoe, Nevada. Their purpose was to come up with a mutually compatible proposal which addressed location, size, structure, and mapping of files on CD-ROM.

High Sierra Standard. A set of rules which address the location, size, structure, and mapping of files on CD-ROM and form the basis of ISO (International Organization for Standardization) 9660.

Homebound modules. Modules on automated library systems which cater to the needs of patrons who are unable to use the library due to physical or mental disability. For example, some homebound modules handle special loan situations, and track visits, deliveries, material preferences, and reading histories.

Hypermedia. A concept that links text, moving images, still images, and sound in an interactive way.

Hypertext. A concept which allows the reader to move rapidly from one part of a document to another, or from one document to another, by means of associative links. These associative links consist of words/phrases. The reader can look into another document that further explains the concept highlighted in the first document. Alternatively, material related to the concept highlighted in the first document is presented in the second document. The reader may return to the initial text and continue reading or go from document to document in this fashion. The sequential pattern of reading familiar to the print world is replaced by this interactive format.

IEEE. Institute of Electronic and Electrical Engineers. The IEEE is responsible for many of the standards used in local area networks.

ILL. See Interlibrary loan.

Implementation. The process of installing the automated library system: putting in the equipment, training the personnel, and establishing the operating policies.

Index. A list of bibliographic information arranged in order, according to some specification such as author, subject, or keyword.

Indicators. Two single-digit numbers (each being a number 0-9) which follow the MARC tag and may be used according to the rules spelled out for each field in MARC format guides. For example in the 260 0o field, the first 0 indicates that a publisher is present; the smaller second o means that the second indicator is undefined and left blank.

INFORMA. An advisory group of information professionals formed in 1989 by IBM Academic Information Systems. The organization addresses technology's role in information access and delivery in the electronic library.

In-house RECON. Performing retrospective conversion in the library, using library staff and MARC records on CD-ROM discs, or MARC records obtained by searching on a bibliographic utility.

Input. Information which is keyed into the computer for processing.

Inquiry. A request to the computer to locate and display data or information.

Installation. The process of actually putting the automated library system in place.

Integrated. Modules working synonymously so that one module shows information input into another module in an automated library system. Acquisitions, serials control, cataloging, circulation, and the online public access catalog (OPAC) modules use a single database made up of a collection of files: such as bibliographic files, authority files, book vendor files, fiscal files, and patron files. All functions are fully interconnected with each other and are kept automatically in synchronization. Any process that is initiated from one terminal is transferred throughout the entire system by a single command.

Integrated Circuit. A system of conductors or semiconductors and related electrical elements etched on a single, small piece of silicon (or chip) through which electrical current passes.

Intelligent system. See Expert system.

Interactive. A continuous dialog between the user and the computer system.

Interlibrary loan. An item secured for a patron from another library.

Internet. A network of over 400 networks. Through the Internet, it is possible to gain access to the online catalogs of many libraries within the U.S. and internationally.

Inventory control. Keeping track of all the material in the library and making sure that it is actually on the shelf or on loan to patrons.

ISBN. International Standard Book Number. Each book published is given a unique number. Part of the number incorporates the publisher's code.

ISO. International Organization for Standardization.

ISSN. International Standards Serial Number.

Item field. A field in MARC records which identifies characteristics such as (1) barcode; (2) call number; (3) copy and volume numbers; (4) holding library; (5) branch or location information; (6) media code (book, cassette, etc.); (7) statistical category code used to generate reports; (8) fine code; and (9) period of circulation code. The item field is specially built by the RECON vendor, using formatting requirements supplied by the automation vendor.

Item record. Data from a collection of item fields. Each copy of a title in the collection has an item record that contains some abbreviated information. Circulation systems link item records to the patrons who check out materials. If more information is needed about an item, the item record can be linked back to the full MARC record.

Jobber. A vendor that buys books, periodicals, or related items in large quantities from publishers and sells them to libraries.

Justification. The process persuading management to approve an automated library system by documenting the reasons why an automated library system would benefit the library and why it would be cost-effective.

K. See kilobyte.

Key players. Persons or groups who represent or have significantly contributed to the growth of automated library systems (e.g., vendors).

Keyword. A specific string of text that can be retrieved and displayed on a computer screen, along with the documents or records in which it is located.

Kilobyte. One thousand bytes or characters.

KWIC. Keyword In Context. A form of indexing whereby key words from the titles of documents are selected and then arranged in an alphabetical sequence, by word.

KWOC. Keyword Out of Context. An index which lists key words separately in a lefthand column, with the corresponding titles appearing to the right.

LAN. See Local Area Network.

Laser disc. A thin, flat, circular plate that is read from or written to by light, generally a laser. The disc may store video, audio, or digital data.

LCCN. Library of Congress Card Number.

Leader. The part of the MARC record which contains information about the length, type, and bibliographic level of the record. For example, the record leader might indicate whether the item is a printed book, manuscript, microform, self-contained monograph, or part of a series.

Library automation. The use of computers and software to perform library tasks.

Local. Any activity which is peculiar to a particular library.

Local area network. A combination of hardware and software which enables several microcomputers in one physical location to "talk" to each other. More precisely, it allows several computers to share resources, such as printers, software programs, and hard disk drives.

Local changes. Modifications to the MARC record that a particular library makes to reflect its own collection or policies.

Locally developed. An automated library system which has been locally designed, programmed, installed, and tested, from scratch. The system meets the exact needs of the library.

Long range plan. A master plan outlining in broad terms the purposes or reasons for automation and any constraints or priorities.

Machine-readable. Able to be read by a computer.

Magnetic tape. A strip of material, coated with a magnetically sensitive substance, which may be used to store computer data.

Mainframe. A large-scale computer which usually comes with peripherals, such as terminals, printers, light pens, etc. Mainframe computers tend to have what is called a "closed architecture." They are compatible only with hardware and software from one or two vendors.

Mandatory specifications. Absolute requirements for the new automated library system as detailed in the RFP.

MARC II. Machine-readable cataloging format which enables a computer to read and interpret the data in the cataloging record. MARC II format is now the recognized national standard for bibliographic records that are exchanged and used by libraries of all types and sizes. It is the communications format recognized by automated library systems.

MARC format. See MARC II.

MARC record. See MARC II.

MARC tag. A three-digit number that identifies fields in a machine-readable record.

Master disc. A thin, flat, circular plate or laser disc that contains bibliographic information, primarily used in conjunction with access on CD-ROM players. The master disc cannot be updated but may be reproduced and copied by the vendor for use on other CD-ROM players.

Matching records. Determining that the fields in bibliographic records of a library and a RECON vendor correspond sufficiently. If a library decides to have a vendor conduct its retrospective conversion process, the vendor matches the library's records against the vendor's MARC databases. When there is a match or "hit," the vendor sells the record to the library.

MB. See megabyte.

Megabyte. One million characters.

MELVYL. The online catalog of the University of California.

Memory. See RAM and ROM.

Merging records. The combining of library records into a single bibliographic file.

Microcomputer. A small-scale desktop, or personal, computer (such as the IBM PC, XT, AT, IBM PS/2 series, Apple Macintosh, etc.).

MICROcomputer Library Interchange Format. See MicroLIF.

MicroLIF. MICROcomputer Library Interchange Format. The MicroLIF committee was created to establish industry-wide standards for MARC records stored on floppy disks (for use in microcomputer based automated library systems).

Migration. A second system installation. This occurs when a library moves from an already installed and working automated library system to a new automated library system. It is also used when a library moves to a new hardware platform in order to make its automated library system function more efficiently.

Minicomputer. A medium-scale centrally located computer to which interactive, dumb terminals are linked. The dumb terminals have no processing capability on their own. Minicomputers normally have an open architecture, which means that they are compatible with hardware and software from many vendors.

Modem. A device which enables digital computers to communicate with analog phone lines. It acts as a middleman to translate the signals back and forth.

Modular. Setting up the component parts of automated library system software (circulation, cataloging, acquisitions, serials, OPAC, etc.) around the concept of building blocks. If only one building block or module is purchased, it is self-contained and will work independently. Two or more are designed to work together to access information that has been keyed into the system only once.

Module committees. Committees comprised of professional librarians and technical staff within the following areas of expertise: acquisitions/serials control, catalog (retrospective conversion), circulation, and online public access catalog. Members of these committees provide valuable information regarding specifications in each area on the RFP.

Monograph. A book on a single subject.

MPE, MPE\XL. Operating system used by Hewlett-Packard.

Multidimensional tool. Hardware and software that can be used to access different kinds of information in a variety of ways. For example, some OPACs may be used to access databases within the library and all over the world through modems, gateways, and networks.

Multi-user license. A permit, paid for by the library to a vendor, which allows the library to install software or CD-ROM products at more than one site.

Natural language. Exact words taken from the title, abstract, or text of a document. These words are typically keyed into a search on a computer screen and highlighted in the displayed text.

NEPHIS. NEsted PHrase Index System. This index system was developed in Canada at the University of Western Ontario.

Network. An interconnected set of computer systems and terminals; two or more libraries which are organized to share or exchange information and other resources.

NISO. National Information Standards Organization.

Nonhit. Nonmatch, which occurs when the vendor conducting the retrospective conversion process is unable to match successfully the library's records against its own MARC databases.

Online. Direct interaction with another computer through local or long-distance telecommunications links.

Online Patron Access Catalog. See OPAC.

Online Public Access Catalog. See OPAC.

Online Public Access Committee. The committee which determines what features/functions the library wants in its automated patron access catalog. Its recommendations are often incorporated into the RFP.

OPAC. The online public or patron access catalog which enables patrons to search the library's holdings from a computer terminal. Status information regarding an item, such as "on the shelf," "on loan," "available at the following branches," is usually also displayed.

Open system. Hardware and software modules from separate vendors that have been linked into a single integrated system.

Open Systems Interconnection. See OSI.

Opening of bids. Unsealing the proposals or bids submitted by automated library system vendors on a specified date and time which is listed on the RFP and open to the public. At this time, the library decides which vendor meets its criteria for the lowest price.

Operating costs. Expenditures necessary to maintain and manage an automated library system so that it will function effectively.

Operating system. A piece of software which supervises the running of other software and controls the hardware platform. It provides an environment within which other programs can function.

Optical disc. See Laser disc.

OSI. Open Systems Interconnection. This is a framework or model within which standards for communication between different types of computer systems are being developed. See also Z39.50.

PAC. Public/patron access catalog; method by which a patron can access the library's holdings through online or via CD-ROM.

Parallel approach. Running the old system and the new automated library system side-by-side for a contracted period of time in order to check the effectiveness of the new system and debug it.

Parallel processing. Using multiple CPUs (central processing units) which share the operating system, the memory, and the disk storage of the hardware platform. Each CPU operates independently. In this mode of operation, tasks assigned to separate CPUs run simultaneously and speed up operations.

Patron Record. See Record. See also Z39.69.

PC. Personal computer.

Periodicals. Journals, magazines, or newspapers that are issued at regular intervals.

Peripheral. An accessory of a computer system, such as a disk drive, a printer, CD-ROM player, or mouse.

Permanent storage. The placing of data into a computer device capable of retaining it for long periods. Examples of such devices are floppy disks, hard disks, magnetic tape, and erasable optical discs. Data placed in permanent storage is not lost when power is turned off.

Phased approach. Installing automated library system modules or subsystems one at a time. For example, a cataloging module might be introduced first, followed by acquisitions, circulation, and finally an online public access catalog (OPAC).

Pick. An operating system.

Pilot approach. Installing an automated library system in one selected branch of a multi-agency or multi-branch system in order to monitor it for problems and debug it prior to placing it in other branches..

Platform. The hardware or computer equipment upon which the software runs.

Port. Electronic circuitry that provides a connection point between the host computer and input/output devices, such as a keyboard, mouse, or modem.

Portability. The capacity to run software on more than one hardware platform and under more than one operating system.

Post-coordinate. A method which allows the user to form a search strategy by combining terms with Boolean operators to express the query need as closely as possible.

PRECIS. PREserved Context Index System. This grammatically based, hierarchical indexing system was developed by Derek Austin at the British National Bibliography in London.

Pre-coordinate. A method in which search terms are determined by indexers, as in a traditional printed index.

Printer. An output device that converts electronic signals from the computer into words printed on paper.

Procedure manual. A step-by-step manual which provides instructions on how to use, operate, and manage an automated library system.

Program. See Computer program.

Project Leader. See Project Manager.

Project Manager. Person in charge of overseeing the planning, selection, and installation of an automated library system.

Protocol. A predetermined and mutually agreed upon step-by-step procedure whereby the parties participating in computer communications understand how the communication process will begin, proceed, and end.

Public Access Catalog. See PAC.

Query. The question around which a search is formulated to elicit an accurate response.

RAM. Random access memory; a temporary working area where data and programs may be stored and processed. Contents of the RAM can be used, erased, and changed under the control of the user. RAM empties when power is withdrawn.

Random access memory. See RAM.

Read-only memory. See ROM.

RECON. See Retrospective conversion.

Record. The complete set of information relating to a particular item in a computer file. Each record consists of a number of constituent elements referred to as fields. A bibliographic record contains data in fields such as author, title, or publisher. A patron record contains data in fields such as name, address, etc.

Record directory. A locational device in a MARC record which pinpoints the address of specific variable fields.

Reliability test. See System reliability test.

REMARC. A database of LC MARC records from 1898-1968.

Request for Information. See RFI.

Request for Proposal. See RFP.

Resolution. The number of pixels or picture elements (small dots) a computer display screen can accommodate. The more pixels, the higher the resolution and the better the picture quality.

Response time. The number of seconds that elapses between the user pressing the <ENTER> or <RETURN> key (after entering a request) and a response appearing on the screen.

Retrospective conversion. The process of changing the library's previously created bibliographic records to MARC (machine-readable cataloging) format. The records being converted may be in one of three formats: (1) catalog cards, (2) paper shelf list; or (3) brief machine-readable records.

Retrospective Conversion Committee. A committee, composed of professional and paraprofessional members of the catalog staff, which makes recommendations for the retrospective conversion process and is instrumental in selecting a RECON vendor.

RFB. Request for Bid.

RFI. Request for Information; an informal document which may be written on headed library stationery. It is sent to a variety of possible vendors initially to find out just exactly what modules make up their automated system, how they interface or interconnect, the functions they perform, and a general cost structure.

RFP. Request for Proposal; a document that (1) includes specific instructions to the bidders, requiring them to seek clarification of any item that is not clear and to check all responses for accuracy before submitting a proposal; (2) lists very precisely all of the specifications required by the library that the vendor must try to match; and (3) enumerates all criteria for evaluation. The name and address of the library where the bids are to be sent is clearly stated on the face of the proposal.

RFP Drafting Committee. The committee which is responsible for drawing up the RFP and listing functional and system requirements that are both mandatory and desirable.

RFQ. Request for quotation; a preliminary procurement document used to solicit ball-park pricing information regarding hardware, software, installation, and maintenance of an automated library system.

Ring configuration. One of the ways in which computer terminals can be connected in a local area network. Each piece of equipment is connected to two others, this being repeated until a loop is formed. Data is transmitted around the loop, always in the same direction.

ROM. Read Only Memory. Instructions are programmed on an integrated circuit at the time of manufacture. They cannot be erased or reprogrammed by normal computer operations, and they are not lost when power is turned off.

ROMCat. See CD-ROMCat or CD-ROM PAC.

Scoping. Allowing users to limit searches by location, date, format, language, etc.

Second-level committee. Secondary committees, often composed of key members of the advisory committee, are responsible to the first-level committee head and project manager. Second-level committees prepare pertinent information for the RFP regarding system requirements and selection, retrospective conversion, and implementation of training.

Selection process. Placing functional, technical, and performance responses submitted by each automated library system vendor side by side and matching their responses against specifications required in the RFP in order to choose the automated library system that best fits the needs of the library.

Serials. Publications, issued in parts, over an indefinite period which includes the subset periodicals. Serials can be issued at regular or irregular intervals.

Shared System. One automated library system that is acquired and accessed through a data communications network by a group of libraries (such as a library consortium or libraries in a particular geographical area).

Shelf List. A list of the books in a library. The entries are brief and arranged on cards or sheets in the order of the books on the shelves.

Site license. A permit, paid for by the library to a vendor, which allows the library to install software or CD-ROM products at several locations within a building.

Site preparation. Making the area(s) in the library ready to accommodate the new automated library system. Site preparation should be contingent on specifications supplied by the vendor which indicate layout guidelines for the new equipment. Typical specifications include hardware installation specifications, electrical power specifications, temperature specifications, humidity specifications, ceiling, floor, and partition specifications, storage facilities specifications, lighting specifications, cabling specifications, floor specifications, safety and fire specifications, and security specifications.

Smart barcoding. The process by which a retrospective conversion vendor assigns barcodes to the items in the database and sends pages of barcodes in shelflist order to the library. Staff affix the related barcode to the item with the correct call number.

Software. Computer programs.

Specifications. See System specifications.

Standard keyboard. A computer input device consisting of 10 function keys, a full set of alphabetical characters, numbers from 0 to 10, punctuation, and a variety of labeled keycaps. It did not originally include a numeric keypad.

Standardization. Conforming to established criteria in order to establish uniform practices and common techniques.

Star configuration. One of the ways in which equipment may be connected in a local area network in which each piece of equipment is wired to a central computer. Its design resembles that of a star.

Steering Committee. See Automation Committee.

Storage. See Permanent storage and RAM.

Straight line configuration. See Bus configuration.

Subcommittee. A committee that is responsible to a higher-level committee.

Subfield code. A subdivision in a MARC record. MARC fields are subdivided into subfields (a, b, c...) which contain related pieces of data (i.e., number of pages, illustrations, and size of the item).

System activation. The process of putting the new automated library system into action once the hardware and software have been installed and tested, supplies have been ordered, essential files have been created and ordered, and staff have been trained.

System capacity. The number of bibliographic items, patron records, vendor files, indexes etc., which can be handled by an automated library system before it is out of storage space and/or processing ability.

System changeover. Moving to the new automated library system in one of four ways: The library may follow a total, module-by-module, branch-by-branch, or parallel system changeover as predetermined by the project team.

System reliability test. An examination of the ability of the new automated library system to function without failure. Typically a system reliability test states that the system is expected to operate reliably for a period of, for example, (20 to) 60 consecutive days at an uptime level of, for example, 98 percent. If the system fails, the period starts again.

System Requirements Committee. A committee that is given the responsibility of gaining input from the work force and developing a list of requirements desired by the new system, based on staff workload, workflow, operating needs, staff reports, and suggestions. Members of the committee may obtain information either directly or indirectly from subcommittees such as those formed in the areas of acquisitions/serials control, cataloging (retrospective or database conversion), circulation, and online public access catalogs.

System specifications. A list of requirements covering capacity, availability, reliability, response time, downtime, compatibility, connectivity, and portability/transportability of an automated library system. System specifications are detailed in the RFP.

System support. The help and advice supplied to a library by a vendor, both on-site and over the telephone.

Systems analysis. Gathering and evaluating data on the work performed in the library for the purpose of deciding whether or not tasks can be undertaken more efficiently and effectively by installing an automated library system.

Systems Selection Committee. A committee which consists of the Project Manager and some of the members of the advisory committee, with the Project Manager generally acting as Chair of the group. This group analyzes results and selects the automated system after the bids have been received.

Tag. See MARC tag.

Telecommunications. The transmission and/or reception of information over a distance by telephone, fax, etc. The information may be in the form of voice, pictures, text, or computer data.

Temporary storage. See RAM.

Terminal. A piece of computer hardware with a keyboard and a cathode ray tube which can send data to and receive data from a mainframe, minicomputer, or supermicro.

Thesaurus. An authority file which defines terms and shows their relationship to broader terms, narrower terms, and related terms.

Third-level subcommittee. See Module committees.

Timeline. A chart which shows the number of hours, days, weeks, or months each task is expected to take when planning for, selecting, and installing the automated library system.

Total approach. Installing an automated library system immediately and simultaneously terminating the old system.

Touch screen. A computer monitor on which a user chooses options by pressing designated areas on the screen with a finger or other object.

Train-the-trainers workshop. A gathering at which designated library staff members are given comprehensive instruction on all the features of an automated library system. These staff members then train other library staff.

Training Committee. A committee which includes a broad base of clerical, paraprofessional, and professional staff and is set up to review the vendor training process; select appropriate staff to attend vendor training sessions; and assign personnel to design complementary training materials, present workshops, and provide ongoing, updated training as new software releases occur and as procedures change.

Transitional catalog. A database of library holdings which is generally used for a short duration. For example, a library might decide to select a CD-ROM patron access catalog as a first step toward automating the card catalog. The final step would be moving from the CD-ROM catalog to a fully integrated OPAC.

Transistor. Electronic switch that controls the flow of electricity in a circuit.

Transparent. Hidden from the user. For example, when the patron searches on a CD-ROM PAC, the information is often transparently accessed from the microcomputer hard disk as well as from the CD-ROM disc and displayed onscreen simultaneously.

Transportability. See Portability.

Truncation. The use of a wildcard character, such as ?, !, or #, as a substitute for a letter or combination of letters in a search term. When the symbol is combined with a word root, the system will search for all terms that contain the root plus any other letter(s) as a replacement of the symbol, i.e. hospit? will search for hospital, hospitalization, hospitals, hospitality, etc.

Turnkey system. An automated library system which has been designed, programmed, and tested by a vendor and then offered for sale to libraries, ready to be installed and operated.

Ultrix. Digital Equipment Corporation's version of the Unix operating system.

Unblocked variable-length record. One of the ways in which MARC records are stored on magnetic tape. In this case a variable-length records format is used in which a blank space of 1/2 to 3/4 inch separates each physical record. Usually called OCLC-MARC format.

Union list. An inventory common to several libraries which lists some or all of their holdings.

Unix. An operating system.

Unspanned variable-length record. See Unblocked variable-length record.

Up and running. Working. Automated library systems are said to be "up" when they are functional; the opposite of "down" or not working.

User group. A gathering of librarians whose libraries have purchased a particular automated library system from a certain vendor which meets to discuss the system, share problems, and solutions, and often makes representations to the vendor for improvements.

Vacuum tubes. Conductors of information used in the earliest computers to process information.

Variable-length records. Combinations of field information in a database which is not fixed or restricted by a limited number of characters or which varies in length, according to need.

Vendor. A commercial company in the business of selling automated library systems or services which support such systems.

Vendor-based RECON. Using a commercial vendor to undertake the retrospective conversion process.

Verify records. The process undertaken by a retrospective conversion vendor to confirm that the MARC records which are being matched are an accurate reflection of the library's holdings.

VGA monitor. Video Graphics Array screen that can display 256 colors and give access to 262,144 tints, tones, and hues.

Virus. A software program which is designed to destroy data, disrupt processing, and replicate itself in other software.

VLSI. Very large scale integration. This refers to the ability to place many thousands of circuits onto a single, tiny silicon chip.

VM. Operating system used on IBM mini and mainframe computers.

VMS. Operating system used on DEC VAX minicomputers.

VSE. Operating system used on IBM mini and mainframe computers.

Workflow. An organized or coordinated movement of activities within the library setting.

Workflow studies. The examination of how work is accomplished, how much time each task takes, and how it is coordinated. When this information is gathered, justification can be made for specific modules in an automated library system, and the proper placement of the hardware and software can be determined.

Z39.2. The standards number assigned to the MARC format.

Z39.50. A standard whose purpose is to allow one computer operating in a client mode to perform information retrieval queries against another computer acting as an information server. See also OSI.

Z39.58. See Common Command Language.

Z39.69. A standard which controls the way in which patron information is stored and accessed in an automated library system.

Index